Ilyushin Il-28 Beagle

Ilyushin Il-28 Beagle

LIGHT ATTACK BOMBER

Yefim Gordon and Dmitriy Komissarov

Airlife

First published in the UK in 2002
by Airlife Publishing Ltd

British Library Cataloguing-in-Publication Data
A catalogue record for this book
is available from the British Library

ISBN 1 84037 351 2

This book contains rare, early colour photographs and the Publisher has made every endeavour to reproduce them to the highest quality. Some, however, have been technically impossible to reproduce to the standard that we normally demand, but have been included because of their rarity and interest value.

Typeset by Rowland Phototypesetting Limited,
Bury St Edmunds, Suffolk
Printed in Hong Kong

Airlife Publishing Ltd
101 Longden Road, Shrewsbury SY3 9EB, England
E-mail: sales@airlifebooks.com
Website: www.airlifebooks.com

Acknowledgements

The authors wish to express their gratitude to Nigel Eastway of the Russian Aviation Research Trust (RART), who, as usual, provided assistance with photos from his extensive archive; to Sergey Komissarov who also supplied several previously unpublished photos; to Andrey Yurgenson for the line drawings and Sergey Yershov for the excellent colour side views.

Contents

The famous Soviet aircraft designer Sergey Vladimirovich Ilyushin, the founder of OKB-240 and the creator of many outstanding aircraft – including the Il-28 tactical bomber. *(Sergey and Dmitriy Komissarov archive)*

INTRODUCTION

Like the other Allied nations, the Soviet Union was very active designing new types of weapons and military technologies in the early years after the Second World War. The advent of the turbojet engine affected first and foremost fighter design. Jet fighters enjoyed top priority, while jet bombers were in effect relegated to second place, although the turbojet inevitably found its way to bombers as well. Having examined German war booty aircraft and the state of Nazi Germany's aeronautical research, US, British and Soviet aircraft designers reached the same conclusion: indigenous jet designs were needed. Research in this field eventually led to masterpieces of aviation engineering, such as the North American F-86 Sabre and Mikoyan/Gurevich MiG-15 (NATO code name *Fagot)* fighters, the English Electric Canberra bomber and, some time later, the Boeing B-52 Stratofortress, Tupolev Tu-16 *Badger* and Tu-95 *Bear* heavy bombers. (The latter is admittedly a turboprop aircraft; however, turboprops are gas turbine engines as well, so the Tu-95 deserves mention, too.)

The well-known Soviet Ilyushin Il-28 tactical bomber can also be regarded as an extraordinary aircraft. Few jet fighters of the time could keep up with the Il-28 in terms of production.

According to contemporary Soviet military strategy, conventional and nuclear strikes against targets in the enemy's tactical area were to be made by tactical (i.e. light) bombers. Development work on jet tactical bombers in the USSR was probably kicked off in 1945 by the design bureau led by Arkhip Mikhailovich Lyulka which was then working on the 1,300 kgp (2,865 lb st) TR-1 axial-flow turbojet – the first indigenous jet engine to reach the hardware stage. (Pre-war projects developed by Lyulka remained paper engines. The only other jets available to Soviet aircraft designers at the time were reverse-engineered versions of the German turbojets – the BMW 003 and Junkers Jumo 004.)

Jet bombers were under development at OKB-156 led by Andrey Nikolayevich Tupolev, OKB-240 led by Sergey Vladimirovich Ilyushin and OKB-51 led by Pavel Osipovich Sukhoi. Even OKB-1 led by the German war booty designer Brunolf W. Baade joined the race.[1]

Early studies by Ilyushin in this direction resulted in the Il-22 (the first aircraft to carry this designation),[2] the first Soviet four-jet bomber. It had a circular-section fuselage, shoulder-mounted straight wings, a conventional tail unit, a tricycle landing

1 OKB = ***op****ytno-kon****strook****torskoye* ***by****u****ro*** – experimental design bureau. The number is a code allocated for security reasons.

2 The designation was reused much later for a purpose-built airborne command post version of the Il-18D turboprop airliner (NATO code name *Coot*; the Il-22 was code-named *Coot-C*).

The Il-22 was the Ilyushin OKB's first jet bomber. Though not a successful design, lessons learned with it accounted in a large degree for the success of the Il-28. *(Sergey and Dmitriy Komissarov archive)*

The experimental 'aircraft 77' (Tu-12) bomber which was a straightforward development of the Second World War-vintage Tu-2. *(Yefim Gordon archive)*

gear with a twin-wheel nose unit and large single mainwheels. The TsAGI[3] 1-A-10 aerofoil was utilized on the inner wings and the TsAGI 1-V-10 aerofoil on the outer wings, with a 12 per cent thickness-to-chord ratio in both cases. The four TR-1 turbojets were carried almost entirely ahead of the wing leading edge on short horizontal pylons; this was a first in world jet aircraft design.

All the bombs were to be carried internally, and the largest weapon carried by the Il-22 was a 3,000 kg (6,613 lb) bomb, which was also the aircraft's maximum ordnance load. The defensive armament comprised a pair of Berezin B-20E 20 mm (.78 calibre) cannon in an electrically powered remote-controlled dorsal barbette and a single 23 mm (.90 calibre) Nudelman/Sooranov NS-23 cannon in an Il-KU-3 tail turret designed in-house.[4] Another NS-23 cannon was mounted on the starboard side of the forward fuselage, firing forward. The five-man crew consisted of two pilots seated side by side in an extensively glazed nose (reminiscent of the Boeing B-29 Superfortress), a navigator/bomb aimer, a gunner/radio operator who worked the dorsal barbette, and a tail gunner.

According to the project the Il-22 was to have a range of 1,250 km (776 miles) with a 2,000 kg (4,409 lb) nominal bomb load. The maximum take-off weight was 24,000 kg (52,910 lb) and the never-exceed speed was set at 800 km/h (432 kt), or Mach 0.75.

Development and prototype construction proceeded extremely fast; piloted by two brothers, Vladimir and Konstantin Kokkinaki, the Il-22 made its maiden flight on 24 July 1947. However, tests quickly showed that its performance was clearly inadequate – mainly because the engines, which suffered from teething troubles, had to be derated to 940 kgp (2,072 lb st). Hence the MTOW had to be limited to 20,000 kg (44,091 lb) for the manufacturer's flight tests. The range turned out to be merely 865 km (537 miles) and the top speed at 7,000 m (22,965 ft) was 718 km/h (388 kt) instead of the required 800 km/h. Hence the Ilyushin OKB chose not to submit the aircraft for State acceptance trials; all further development work was discontinued and the sole prototype was relegated to the Bureau of New Hardware (a division of the Ministry of Aircraft Industry), where it could be studied by leading industry experts. The Il-22 was no more than a stepping stone to more efficient designs.

Meanwhile, Tupolev came up with the Tu-77 experimental bomber (aka Tu-12), a heavily modified Second World War-vintage Tu-2 with two turbojets and a tricycle landing gear, and later the Tu-73/Tu-78/Tu-81/Tu-89 family. The last aircraft in the series was eventually to see limited production and service as the Tu-14 (NATO code name *Bosun*). The German team led by Baade refined the Junkers EF 131 project which culminated in the Type 140, an experimental bomber with forward-swept wings.

Sukhoi built a prototype of the Su-10 four-jet light bomber, but it was scrapped without ever being flown when OKB-51 was dissolved in 1949. There was yet another contender, Vladimir Mikhailovich Myasischchev with his VM-24 (aka RB-17) four-turbojet bomber project. However, it never materialized because Myasischchev was out of favour with Soviet leader Josef Stalin and consequently his projects received a thumbs-down at the time. This was basically the situation in which the Il-28 was born – the Soviet Union's first operational jet bomber, which entered service with the VVS (*Voyenno-vozdooshnyye seely* – [Soviet] Air Force) in 1949.

3 TsAGI = *Tsentrahl'nyy aero- i ghidrodinamicheskiy institoot* – Central Aerodynamics & Hydrodynamics Institute, named after Nikolay Yegorovich Zhukovskiy.

4 KU stands for *kormovaya [strelkovaya] oostanovka* – tail barbette.

•1

BREEDING THE *BEAGLE*

The Il-28 project was conceived in late 1947. On 31 October that year Sergey V. Ilyushin wrote to the then Minister of Aircraft Industry, Nikolay A. Bulganin, proposing a tactical bomber powered by two Rolls-Royce Nene 1 centrifugal-flow turbojets, with a first flight date tentatively set for July 1948. This tight schedule was due in no small part to the experience accumulated with the Il-22 which would allow the new bomber to be developed quickly. The objective was to achieve a performance far superior to that of the Il-22 and the projected Il-24 bomber (again the first aircraft to use this designation).[1] This was made possible by reducing the crew and rethinking the defensive armament concept.

The Il-28's general arrangement was similar to its predecessor's. However, the aircraft was rather smaller and differed in a number of important respects. This was because of the new bomber's higher speed and different service conditions: unlike the Il-22, the Il-28 was designed to operate mainly from tactical airfields with unpaved strips.

The crew was reduced to three – pilot, navigator/bomb aimer and tail gunner/radio operator. The decision to eliminate the co-pilot and forward gunner was dictated first of all by the limited mission time of a tactical bomber. At a cruising speed of 650–750 km/h (361–416 kt) a sortie would typically last 2 or 2.5 hours – four hours at the most. An autopilot would be installed to ease the pilot's workload during cruise.

The armament would probably best be described now, because the Il-28 was, as one Russian writer put it, 'designed around the tail' – or, to be precise, the tail turret. Trials of the Il-22 had shown that the remote-controlled dorsal barbette was inefficient because the tail unit created large blind sectors. Also, the gunner's station was located well away from the barbette; hence some areas where the cannon could be brought to bear on the target were concealed from the gunner's view by the wings and fuselage. Various armament arrangements were studied. Eventually the engineers decided that a single tail turret offered adequate protection against enemy fighter attacks from the rear hemisphere, providing the traversing/elevating angle and speed of the cannon were increased and the bomber made appropriate defensive manoeuvres. Besides, the use of only a single tail turret reduced empty weight and improved aerodynamic efficiency.

Yet designing a new tail turret turned out to be quite a challenge; the engineers had to meet stringent specifications while keeping the unit's weight to a minimum. The Il-22's tail turret turned out to be too sluggish; a new power drive and remote control system had to be developed. The result was the highly efficient Il-K6 ball turret[2] – originally mounting the same NS-23 cannon which were later replaced by Nudelman/Richter NR-23s with 225 rpg. The new weapons had the same calibre but a much higher rate of fire (850 rounds per minute versus 550 rpm for the earlier model).

The Il-K6 was the first Soviet electrohydraulically powered remote-controlled turret; it had a traversing angle of ±70° and an elevating angle of +60° to –40°. In normal mode the cannon moved at a rate of 15–17° per second, the motion increasing to up to 36° per second in boost (emergency) mode. The power drive enabled the turret to operate adequately at airspeeds in excess of 1,000 km/h (555 kt). At 340 kg (750 lb), the turret was relatively lightweight. By comparison, the DK-3 turret used on the Tu-4 *Bull* bomber (a reverse-engineered Boeing B-29) had traversing and elevating angles of only ±30°, while weighing nearly 390 kg (860 lb).

The power drive of the Il-K6 turret was built around an unorthodox swivelling hydraulic pump unit driven by two 5 kW electric motors. The output of the pumps and hence the motion speed of the cannon depended on the angle at which the pump unit was tilted; with the pump unit in a neutral position the turret remained motionless. This made it possible to dispense with slide valves, reservoirs and other unreliable components, resulting in a simple and safe hydraulic system. The ammunition boxes were built into the body of the turret, allowing the

1 A derivative of the Il-22 powered by four 3,300 kgp (7,275 lb st) Mikulin AM-TKRD-01 turbojets and equipped with an Il-KU-4 twin-cannon tail turret. The designation was later reused for the Il-24N long-range ice reconnaissance aircraft – another spin-off of the Il-18D.

2 Once again, K stands for *kormovaya strelkovaya oostanovka* – tail barbette.

customary belt feed and tightening mechanisms to be dispensed with, which again made for higher reliability.

The turret was electrically controlled by means of a highly reliable and precise potentiometric tracking system. Targeting was done by a computing gunsight which automatically made adjustments for the target's motion, shell velocity and trajectory, cannon traversing angle, flight altitude and airspeed. The sight received feedback from the turret to minimize miscoordination between the two. Thus, miscoordination in the horizontal plane was three times less than the limit set by general operational requirements of the time.

The Il-28 also featured two fixed forward-firing NR-23 cannon with 100 rpg installed on both sides of the nose on quick-release mounts. These were fired by the pilot and could be removed by simply disconnecting an electrical connector and turning a locking lever.

The decision to use only a single power turret and reduce the crew to three enabled the designers to make the Il-28's fuselage nearly 3.5 m (11 ft 5.79 in.) shorter than that of the Il-22 and reduce wing area by 13.7 m^2 (147.3 sq. ft), which led to a significant reduction in empty weight. Hence the second major difference was the powerplant. The basic projected size and weight allowed the new bomber to be powered by two Rolls-Royce Nenes rated at 2,270 kgp (5,000 lb st).

The Nene, which entered licence production in the USSR in 1947 as the Klimov RD-45,[3] had by then reached a high degree of reliability and boasted a 25–30 per cent lower specific fuel consumption as compared to the TR-1. On the other hand, a major drawback of this engine was its large diameter, caused by the centrifugal compressor. This, and the necessity to keep the air intakes as far away from the ground as possible in order to avoid foreign-object damage (FOD) – a must since the aircraft was to operate from dirt airstrips – led the designers to mount the engines in nacelles adhering directly to the lower surface of the wings (i.e. without pylons).

For centre-of-gravity reasons the engines were located well forward in the nacelles. Thus, the large diameter of the engine's compressor and the small jetpipe allowed the main gear units to be relocated from the fuselage to the engine nacelles, giving a wide track which was a bonus on semi-prepared strips. The shock struts were attached to the nacelles' main frames, and as they retracted forward the single mainwheels turned through 90° by means of a simple mechanical link to lie flat in the bottom of the nacelles beneath the jetpipe (behind the combustion chambers). Incidentally, here the Ilyushin OKB made a virtue out of necessity: the landing gear struts were noticeably longer than on the Il-22, giving a large ground clearance under the fuselage and easing the bomb-loading procedure. In contrast, the Il-22 had a very small ground clearance, needing to be jacked up when 2,500 kg (5,511 lb) and 3,000 kg (6,613 lb) bombs were hooked up.

To meet the high speed requirement the Il-28's wings employed a new TsAGI SR-5S high-speed aerofoil developed under the guidance of Yakov M. Serebriyskiy and Maria V. Ryzhova – again with a 12 per cent thickness-to-chord ratio. This enabled the bomber to reach a maximum speed of Mach 0.82 at 7,000–8,000 m (22,965–26,246 ft) without any adverse effects on stability and control characteristics caused by shock wave formation. The provision of simple slotted flaps assured the Il-28 good field performance.

The high design speeds called for a swept tail unit which ensured good stability and handling throughout the speed range. The tail unit employed symmetrical aerofoil sections with a slightly higher thickness-to-chord ratio than that of the Il-22. The fin was swept back 41° at quarter-chord, while the stabilizers were swept back 30°; this delayed dangerous Mach buffeting to a speed well above the aircraft's never-exceed speed. In addition, the sweepback increased the rudder and elevator arm, which allowed the area and weight of the tail surfaces to be reduced.

One of the complaints voiced by the Il-22's pilots during flight tests concerned the flight deck glazing (which was blended entirely into the nose contour *à la* B-29). The curved glazing panels distorted the view and generated annoying reflections, and the heavy framework created numerous blind spots. Since the Il-28 would be flown by a single pilot, the engineers provided him with a fighter-type cockpit enclosed by a sideways-opening bubble canopy with a bullet-proof windscreen. The extensive nose glazing was still there of necessity, but now the navigator/bomb aimer had the glazed nose all to himself.

The crew was seated in two pressurized compartments – one for the pilot and navigator/bomb aimer, the other for the gunner/radio operator. At low altitudes these were pressurized by the slipstream; from 1,700 m (5,580 ft) upwards the compartments were sealed off and pressurized by engine bleed air via filters. The pressurization system was combined with the heating and ventilation systems. The cockpit

3 RD = *reaktivnyy dvigatel'* – jet engine.

and navigator's compartment were equipped with upward-firing ejection seats; ejection was triggered by jettisoning the canopy or entrance hatch respectively. The gunner baled out via the ventral entrance hatch; the hatch cover doubled as a shield protecting him from the slipstream.

As had been the case with the Il-22, the Il-28's wing panels and tail surfaces had a manufacturing joint running along the chord line. Each half of the unit consisted of a number of panels incorporating stringers and ribs. This allowed different panels to be manufactured simultaneously at different workstations while improving working conditions; noisy and labour-intensive manual riveting was replaced with high-quality machine riveting.

The fuselage was also designed in two halves with a manufacturing joint running the full length of it: it went together just like a plastic model kit! For the first time in Soviet aircraft production, all structural members of the fuselage were readily accessible, allowing riveting and assembly operations to be mechanized and various internal equipment to be fitted quickly and efficiently. The fuselage was also divided lengthwise into four sections, facilitating the installation of equipment in bays which would not be accessible once the structure was fully assembled. Finally, the fuselage had longitudinal recesses on both sides covered by removable skin panels. These facilitated installation of all wiring and pipelines during manufacturing, as well as checking them and replacing faulty components in service. This feature reduced pre-flight check time and enhanced combat efficiency.

The slight weight penalty (about 4 per cent) incurred by the new technology more than paid off. The surface finish was significantly improved; labour intensity was cut by 25–30 per cent for production airframes and by 30–40 per cent for internal equipment installation. As a result, the twinjet bomber was hardly more complicated to build than a tactical fighter. Also, this allowed Ilyushin to avoid a problem which affected some early Soviet jets – the propensity to uncommanded bank at high airspeeds, called *val'**o**zhka* in Russian. (This problem, which had manifested itself on the Mikoyan/Gurevich MiG-9 *Fargo* and the MiG-15 *Fagot-A*, was caused by aerodynamic asymmetry caused by the wings having slightly different aerofoil sections because of insufficiently high manufacturing accuracy. This structural asymmetry meant that the wings produced different amounts of lift; this was not critical at low speeds, but as airspeed increased the difference became appreciable.)

The Ilyushin OKB had accumulated a lot of design and operational experience with hot air de-icing systems and put it to good use when working on the Il-28. The turbojet engines powering the aircraft supplied lots of bleed air, enabling the engineers to quickly create the most efficient de-icing system of the time. This was the Soviet Union's first automatic hot air de-icing system; it was lightweight, reliable and simple to operate and had no parts disrupting the airflow. This feature greatly improved the bomber's combat efficiency and flight safety in adverse weather – particularly because the relatively thin aerofoils used in the wings and tail unit made icing much more dangerous than in the case of slower piston-engined aircraft utilizing thick aerofoils.

All-weather and night-flying capability was ensured by the provision of a comprehensive avionics and communications suite which enabled the crew to navigate the aircraft and detect, identify and destroy ground targets without maintaining visual contact with the ground. The avionics suite included an OSP-48 instrument landing system (ILS) for use in instrument meteorological conditions (IMC). The ground part of the system included two range beacons, three marker beacons, communications radios and an HF or VHF radio direction finder to facilitate approach and landing in bad weather. The system's components installed on the aircraft comprised an ARK-5 Amur (a river in the Soviet Far East; pronounced like the French word *amour*) automatic direction finder, an RV-2 Kristall (Crystal) low-altitude radio altimeter and an MRP-48 Dyatel (Woodpecker) marker beacon receiver.[4] The OSP-48 was fairly simple and had few components, which rendered the ground part suitable for use on *ad hoc* tactical airfields (in truck-mounted form). The aircraft was also equipped with an AP-5 autopilot and an identification friend-or-foe (IFF) transponder.

Unlike the Il-22, the Il-28's normal bomb load was 1,000 kg (2,204 lb); the maximum bomb load in overload condition remained the same at 3,000 kg (6,613 lb). The bomb bay located in the centre fuselage featured four bomb cassettes and one beam-type bomb cradle. The former could carry bombs of 50–500 kg (110–1,102 lb) calibre, while the latter was designed for bombs weighing from 1,000 to 3,000 kg (2,204–6,612 lb).

In visual meteorological conditions (VMC) the navigator/bomb aimer used an OPB-5S optical

4 OSP = *obo**roo**dovaniye sle**poy** po**sahd**ki* – blind landing equipment; ARK = *automa**tich**eskiy **rah**dio**kom**pas* – ADF; RV = ***rah**diovysoto**mer*** – radio altimeter; MRP = ***mar**kernyy **rah**dio-preeyomnik*. The MRP-48 has also been designated Khrizantema (Chrysanthemum) in some sources.

bomb sight (***opticheskiy pritsel bombardirovochnyy***) which enabled him to take aim automatically at stationary and moving targets in level flight. Interestingly, the navigator had to leave his ejection seat and sit sideways on a special jump seat in the extreme nose on the starboard side to use the sight. The OPB-5S computed the sighting angles and dropped the bombs automatically at the correct moment by means of an electric release mechanism. The sight was gyrostabilized to prevent the aircraft's manoeuvres from affecting bombing accuracy and linked to the autopilot, enabling the navigator to set the aircraft's course on its bombing run. In IMC, bomb-aiming was assisted by the PSBN-M search/bomb-aiming radar (*pribor slepovo bombometahniya i navigahtsii* – blind-bombing and navigational device) with a 360° field of view. The radar was located in the aft fuselage just ahead of the gunner's station and enclosed by a flush dielectric fairing.

Taking a risk

General Designer[5] Sergey V. Ilyushin approved the Il-28 advanced development project on 12 January 1948, giving the go-ahead to complete a set of manufacturing drawings and start prototype construction. By then, however, Tupolev's OKB-156 – the Soviet Union's leading authority in bomber design – had received an assignment to design and build a similar jet-powered tactical bomber. OKB-240 had no such assignment. Still, Ilyushin's belief in his aircraft was so strong that he decided to carry on with the Il-28 and build a prototype at his own risk – all the more so because the Soviet Air Force was in desperate need of a tactical bomber meeting the stringent new requirements. (It is worth noting here that Ghenrikh Vasilyevich Novozhilov, who succeeded Ilyushin as the OKB's head in 1970, started his career at the Ilyushin OKB by taking part in the preparation of the Il-28 prototype's manufacturing drawings.) The Il-28 was not officially included in the Ministry of Aircraft Industry's experimental aircraft construction plan until 12 June 1948, when the Soviet Union's Council of Ministers issued directive No. 2052-804 to this effect – one month before the prototype was rolled out.

Bearing no serial or even national insignia, the prototype (powered by authentic Rolls-Royce Nene turbojets imported from the UK) commenced ground tests at Moscow-Khodynka on 29 May 1948. On 1 July the aircraft was dismantled and trucked to the Flight Research Institute named after Mikhail M. Gromov (LII – *Lyotno-issledovatel'skiy institoot*) in Zhukovskiy, south of Moscow, where most Soviet aviation OKBs had their flight test facilities. V. N. Boogaiskiy was assigned engineer in charge of the flight tests.

The company chief was as good as his word: the bomber took to the air for the first time on 8 July 1948 with Ilyushin OKB chief test pilot Vladimir K. Kokkinaki at the controls; N. D. Sorokin was the *flight engineer* (*sic* – obviously the navigator) and B. A. Yerofeyev was the radio operator. Kokkinaki

The Rolls-Royce Nene-powered first prototype of the Il-28 was totally devoid of markings. Note the complex framework of the cockpit canopy and the flush installation of the navigation/bomb-aiming radar. *(Yefim Gordon archive)*

Tupolev's 'aircraft 73', the three-engined forerunner of the Tu-14 bomber; note the air intake and nozzle of the centre engine. This configuration was to change soon... *(Yefim Gordon archive)*

was pleased with the aircraft's handling, saying that the Il-28 was easy to fly, both during take-off and in cruise, and climbed well.

Speaking of serials, until the mid-1950s Soviet military aircraft had three- or four-digit *serial numbers*. These allowed more or less positive identification, since they tied in with the aircraft's construction number – usually the last one or two digits of the batch number plus the number of the aircraft in the batch.

In 1955, however, the VVS switched (probably for security reasons) to the current system of two-digit *tactical codes* which, as a rule, are simply the aircraft's number in the unit operating it, making positive identification impossible. Three- or four-digit tactical codes are rare and are usually worn by development aircraft only, in which case they still tie in with the c/n or fuselage number (manufacturer's line number).[6] At the same time the star insignia on the aft fuselage were deleted, remaining on the wings and vertical tail only. So far, however, no Soviet Air Force Il-28s with pre-1955 serials related to the c/n have been identified.

The Il-28 had good directional and lateral stability throughout its operational envelope. When properly trimmed the aircraft flew stably in level flight even when the controls were released. Low-speed handling was quite good, with no tendency to stall or spin. Straight and level flight with one dead engine was no problem either, the yaw being easily countered without excessive loads on the rudder pedals.

The aircraft had good field performance and could operate from existing airbases and tactical airfields. At a normal gross weight of 17,220 kg (37,963 lb), the take-off run was just 560 m (1,837 ft) if the aircraft was fitted with two PSR-1500-15 jet-assisted take-off (JATO) rockets[7] with a 13-second burn time developing 1,600 kgp (3,527 lb st) each. The Il-28 could easily operate from dirt strips; in fact, the test pilots expressly recommended operating the bomber from dirt strips in order to prolong the tyres' service life.

During manufacturer's flight tests the Nene-powered first prototype attained a top speed of 833 km/h (462 kt) at 5,000 m (16,404 ft), and reached Mach 0.79 at 7,000–8,000 m (22,966–26,246 ft). The test pilots reported that the aircraft behaved normally at these speeds and could go even faster if appropriate changes were made. Hence the OKB set about streamlining the airframe and installing more powerful engines.

The Tu-73 and Tu-78 trijet bomber prototypes[8] were undergoing manufacturer's flight tests at the same time. One day General Designer Andrey N. Tupolev saw the Il-28 prototype at the airfield of LII. Being, by many accounts, an ill-tempered person and a man who did not care about competition

5 The official title of Soviet OKB heads.

6 On military *transport* aircraft, however, three-digit tactical codes do not relate to the c/n or f/n; they are the last three of the former civil registration (many Soviet/Russian Air Force transports were, and still are, quasi-civilian).

7 PSR = *porokhovaya startovaya raketa* – solid-fuel rocket booster.

8 The Tu-73 was powered by two RR Nenes in wing-mounted nacelles and one RR Derwent V in the rear fuselage. On the otherwise identical Tu-78 these were replaced by two RD-45Fs and one RD-500 respectively (the RD-500 was the licence-built version of the Derwent).

(to say the least), Tupolev was openly scornful at first. 'Humph! Whose bastard child is this?' he asked the technicians working on the aircraft. However, after examining the competitor's product closely and studying the specifications he had a long talk with his aides, and it was easy to see that he was very displeased. The reason for Tupolev's displeasure was obvious: on their jet bombers the Tupolev engineers had copied the defensive weapons arrangement of the piston-engined Tu-2, which led to excessively large overall dimensions, an excessively large crew and hence excessive weight, not to mention the decidedly complex powerplant. The ultimate Tu-81 (Tu-14) and Tu-89 (Tu-14T) dispensed with the centre engine and two remote-controlled gun barbettes in favour of a single tail gunner's station – inspired by the Il-28, no doubt.

On 30 December 1948 the second prototype Il-28 powered by production RD-45F engines[9] entered flight test, again flown by Vladimir Kokkinaki. New models of tyres were tested concurrently with the aircraft itself, as the original ones were totally worn out after just ten landings on concrete strips. The best results were attained with tyres made of perlone, a synthetic rubber, which lasted for more than 100 landings.

Apart from the powerplant, the second prototype differed from future production Il-28s in avionics and equipment fit. The aircraft was equipped with RSB-5 and RSU-10 radios, an SPUF-3 intercom, an MRP-46 marker beacon receiver, AFA-BA and AFA-33/50 or AFA-33/75 aerial cameras, two GSN-3000 generators, three sets of KP-14 breathing apparatus with 8-litre (1.76 imp. gal.) liquid oxygen bottles, an RUSP-48 ILS, etc.[10]

After the successful completion of the initial flight test programme, the second prototype was turned over to the Soviet Air Force Research Institute (NII VVS – *Naou**ch**no-iss**led**ovatel'skiy institoot vo**yen**no-voz**dooshn**ykh seel*) for State acceptance trials, which lasted from February to April 1949. The formal act of acceptance was signed on 18 May.

The specifications of the RD-45F-powered second prototype Il-28 attained at the State acceptance trials are detailed in Table 1.

Table 1. RD-45F-powered second prototype; specifications attained in State acceptance trials

Length overall		17.45 m (57 ft 3 in.)
Height on ground		6.0 m (19 ft 8.22 in.)
Wing span		21.45 m (70 ft 4.48 in.)
Wing area		60.8 m² (653.76 sq. ft)
Wing loading		288 kg/m² (1,400 lb/ft²)
Power loading at sea level		3.38 kg/kgp (lb/lb st)
Normal all-up weight		17,500 kg (38,580 lb)
Maximum all-up weight		20,000 kg (44,091 lb)
Fuel load		6,300 kg (13,888 lb)
Top speed:	at sea level	750 km/h (405.4 kt)*
	at 5,750–6,000 m (18,864–19,685 ft)	843 km/h (455.67 kt)
	at 10,000 m (32,808 ft)	820 km/h (443.24 kt)
Landing speed		178 km/h (96.2 kt)
Rate of climb:	at sea level	10.9 m/sec (2,145 ft/min)
	at 5,000 m (16,404 ft)	8.3 m/sec (1,633 ft/min)
	at 10,000 m (32,808 ft)	3.6 m/sec (708 ft/min)
Time to height:	5,000 m	8.6 min
	10,000 m	22.6 min
Range:	at 20,000 kg TOW, 5,000 m and 542 km/h (293 kt)	1,815 km (1,127 miles)
	at 20,000 kg TOW, 10,000 m and 546 km/h (295 kt)	2,370 km (1,472 miles)
Endurance at 10,000 m cruising altitude and 546 km/h cruising speed		4 hr 13 min
Take-off run		1,150 m (3,773 ft)/650 m (2,132 ft)**
Take-off distance		2,540 m (8,333 ft)/990 m (3,248 ft)**
Landing distance		1,730 m (5,678 ft)***

Notes:

* Speed limited at altitudes up to 1,750 m (5,741 ft) owing to 2,700 kg/m² (13,122 lb/ft²) dynamic strength limit.

** Without boosters/with two PSR-1500-15 JATO bottles.

*** With a 13,500 kg (29,762 lb) landing weight.

Table 2. Performance comparison between the Il-28 and Tu-14

	Tu-14	Il-28
Empty weight, kg (lb)	14,940 (32,936)	12,795 (28,207)
All-up weight, kg (lb):		
normal	21,000 (46,296)	18,400 (40,564)
in overload configuration	25,350 (55,886)	21,069 (46,448)
maximum	25,350 (55,886)	23,069 (50,875)
Top speed at take-off power/normal AUW, km/h (kt):		
at 5,000 m (16,404 ft)	845 (456.75)	893 (482.7)
at 10,000 m (32,808 ft)	811 (438.37)	850 (459.45)
Top speed at take-off power/maximum AUW, km/h (kt):		
at S/L	774 (418.37)	800 (432.43)
at 5,000 m (16,404 ft)	823 (444.86)	857 (463.24)
at 10,000 m (32,808 ft)	773 (417.83)	823 (444.86)
Service ceiling at normal AUW, m (ft)	11,200 (36,745)	12,300 (40,354)
Maximum range at 10,000 m/normal AUW, km (miles)	2,870 (1,782)	2,415 (1,500)
Take-off run, m (ft)	1,200 (3,937)	965 (3,166)
Landing run, m (ft)	1,100 (3,609)	960 (3,149)
Bomb load, kg (lb):		
normal	1,000 (2,204)	1,000 (2,204)
maximum	3,000 (6,613)	3,000 (6,613)

Table 2 gives a performance comparison of the Il-28 and Tu-14. **Note that the figures stated for the Il-28 differ from those in Table 1; however, in both cases they originate from official documents.** A possible explanation is that different examples of the *Beagle* were involved – or that whoever prepared the comparative table was not very honest, doctoring the figures to benefit the Il-28.

The Tu-14 was being tested concurrently; the Powers That Be were to choose between the two, so that in effect Ilyushin and Tupolev had a flyoff, even though the term was unknown in the Soviet Union at the time. Hence the VVS top brass was in a turmoil; some of the generals and marshals lobbied for the Tu-14, which had somewhat longer range, while others supported the Il-28, which was much easier to build and operate. The discussion raged on at ministerial level; the chief of NII VVS denounced the Il-28 and strongly urged the Minister of Aircraft Industry, Nikolay A. Bulganin, to give the go-ahead for the Tu-14. Still, even Bulganin failed to resolve the issue.

Finally, on 14 May 1949 a special commission chaired by Stalin himself analysed the test results and compared the performance of the two types. According to Ilyushin, after examining the reports carefully and listening to his military advisers, Stalin picked the Il-28. However, Ilyushin was requested to increase the speed of production aircraft immediately to 900 km/h (486 kt) by re-engining the Il-28 with more powerful and fuel-efficient Klimov VK-1 turbojets; Council of Ministers directive No. 1890-700 to this effect appeared on the same day. (It makes you wonder if the pro-Ilyushin lobby had prepared the directive in advance, foreseeing this victory!) The VK-1 was a version of the RD-45F uprated to 2,700 kgp (5,950 lb st). As a consolation prize, Tupolev was requested to develop a version of the Tu-14 (likewise powered by VK-1s) for the Naval air arm.

Defining and refining

Building on the results of numerous wind tunnel tests at TsAGI, the Ilyushin OKB developed new engine nacelles for the production VK-1-powered form of the Il-28. Unlike the prototypes' nacelles, which were bulged around the middle, the new ones were distinctly area-ruled, the waist being narrowest

9 F = *for**seer**ovannyy* – uprated.
10 AFA = ***aero**foto**apparaht*** – aircraft camera; KP = *kis**lorod**nyy pree**bor*** – oxygen equipment.

In designing the 'aircraft 81', a derivative of the '73' and '78' trijets which entered production as the Tu-14, the Tupolev OKB clearly borrowed Ilyushin's defensive armament concept employed on the Il-28. *(Yefim Gordon archive)*

where the wing section was at its thickest. This significantly reduced harmful interference between wing and nacelle, especially at transonic speeds, resulting in a major improvement in the Il-28's performance. (As a point of interest, in the USA the area rule was formulated in parallel by R. Whitcomb, but did not find practical use until 1954, when Convair brought out the F-102 Delta Dagger interceptor.)

Other changes were made after the initial flight tests and State acceptance trials. The PSBN-M radar was relocated from the aft fuselage to a position immediately after the nosewheel well in order to improve its operating conditions and enclosed by a teardrop-shaped radome. The rudder's horn balance was enlarged to reduce rudder forces. Some minor changes were made to the hydraulic system and the nosewheel steering actuator/shimmy damper. The fuselage fuel cells were equipped with a nitrogen pressurization system to reduce the danger of explosion if hit by enemy fire, enhancing survivability. The angular cockpit windscreen of the prototypes gave way to a more streamlined one featuring an elliptical Triplex windshield and curved sidelights, and the frame of the hinged canopy portion was simplified by introducing a two-piece blown transparency. The navigator's glazing was also modified.

The pre-production Il-28 powered by VK-1s commenced flight tests on 8 August 1949; the crew was the same as on the day of the type's maiden flight a year earlier. At a normal gross weight of

An uncoded pre-production Il-28 powered by Klimov VK-1 engines in area-ruled nacelles. This view illustrates well the sleek lines of Ilyushin's jet bomber. *(Yefim Gordon archive)*

Three-quarters rear view of the same aircraft, showing the Il-K6 ball turret. *(Yefim Gordon archive)*

18,400 kg (40,564 lb), the aircraft had a top speed of 906 km/h (503 kt) at 4,000 m (13,123 ft). The pilots noted the aircraft was stable at any speed; control forces could be trimmed down easily. At the maximum allowed speed of Mach 0.78 the back pressure on the control column gradually increased; then, if elevator trim remained unchanged, the load reversed, the control column would move forward and the aircraft would tend to go into a dive. If elevator trim was selected up, the aircraft could reach Mach 0.81 or 0.82, but this caused severe Mach buffet, warning the pilot to slow down. The production-standard Il-28's top speed at various altitudes is indicated in Table 3.

With a 1,000 kg (2,204 lb) normal bomb load and a 21,000 kg (46,296 lb) MTOW, the Il-28 had a maximum range of 2,455 km (1,525 miles) and was generally superior in performance to the piston-engined Tu-2 which was the mainstay of the VVS's tactical bomber force at the time.

On 24 August 1949 the production-standard VK-1-powered aircraft was handed over for State acceptance trials and passed them with flying colours. On 16 September the State Commission recommended that production be started forthwith, and so it was. Starting in September 1949, it entered production at three major aircraft factories: No. 30 Znamya truda (Banner of Labour, pronounced

Table 3. Production-standard Il-28's top speeds at various altitudes

	Indicated airspeed		Mach number	
	at cruise power	at full military power	at cruise power	at full military power
sea level	786 km/h (424.86 kt)	800 km/h (432.43 kt)	0.642	0.655
4,500 m (14,763 ft)	846 km/h (457.29 kt)	900 km/h (486.48 kt)	0.73	0.776
5,250 m (17,224 ft)	848 km/h (458.37 kt)	897 km/h (484.86 kt)	0.738	0.782
8,000 m (26,246 ft)	837 km/h (452.43 kt)	876 km/h (473.51 kt)	0.759	0.79
12,000 m (39,370 ft)	710 km/h (383.78 kt)	805 km/h (435.15 kt)	0.67	0.757

Individual factory construction number systems

System 1: 4 Red, c/n 50301106:	50	year of manufacture (1950);
	30	= Moscow Machinery Plant (MMZ) No. 30;
	11	batch number;
	06	number of aircraft in the batch (up to 100?).

The c/n is stencilled on the fuselage nose and sometimes under the horizontal tail as well.

System 8: unknown, c/n 430512301:	4	in-house version designator: *izdeliye* (product) 4 = Il-28R;
	30	= MMZ No. 30;
	51	year of manufacture (1951);
	23	batch number;
	01	number of aircraft in the batch.

System 3: 12 Red, c/n 53005112:	5	in-house version designator: *izdeliye* (product) 5 = Il-28, *izdeliye* 6 = Il-28U;
	3	year of manufacture (1953);
	0	= MMZ No. 30 (the first digit is omitted for security reasons to confuse would-be spies);
	051	batch number;
	12	number of aircraft in the batch (up to 100?).

The c/n is sometimes stencilled on the fuselage nose and under the horizontal tail.

System 4: 184 Black, c/n 5901207:	5	year of manufacture (1955);
	9	= Irkutsk aircraft factory No. 39 (the first digit is omitted for security reasons);
	012	batch number;
	07	number of aircraft in the batch.

System 5: code unknown, c/n 6450301:	64	factory number (Voronezh aircraft factory);
	50	year of manufacture (1950);
	3	batch number;
	01	number of aircraft in the batch.

System 6: 01 Red, c/n 2402101:	2	year of manufacture (1952);
	4	= Voronezh aircraft factory No. 64 (the first digit is omitted for security reasons);
	021	batch number;
	01	number of aircraft in the batch.

The c/n is sometimes stencilled on the fin or under the horizontal tail.

System 7: unknown, c/n 0416601:	04	batch number;
	166	factory number (Omsk aircraft factory);
	01	number of aircraft in the batch.

System 8: 33 Red, c/n 56605702:	5	year of manufacture (1955);
	66	= Omsk aircraft factory No. 166 (the first digit is omitted for security reasons);
	057	batch number;
	02	number of aircraft in the batch.

The c/n is sometimes stencilled under the horizontal tail.

The Il-28 was built by several Soviet aircraft factories. These two *Beagle*s, 26 Blue and 27 Blue, were manufactured by the Moscow Machinery Factory No. 30; the former aircraft carries the c/n 55006424 on the nose. *(Yefim Gordon archive)*

***z**nah**mya troo**dah*) at Khodynka airfield right in the centre of Moscow, No. 64 in Voronezh and No. 166 in Omsk – started gearing up to build the Il-28. A fourth factory, No. 39 in Irkutsk, also began Il-28 production shortly afterwards (see next chapter).[11] Each factory had its own construction number system(s), explained on page 20:

After the type's first public appearance at the 1950 May Day parade in Moscow, NATO's Air Standards Co-ordinating Committee (ASCC) initially allocated the code name *Butcher* to the Il-28. However, this was promptly changed to *Beagle* to avoid confusion with the Tupolev Tu-16 medium bomber, which was code-named *Badger*.

11 Some sources state the Il-28 was also built by plants No. 1, No. 18 (both in Kuibyshev, now Samara) and No. 23 in Fili, then a suburb of Moscow, but this appears highly unlikely.

2.

The Il-28 Family

Il-28 *Beagle* bomber

The basic bomber version was built in Moscow, Voronezh and Omsk; the first production aircraft left the Moscow production line in March 1950. The aircraft was built in huge numbers (no fewer than 6,316 copies of all versions were built in the USSR alone in 1950–5!), becoming one of the most prolific types in service with the VVS. MMZ No. 30 in Moscow, which was the main manufacturer of the type, turned out more than 100 aircraft per month at peak periods.

Various improvements were introduced in the course of production. Among other things, the Il-28 received more effective formation lights for station-keeping during flights of bomber formations at night. The cockpit windshield received an electric de-icing system, and hot air de-icing was introduced on the engine air intake leading edges. Optically flat windshield sidelights were tested (probably on an uncoded example with the c/n 52005714) in an effort to reduce distortions and improve cockpit visibility, but this feature was apparently not fitted to standard production aircraft.

Four shut-off valves were introduced in the fuel system to seal off a punctured tank in the event of battle damage, preventing loss of fuel (eventually the *Beagle* got self-sealing fuel tanks, which theoretically took care of the problem). Fuel cell No. 3 was divided into cells Nos. 3A and 3B; the capacity of these cells was carefully calculated in order to preserve the CG position as the fuel was burned off, obviating the need for fuel transfer.

(**Note:** Some sources claimed that the CG shift problem associated with fuel burn-off was still there and was, in fact, the Il-28's only major shortcoming which was never eliminated, because of the lack of an automatic fuel transfer system maintaining CG position. Since the forward fuel cells accommodated more fuel than the rear fuel cells, the Il-28's CG gradually shifted forward. This was especially unwelcome during landing; the pilot had to keep an eye on the fuel meters and activate the fuel transfer pump at the right moment. The pump worked slowly, and as the pilot had to concentrate on flying the aircraft during the landing approach he often

The Il-28 incorporated various changes made in the course of production; among other things, the transparency immediately aft of the cockpit where the DF aerial was located was replaced by an opaque dielectric fairing. *(Yefim Gordon archive)*

A trio of red-coded *Beagles* cruises in V formation. *(Yefim Gordon archive)*

51 Blue, a production Il-28, in flight. Note that the tail cannon are in the fully raised position. *(Yefim Gordon archive)*

This view illustrates the clean lines of the *Beagle*, as well as the large diameter of the engine nacelles. *(Sergey and Dmitriy Komissarov archive)*

This Il-28, 30 Red, is unusual in having three non-standard rod aerials under the aft fuselage. *(Yefim Gordon archive)*

10 Red, another Il-28 bristling with non-standard aerials. *(Sergey and Dmitriy Komissarov archive)*

forgot to turn it off in time. As a result, the CG would now be too far aft and the aircraft assumed an excessively nose-high attitude, with high angles of attack which were difficult to counter by elevator input. To make up for the missing system, Il-28 pilots would ask the navigators to remind them to switch off the pump in time.)

New ejection seats were fitted, replacing the earlier model; these featured leg restraints, a face protection visor and a seat belt tightening mechanism. Finally, a brake parachute was provided to shorten the landing run; this feature was tested on Il-28 c/n 2007[1] pursuant to a Ministry of Aircraft Industry (MAP) order of 11 January 1951. However, everything comes at a price, and these modifications were expected to increase empty weight by 240 kg (529 lb). Hence Ilyushin engineers took measures to achieve an identical weight reduction, lightening the rear fuselage structure, tail unit and Il-K6 turret, removing the anti-flutter weights from the wings, etc. Additionally, air bleed valves were incorporated in the engine nacelles to prevent engine surge, and the OSP-48 ILS was replaced by a more advanced SP-50 *Materik* (Continent) ILS.

Table 4 details the changes introduced at the production lines.

For the development of the Il-28 bomber, Sergey V. Ilyushin, M. F. Astakhov, Valeriy A. Borog, V. N. Boogaiskiy, N. F. Zotov, A. Ya. Levin, G. M. Litvinovich, M. I. Nikitin, B. V. Pavlovskiy, K. V. Rogov, Ye. I. Sankov and V. A. Fyodorov were awarded the prestigious Stalin Prize (2nd Class) on 12 March 1951 for outstanding inventions and improvements in the field of machinery design.

The basic bomber soon evolved into a range of specialized versions which expanded the *Beagle*'s combat potential perceptibly.

1 Only the batch number and number of aircraft in the batch were stated in MAP documents; however, considering the time when the order was issued, the aircraft was probably Moscow-built and the full c/n may be 50302007.

Table 4. Manufacturing changes introduced at production lines

Modification	Incorporated (starting with aircraft c/n ...)		
	Plant No. 30	Plant No. 64	Plant No. 166
Round ventilation window moved from hinged canopy section to port windshield sidelight to improve visibility and canopy strength; ventilation window reduced in diameter and glazing thickness reduced for better transparency	50301408	all aircraft (from c/n 6450001 onwards)	all aircraft (from c/n 0016601 onwards)
Anti-flutter weights between wing ribs 28 and 32 deleted	53005005	3402701	36603509
Anti-surge bleed valves installed	50301801	6450301	0416601

A night-time shot of a typical production *Beagle*. *(Yefim Gordon archive)*

The unserialled prototype of the Il-28U trainer undergoing evaluation with the Soviet Air Force in early 1950. *(Yefim Gordon archive)*

Another unserialled example, this time a production *Mascot*. *(Yefim Gordon archive)*

Il-28U *Mascot* trainer

Specialized versions began appearing before long. Predictably, the first of these was a conversion trainer easing the transition from Second World War-vintage piston-engined types to the jet bomber. The OKB was immediately tasked with creating such an aircraft; development work began in September 1949, and on 14 October Sergey V. Ilyushin approved the advanced development project of the Il-28U trainer (*oo**cheb**nyy* – training, used attributively) powered by VK-1 engines.

Soviet Air Force Il-28U 85 Red comes in to land. *(Yefim Gordon archive)*

The Il-28U – erroneously called UIl-28 in some sources – differed from the basic bomber primarily in having a new nose grafted on in place of the extensively glazed navigator's station (up to fuselage frame No. 6). It incorporated the instructor's cockpit with a stepped windscreen, rather like the flight deck of an airliner *en miniature*; the trainee pilot sat in the standard cockpit. According to some Western authors, what Ilyushin did was the best way to ruin the sleek lines of the Il-28; the result certainly looked bizarre, but both the trainee and the instructor enjoyed an unrestricted field of view.

The trainee's cockpit was virtually identical to that of the standard bomber except for a cut-out in

This view of 87 Red shows clearly that the *Mascot* lacked armament and radar. *(Yefim Gordon archive)*

the instrument panel permitting visual contact with the instructor, which required some of the flight instruments to be relocated. The front cockpit featured a complete set of flight controls and instruments; the instructor had complete control over the trainee's actions and could take over if necessary by flipping some switches, barring the trainee from flying the aircraft.

All armament and bomb-aiming equipment, including the radar, were deleted. Still, the Il-28U could be used for training gunners/radio operators, for which the former gunner's station was suitably equipped. The capacity of the fuel system was reduced to 6,600 lit. (1,452 imp. gal.) and the fuel load to 5,500 kg (12,125 lb). To maintain CG position the Il-K6 tail turret was substituted by 250 kg (551 lb) of ballast on the prototype. According to OKB calculations, production aircraft were to have 200 kg (440 lb) of ballast, but it was found possible to reduce this to 130 kg (286 lb).

Other changes included removal of the RV-10 radio altimeter and the fuel tank inert gas pressurization system. The Il-28U was equipped with an RSIU-3B radio (instead of the bomber's RSU-5), an AP-5 autopilot, a Bariy-M (Barium-M) IFF transponder, an SPU-5 intercom, an RV-2 radio altimeter and a Materik-B ILS with SD-1 distance-measuring equipment.

On 21 February 1950 a standard *Beagle* was delivered to Ilyushin's experimental shop at Khodynka (MMZ No. 240), straight off the MMZ No. 30 production line, for conversion into the Il-28U prototype. Piloted by Vladimir K. Kokkinaki, the trainer took to the air on 18 March, with B. A. Goloobev as flight engineer and B. A. Yerofeyev as radio operator; A. P. Vinogradov was the engineer in charge of the flight tests.

It was soon discovered that performance and handling were virtually identical to that of the standard bomber, except for the marginally better climb rate. The Il-28U was stable throughout its flight envelope, remaining well balanced at Mach 0.78. It performed all manoeuvres the bomber version was to make; turns with 70–80° bank could be made without any trouble and the aircraft gained 2,000 m (6,560 ft) during a yo-yo manoeuvre. Flying the aircraft from the instructor's seat was just as simple and enjoyable as from the rear cockpit. Like the other versions, the trainer could be fitted with PSR-1500-15 JATO boosters.

The specifications of the Il-28U prototype obtained at the manufacturer's flight tests are indicated in Table 5.

The manufacturer's flight test programme was completed on 30 March 1950. By then a bomber regiment commanded by Lt-Col A. A. Anpilov, Hero of the Soviet Union, was taking delivery of production Il-28 bombers. Therefore it was decided to hand over the Il-28U prototype to that unit for evaluation in order to speed up conversion training. This enabled Anpilov's unit to achieve initial operational

Table 5. Il-28U prototype specifications obtained at manufacturer's flight tests

Length overall	17.65 m (57 ft 10.88 in.)
Height on ground	6.0 m (19 ft 8.22 in.)
Span	21.45 m (70 ft 4.48 in.)
Wing area	60.8 m² (653.76 sq. ft)
Wing loading	288 kg/m² (1,400 lb/ft²)
Power loading at sea level	3.25 kg/kgp (lb/lb st)
Operating empty weight	11,760 kg (25,925 lb)*
Normal all-up weight	17,560 kg (38,712 lb)
Payload	5,800 kg (12,786 lb)
Fuel load	5,500 kg (12,125 lb)
Top speed: at 3,000 m (9,842 ft)	843 km/h (455.67 kt)
at 5,000 m (16,404 ft)	820 km/h (443.24 kt)
Rate of climb at sea level with a 17,020 kg (37,522 lb) TOW	17.0 m/sec (3,345 ft/min)
Climb time to 5,000 m with a 17,020 kg TOW	5.5 min
Maximum range with a 17,020 kg TOW	2,400 km (1,490 miles)
Take-off run	800 m (2,624 ft)**
Landing run	1,170 m (3,838 ft)**

Notes:

* With 250 kg (551 lb) of ballast.

** Ilyushin OKB data.

An Il-28U makes a flypast during a military parade, flanked by two MiG-19P *Farmer-B* all-weather interceptors. *(Boris Vdovenko)*

An Il-28U about to become airborne. The picture does not show how close the bird on the right is to the aircraft. *(Yefim Gordon archive)*

capability in time to participate in the 1950 May Day parade in Moscow (which of course was largely a matter of prestige); the trainer prototype took part in this parade, together with production *Beagle*s. Then the Il-28U was turned over to NII VVS for State acceptance trials which took place on 13–27 May; the act of acceptance was signed by Soviet Air Force C-in-C Air Marshal P. F. Zhigarev on 8 June.

The type entered large-scale production at MMZ No. 30 pursuant to an MAP order of 21 July 1950 (all Il-28Us were built in Moscow), and remained the principal trainer for Soviet and WarPac tactical bomber pilots well into the 1970s. Soviet trainers were assigned NATO code names in the miscellaneous aircraft category at the time – a practice later discontinued; accordingly the Il-28U was codenamed *Mascot*. On production Il-28Us the empty operating weight rose to 11,900 kg (26,234 lb) and the all-up weight to 17,700 kg (39,021 lb), reduction in ballast notwithstanding.

The transition from the Il-28U to the bomber version did not require additional training. The report of the State commission said that a pilot with 350–400 hrs' total time on anything from the Polikarpov Po-2 *ab initio* trainer to the Tu-2 bomber could fly the Il-28 solo after only two to four flights on the trainer version. The Naval Air Arm (AVMF

Stills from a motion picture showing an Il-28U in action. *(Sergey and Dmitriy Komissarov archive)*

– *Aviahtsiya voyenno-morskovo flota*) also operated the *Mascot*; the first naval aviation unit to receive the Il-28U in October 1951 was the 943rd MTAP (*minno-torpednyy aviapolk* – minelaying and torpedo-bomber regiment).

Il-28U ejection trainer version

On 10 December 1953 the Minister of Aircraft Industry issued an order concerning the development of a version of the Il-28U specially modified for training *Beagle* crews in ejection techniques. This aircraft's *raison d'être* was that the crews were apprehensive about the bomber's first-generation ejection seat, fearing serious injuries in the event of an ejection at low altitude or on landing, when most accidents happen. It was necessary to overcome this psychological obstacle and build up the pilots' confidence in the aircraft.

The Ilyushin OKB delivered a set of manufacturing documents for the ejection trainer to MMZ No. 30 on 5 March 1954. Unfortunately it is not known how many *Mascots*, if any, were built in this configuration.

Il-28R tactical reconnaissance aircraft

On 5 March 1950 another Moscow-built Il-28 powered by VK-1 engines was delivered to MMZ No. 240 for conversion into the prototype of the Il-28R ([*samolyot-*] *razvedchik*) reconnaissance aircraft. The unserialled aircraft entered flight test on 19 April 1950, one month and one day after the first flight of the Il-28U, flown by pilot Vladimir K. Kokkinaki, flight engineer I. B. Küss and radio operator B. A. Yerofeyev. Once again A. P. Vinogradov was in charge of the flight tests.

The Il-28R was intended for tactical photo

The prototype of the Il-28R photo reconnaissance aircraft. *(Yefim Gordon archive)*

Another view of the Il-28R prototype. Note the twin rod aerials on the upper fuselage. *(Yefim Gordon archive)*

reconnaissance (PHOTINT) to meet the objectives of fronts (in a war scenario), fleets and air armies. For day reconnaissance the aircraft could carry a PHOTINT suite comprising two AFA-33/100 or AFA-33/75 cameras on AKAFU mounts in the forward and centre parts of the (former) bomb bay for high/medium-altitude photography, one AFA-33/20 or AFA-42/20 (AFA-RB/20) downward-looking camera in the rear part of the bomb bay and one AFA-33/50 or AFA-33/75 camera mounted obliquely on the port side in a special camera bay in the aft fuselage. Alternatively, some aircraft were fitted with two AFA-42/100 or AFA-42/75 cameras on the forward mount.

For night reconnaissance the Il-28R carried either two NAFA-3S/50 cameras or one NAFA-MK-75 (or NAFA-MK-50) camera in the forward part of the bomb bay. The rest of the bay was occupied by twelve 50 kg (110 lb) FotAB-50-35 flare bombs;[2] this number was reduced to six if a long-range fuel tank was fitted. The bombs were dropped using an NKPB-7 bomb sight which could be used at up to 11,500 m (37,729 ft). (It should be noted that one Russian source gives rather different data: three AFA-33 cameras with varying focal lengths (100, 75 and 20 cm) and one AFA-RB camera for day sorties and two NAFA-3S cameras for night sorties, assisted by FotAB-100-60, FotAB-50-35, SAB-100-55 or SAB-100-35 flare bombs.) The cameras were installed in special containers heated by air from the cockpit heating and pressurization system to prevent the lubricant from freezing at high altitude; the night cameras, however, did not have such containers.

To extend range the capacity of the fuel system was increased to 9,550 lit./8,000 kg (2,101 imp. gal./17,636 lb). This was done by installing a 750 lit. (165 imp. gal.) long-range tank in the aft portion of the bomb bay, which required the standard fuel cell No. 3 to be removed, and two 950 lit. (209 imp. gal.) drop tanks at the wingtips. As compared to the standard bomber, this amounted to 1,650 lit. (363 imp. gal.) of additional fuel.[3] The increased mission time (up to five hours) necessitated the provision of additional oxygen for the crew.

Depending on the equipment fit the reconnaissance version's MTOW was 22,685–22,720 kg (50,011–50,088 lb). Therefore the main landing gear units were reinforced and fitted with bigger wheels measuring 1,260 × 390 mm (49.6 × 15.35 in.) instead of the usual 1,150 × 355 mm (45.27 × 13.97 in.); besides, the landing gear was actuated hydraulically, not pneumatically, and retracted in just eight

2 NAFA = *nochnoy* ***aero******foto****appar****aht*** – aircraft camera for night operations; AKAFU = *avtomati****ch****eskaya ka****ch****ayusch-chayasya* ***aero******foto****oust****an****ovka* – automatic tilting mount for aircraft cameras; FotAB = *fotogra****fich****eskaya* ***avia******b****omba* – photo bomb (i.e. flare bomb for aerial photography); SAB = *svetyaschchaya* ***avia******b****omba* – flare bomb.

3 Some sources quoted a figure of 2,660 lit. (585.2 imp. gal.) of additional fuel. Also, some documents state that the additional fuselage tank held 760 lit. (167.2 imp. gal.), making for a total internal fuel volume of 9,560 lit. (2,103.2 imp. gal.), and the drop tanks each held 900 lit. (198 imp. gal.).

A production Il-28R operated by the Polish Air Force. Note the black anti-glare panels on the wingtip tanks. *(Wojskowa Agencja Fotograficzna)*

Close-up of the wingtip drop tanks on the same aircraft, 03 Red; the drop tanks were the chief recognition feature of the reconnaissance version. *(Wojskowa Agencja Fotograficzna)*

seconds – much faster than on the standard bomber. The higher gross weight of the Il-28R also led the designers to introduce a unique feature minimizing wear and tear on the tyres: the mainwheels were spun up automatically by hydraulic motors when the gear was extended. According to the crews, this resulted in an exceptionally smooth touch-down.

Owing to the installation of camera controls the starboard fixed NR-23 cannon had to be deleted as a weight-saving measure. The PSBN-M radar was sometimes removed as well; in that case 110 kg (242.5 lb) of ballast was carried in the navigator's compartment for CG reasons. Some changes were made to the avionics fit; the reconnaissance version featured a Magniy-M (Magnesium-M) IFF interrogator, an RSB-5 communications radio with a US-P receiver, an RSIU-3 command radio, an SPU-5 intercom, RV-2 and RV-10 radio altimeters, an SP-50 Materik ILS, etc. For overwater flights the Il-28R could carry an LAS-3 inflatable rescue dinghy (***lod**ka avareeyno-spasahtel'naya*) in the bomb bay; this could be dropped by either the pilot or the gunner and inflated automatically by a rip cord.

The performance of the Il-28R was broadly similar to that of the basic bomber, except that range in high-altitude cruise increased to 3,150 km (1,702 nm); the combat radius 740 km (400 nm) at 5,000 m (16,404 ft) and 1,140 km (616 nm) at 10,000 m (32,808 ft). Indicated airspeed was limited to 750 km/h (416 kt) at up to 4,000 m (13,123 ft), and Mach 0.78 above that altitude. Kokkinaki reported that handling and cockpit visibility remained unchanged. High-speed aerial photography at various altitudes did not affect piloting techniques. The autopilot, as well as the heated and pressurized cockpits, reduced crew fatigue, which is especially important for a reconnaissance aircraft.

Initial flight testing was completed on 29 June 1950. After passing the State acceptance trials on 23 November, the Il-28R was ordered into production on 8 December 1951 and joined the VVS inventory. Initially the reconnaissance version was built in Moscow, but from 1953 onwards Il-28R production was passed on to aircraft factory No. 39 in Irkutsk, which had previously built the Tu-14T.

The performance of the production Il-28 and Il-28R is compared in Table 6.

The field performance of the bomber and reconnaissance versions is compared in Table 7.

Table 6. Performance comparison: production Il-28 and Il-28R

	Il-28	Il-28R
Empty weight, kg (lb)	12,720 (28,042)	13,250 (29,210)
All-up weight, kg (lb):		
normal	18,400 (40,564)	20,020 (44,135)
in overload configuration	22,000 (48,500)	22,490 (49,581)
Fuel capacity, lit. (imp. gal.)	8,000 (1,760)	9,550 (2,101)
Top speed, km/h (kt)	902 (487)	876 (473)
at altitude, m (ft)	4,500 (14,763)	5,000 (16,404)*
Service ceiling, m (ft)	12,400 (40,682)	12,300 (40,354)
Time to service ceiling, min	37	42
Range, km (miles):		
at 5,000 m (16,404 ft)	1,790 (1,111)	2,020 (1,242)
cruising at, km/h (kt)	556 (300)	547 (295)
at 10,000 m (32,808 ft)	2,450 (1,521)	2,780 (1,726)
cruising at, km/h (kt)	698 (377)	670 (362)
at 10,000 m (32,808 ft)	2,580 (1,602)	3,040 (1,888)
cruising at, km/h (kt)	690 (373)	670 (362)

Note:

* The Il-28R's indicated airspeed below 4,000 m (13,123 ft) was limited to 750 km/h (405 kt); the Mach limit above 4,000 m was 0.78.

Table 7. Comparison of field performance: bomber and reconnaissance versions

	TOW, kg (lb)	Unstick speed, km/h (kt)	Take-off run, m (ft)	Landing speed, km/h (kt)	Landing run, m (ft)
a) paved runway					
Il-28	20,100 (44,312)	240 (129)	1,400 (4,593)	200–205 (108–110)	1,500 (4,921)
Il-28R	19,800/22,200 (43,650/48,941)	259/274 (140/148)	1,610/2,150 (5,282/7,053)	220–225 (119–121)	1,620 (5,315)
b) unpaved runway (dirt strip)					
Il-28	20,100 (44,312)	240 (129)	1,700 (5,577)	200–205 (108–110)	1,200 (3,937)
Il-28R	19,800/22,200 (43,650/48,941)	259/274 (140/148)	1,720/2,300 (5,643/7,546)	220–225 (119–121)	1,300 (4,265)

Il-28RTR ELINT aircraft

Apart from the Il-28R PHOTINT aircraft, the *Beagle* also had an electronic intelligence (ELINT) version designated Il-28RTR ([*samo**lyot***] ***rah**diotekh**nich**eskoy razve**dk**i*) reconnaissance aircraft powered by VK-1 engines. Outwardly it could be identified by a second teardrop-shaped dielectric fairing installed in lieu of the faired-over bomb bay doors. The Il-28RTR was supplied to both the VVS and the air forces of some of the Soviet Union's allies, including Czechoslovakia and Hungary.

Il-28REB (?) ECM aircraft

Another specialized version was intended for electronic countermeasures (ECM). Some sources claim the aircraft was designated Il-28REB (***rah**dioelek**tron**naya bor'**bah*** – ECM). The main identification feature of this version was the cylindrical wingtip pods reminiscent of the Il-28R's drop tanks, but featuring dielectric front and rear portions concealing emitter antennas. The ECM version was also supplied to Czechoslovakia.

A Hungarian Air Force Il-28RTR ELINT aircraft, showing clearly the dielectric teardrop fairing over ELINT equipment aft of the standard radome. *(Yefim Gordon archive)*

A Czech Air Force example of the ECM version sometimes referred to as Il-28REB. *(Yefim Gordon archive)*

Il-28 radiation reconnaissance aircraft

The Soviet Air Force's 647th Special Composite Support Air Regiment operating in support of the 71st Nuclear Weapons Proving Ground in Totskoye, Orenburg Region, operated two Il-28s fitted with air sampling pods for radiation reconnaissance. Compressed-air bottles were installed in the bomb bays to pressurize the cockpits, ensuring that radioactive products would not enter. As an additional protective measure the cockpit walls were lined with lead, and radiometers were provided for the crew. Together with similarly modified aircraft and helicopters of various types, these *Beagle*s flew through radioactive clouds in the wake of nuclear tests, measuring radiation levels.

Il-28 torpedo-bomber conversion

The AVMF also operated the *Beagle* after August 1951; this aircraft suited the Soviet Navy better than the Tu-14, being lighter and more agile. Initially the naval Il-28s were operated in standard bomber configuration; however, as early as 1 June 1950 the Council of Ministers ordered the development of a torpedo-bomber version. The bomb bay was modified to carry one RAT-52 rocket-propelled torpedo internally. Developed by NII-2,[4] this weapon was conceived as a homing torpedo, but the guidance system was considered too complicated and was deleted in the production version. The torpedo weighed 627 kg (1,382 lb) and had a 243 kg (535 lb) warhead.

Before dropping the torpedo the navigator set its travel depth (2–8 m/6.5–26 ft), charged the torpedo's condensers and began the run-in to the target as usual. At the appropriate moment the bomb sight automatically triggered the drop mechanism. One second later the small propeller-shaped drag parachute deployed and the torpedo descended vertically, dropping quickly like a bomb. The main parachute deployed at 500 m (1,640 ft), reducing descent speed. It separated after the torpedo entered the water, then the foreplanes were brought into play to turn the torpedo horizontally and were jettisoned immediately afterwards. Then the solid-fuel rocket motor fired and the torpedo accelerated to 58–68 kt (107–130 km/h); by comparison, conventional torpedoes with steam turbines could not travel faster than 40–45 kt. Time from drop to impact was only about 35 seconds, which left the target no time for evasive action.

The chief shortcoming of the RAT-52 was the rocket motor's short burn time, resulting in a range of only 550–600 m (1,804–1,968 ft), which took the bomber uncomfortably close to the target (within range of the ship's air defences). On the other hand,

4 Later became the State Research Institute of Aircraft Systems (GosNII AS – *Gosoo**dahr**stvennyy naoo**ch**no-issle-dovatel'skiy insti**toot** aviatsee**on**nykh sis**tem***).

An Il-28 converted into a torpedo-bomber is about to be loaded with a RAT-52 torpedo. Note the foreplanes on the weapon's nose bringing the torpedo into level attitude after splashdown. *(Yefim Gordon archive)*

10 Red, another *Beagle* converted for torpedo-bomber duties, is prepared for a mission (note fuel hoses). *(Yefim Gordon archive)*

The second prototype of the purpose-built Il-28T torpedo-bomber. The non-standard nose glazing is clearly visible, as are the angular cockpit windshield and undernose blister for the PTN-52 optical sight. *(Yefim Gordon archive)*

the torpedo could be dropped at any altitude between 1,500 m (4,920 ft) and the aircraft's service ceiling at a speed of up to 800 km/h (444 kt), which was of particular importance for jet torpedo-bombers. Live drops at the Soviet Navy's test range showed a kill probability of 17–38 per cent in a single-torpedo attack.

During trials held on the Black Sea in September–November 1952, Tu-14T and modified Il-28 torpedo-bombers successfully dropped 54 RAT-52 torpedoes, both inert and live; targeting was done using an OPB-6SR sight on both aircraft. The RAT-52 was officially included in the AVMF inventory on 4 February 1953. It could be carried by Tu-14T torpedo-bombers and converted Il-28s (deliveries of the latter began the same year). With one torpedo the modified Il-28T had an 18,400 kg (40,564 lb) TOW and a top speed of 906 km/h (503 kt); service ceiling and range were 12,500 m (41,010 ft) and 2,400 km (1,490 miles) respectively.

However, the converted Il-28 had some serious deficiencies. It carried only about one third of its design payload and could not carry other models of torpedoes internally, as they were too long to fit into the standard bomb bay. Also, the Soviet Naval Air Arm had large stocks of pre-war 45-36MAN torpedoes (i.e. 450 mm/17.7 in. calibre, 1954 model; MAN = [*torpeda*] *modernizeerovannaya, aviatsion***-***naya,* ***ni****zkovysotnaya* – updated aircraft torpedo for low-altitude attacks) which it wished to use on the Il-28. However, it turned out that the bomber's high speed rendered these torpedoes unsuitable. The weapon had to undergo a lengthy upgrade programme, emerging in 1956 as the 45-56NT torpedo (NT = ***n****izkoye* ***t****orpedometahniye* – low-altitude torpedo attack) which could be dropped at 120–230 m (393–754 ft) and 550–600 km/h (297–324 kt).

Il-28T torpedo-bomber (first use of designation)

Apparently the engineers were aware of the shortcomings of the quick-fix torpedo-bomber conversion all along, because development of a dedicated torpedo-bomber, designated Il-28T (*torpedonosets*), also began in 1950. The mock-up review commission signed the act of acceptance on 7 July that year.

The aircraft was intended for high- and low-altitude torpedo attacks and minelaying. It differed from standard Il-28s and those converted into torpedo-bombers primarily in having a weapons bay lengthened from 4.18 m (13 ft 8.56 in.) to 6.66 m

The same aircraft, pictured most probably at Moscow-Khodynka, with an Il-12 airliner in the background. The c/n 50301104 is visible on the nose. *(Yefim Gordon archive)*

(21 ft 10.2 in.) and having the wings moved back 100 mm (3.93 in.), with appropriate changes to the fuselage structure. The modification of the weapons bay and the provision of an LAS-3 rescue dinghy required changes to fuel cells Nos. 2, 3 4 and 5. This reduced internal fuel capacity from 8,000 lit. (1,760 imp. gal.) to 4,770 lit. (1,269.4 imp. gal.) and the fuel load from 6,600 kg (14,550 lb) to 5,080 kg (11,199 lb). To compensate for this the Il-28T had provisions for 950 lit. (209 imp. gal.) tip tanks, each holding 750 kg (1,653 lb) of fuel, as on the Il-28R.

The starboard fixed NR-23 cannon and its round counter were deleted, as was the AFA-33/75 (or NAFA-MK) camera. Instead, two AFA-BA/400 vertical cameras and an AKS-1 hand-driven cine-camera were installed to record the strike results. Other new equipment items included a Magniy IFF interrogator, a PTN-45 low-altitude sight (***pritsel** torpednyy **nizkovysotnyy*** – sight optimized for low-level torpedo drops) and a separate PP-1 high-altitude sight also used for dropping anti-shipping mines; a Model 1010 electric heater was provided to defrost the sighting window of the PTN-45. Some of the existing equipment items were relocated, and additional armour protection was provided for the pilot and navigator.

The normal ordnance load was 1,000 kg (2,204 lb), which permitted carriage of one torpedo of various models (45-36AVA, TAS, TAV, RAT-52 or A-2), or two AMD-500 anti-shipping mines, or one AMD-1000, AMD-M or Type A mine. If necessary the Il-28T could carry up to 3,000 kg (6,613 lb) of weapons at the expense of a reduced fuel load and hence shorter range. In that case possible weapons configurations were two 45-46AMV torpedoes totalling 1,940 kg (4,276 lb), or one 1,500 kg (3,306 lb) TOZ torpedo, or one 1,100 kg (2,425 lb) AMD-1000 mine, or four AMD-500 mines (2,000 kg/4,409 lb), or two Serpey mines (2,500 kg/5,511 lb), or two Lira (Lyre) mines (1,940 kg/4,276 lb), or two Desna mines (1,500 kg).[5]

Despite the relocated wings, the external dimensions were identical to those of the Il-28R. The Il-28T could be refitted and used as a conventional bomber with a bomb load equal to that of the standard *Beagle*.

Prototype conversion was completed in 1950. The first prototype Il-28T (c/n 50301106) first flew on

5 The meaning of the name *Serpey* is not known but it sounds suspiciously like an anagram of *Persey* (Perseus).

Table 8. Il-28T specifications

	Manufacturer's estimates	Manufacturer's flight tests	State acceptance trials
Wing loading, kg/m² (lb/sq. ft)	308 (1,497)	308 (1,497)	308 (1,497)
Power loading at S/L, kg/kgp (lb/lb st)	3.4	3.48	3.48
Empty weight, kg (lb)	13,085 (28,847)	13,370 (29,475)	13,370 (29,475)
Normal AUW, kg (lb)	18,400 (40,564)	18,760 (41,358)*	18,763 (41,364)*
Maximum AUW, kg (lb)	21,330 (47,023)	21,620 (47,663)*	21,630 (47,685)*
Landing weight, kg (lb)	13,840 (30,511)	n.a.	n.a.
Internal fuel load, kg (lb)	3,600 (7,936)	3,800 (8,377)	3,800 (8,377)
Fuel load with tip tanks, kg (lb)	6,580 (14,506)	6,475 (14,274)	6,485 (14,296)
Payload, kg (lb): normal	5,315 (11,717)	5,390 (11,882)	5,390 (11,882)
maximum	8,245 (18,176)	8,250 (18,187)	8,260 (18,209)
Top speed (with tip tanks), km/h (kt):			
at 1,000 m (3,280 ft)	n.a.	802 (433.5)	785/800** (424.3/432.4)
at 5,000 m (16,404 ft)	n.a.	874 (472.4)	827/877** (447.0/474.0)
at 10,000 m (32,808 ft)	n.a.	836 (451.8)	802/840** (433.5/454.0)
Landing speed, km/h (kt)	n.a.	n.a.	178 (96.2)
Rate of climb, m/sec (ft/min):			
at S/L	n.a.	13.4 (2,637)	14.7 (2,893)
at 5,000 m	n.a.	7.8 (1,535)	9.05 (1.781)
at 10,000 m	n.a.	2.3 (452)	3.3 (649)
Climb time, min: to 5,000 m	n.a.	8.0	7.1
to 10,000 m	n.a.	26.4	21.4
Service ceiling, m (ft)	n.a.	11,500 (37,729)	11,950 (39,206)
Maximum range with tip tanks and one 45-36AMV torpedo, km (miles)	2,200 (1,366)***	1,644/2,221 # (1,021/1,379)	2,149 (1,334) ##
Endurance with tip tanks and one 45-36AMV torpedo, km (miles)	n.a.	3 hr 03 min/ 3 hr 33 min #	3 hr 29 min/ 3 hr 41.5 min ‡‡‡
Take-off run, unassisted, m (ft)	n.a.	875/1,450 † (2,870/4,757)	950/1,395 †† (3,116/4,576)
Take-off run with JATO bottles, m (ft)	n.a.	770 (2,526) ‡	1,020 (3,346) ‡
Take-off distance, unassisted, m (ft)	n.a.	1,570/2,460 † (5,151/8,070)	2,000/2,630 †† (6,561/8,628)
Take-off distance with JATO bottles, m (ft)	n.a.	1,300 (4,265) ‡	2,410 (7,906) ‡
Landing run, m (ft)n.a.	n.a.	940 (3,084) ‡‡	
Landing distance, m (ft)	n.a.	n.a.	2,125 (6,971) ‡‡

Notes:

* With one 45-36AMV torpedo.

** At N (engine speed) = 11,200 rpm/11,560 rpm respectively.

*** With a 1,000 kg (2,204 lb) weapons load at 10,000–12,700 m (32,808–41,666 ft).

At 5,000 m (16,404 ft)/543 km/h (293 kt) and 10,000 m (32,808 ft)/645 km/h (348 kt) respectively.

At 10,000 m (32,808 ft) and 652 km/h (352 kt) with a 21,632 kg (47,689 lb) AUW.

† With an 18,768 kg (41,375 lb) normal AUW and a 21,620 kg (47,663 lb) maximum AUW.

†† With an 18,760 kg (41,357 lb) normal AUW and a 21,620 kg (47,663 lb) maximum AUW.

‡ With a 22,100 kg (48,721 lb) TOW.

‡‡ With a 15,000 kg (33,068 lb) landing weight.

‡‡‡ At 10,000 m (32,808 ft) and 652/569 km/h (352/307 kt) respectively with a 21,632 kg (47,689 lb) AUW.

Table 9. Torpedo attack configuration

Ordnance type	45-36AM	TAS	A-2	45-36AMV
Quantity	1	1	1	2
Ordnance weight, kg (lb)	1,043 (2,299)	1,533 (3,379)	615 (1,355)	2,128 (4,691)
Fuel load, kg (lb)	6,485 (14,296)	6,485 (14,296)	6,485 (14,296)	5,550 (12,235)
Take-off weight, kg (lb)	21,600 (47,619)	22,090 (48,699)	21,063 (46,435)	21,635 (47,696)

Table 10. Minelaying configuration

Ordnance type	AMD-500		AMD-1000	Lira		Serpey		Desna (on BD-4 rack)		IGDM
Quantity	2	4	1	1	2	1	2	1	2	1
Ordnance weight, kg (lb)	1,018 (2,244)	2,018 (4,448)	1,018 (2,244)	988 (2,178)	1,958 (4,316)	1,268 (2,795)	2,518 (5,551)	768 (1,693)	1,518 (3,346)	1,268 (2,794)
Fuel load, kg (lb)	6,485 (14,296)	5,550 (12,235)	6,485 (14,296)	6,485 (14,296)	5,700 (12,566)	6,485 (14,296)	4,800 (10,582)	6,485 (14,296)	6,150 (13,558)	6,485 (14,296)
TOW, kg (lb)	21,575 (47,564)	21,640 (47,707)	21,575 (47,564)	21,545 (47,497)	21,616 (47,654)	21,825 (48,115)	21,094 (46,503)	21,325 (47,012)	21,626 (47,676)	21,825 (48,115)

8 January 1951 with Vladimir K. Kokkinaki at the controls; N. D. Sorokin was the flight engineer and A. P. Vinogradov was the engineer in charge of the flight tests. The second prototype (c/n 50301104) joined the programme on 12 March 1951, making its maiden flight from Khodynka – again at the hands of Vladimir K. Kokkinaki. Outwardly the Il-28T prototypes differed from standard *Beagle*s in having a small Perspex blister under the nose accommodating the lower part of the PTN-45 sight, a non-standard navigator's glazing framework and a non-standard angular cockpit windshield with a rectangular windscreen and optically flat sidelights.

The manufacturer's tests were completed on 17 April 1951 (the test report was endorsed six days later). Then the Il-28T was submitted to the Soviet Navy's Research Institute No. 15 for State acceptance trials, which proceeded from 7 June to 25 July 1951 and also went successfully. In August 1951 the complete set of manufacturing documents was transferred to one of the production factories; the type entered limited production and service with the AVMF.[6] For this achievement a group of OKB-240 employees was again nominated for the Stalin Prize.

The specifications of the Il-28T are given in Table 8.

Tables 9 and 10 detail the Il-28T's weapons options.

Il-28T torpedo-bomber conversion (second use of designation)

In 1954 the improved 45-54VT torpedo (i.e. 450 mm calibre, 1954 model, VT = *vysotnoye torpedometahniye* – high-altitude torpedo attack) was included in the AVMF arsenal, followed by the 45-56NT torpedo two years later. Both types were powered by steam engines and were carried by the Tu-14T along with the RAT-52. In order to standardize the armament carried by Soviet torpedo-bombers and increase their punch, it was decided to upgrade the Il-28s then in service.

To this end a standard Il-28 torpedo bomber was retrofitted with two external BD-4T torpedo racks (***bah**lochnyy **der**zhahtel'* – beam-type [weapons] rack). The increased payload meant that the centre fuselage frames had to be reinforced. The aircraft was also fitted with the new PTN-55 low-altitude sight, albeit incomplete, which was concurrently being tested on a modified Tu-14T. This allowed the navigator to programme the torpedo to move in a zigzag (this feature was believed to increase kill probability but demanded a substantial increase in the torpedo's range) and feed target data into the torpedo's control module up to the moment of release.

The modified aircraft – which, rather confusingly, was again designated Il-28T – could carry three RAT-52 torpedoes (two externally and one internally) or two 45-54VT or 45-36NT torpedoes externally; alternatively, two AMD-500 anti-shipping mines could be carried externally. The weapons were dropped at altitudes of 40–400 m (131–1,312 ft) and speeds of 360–800 km/h (200–444 kt).

However, the Navy was displeased, claiming the

6 Some sources, though, claim the Il-28T did not enter production because of the protracted development of the 45-56NT torpedo and the inability to carry two RAT-52 torpedoes internally.

required modifications were too extensive. Besides, the high-drag external stores impaired the aircraft's performance and caused some restrictions on piloting techniques. Rotation at take-off became very difficult; the aircraft experienced severe vibration at high speed, almost certainly caused by the turbulence generated by the external torpedo racks. Tailplane buffet was commonly encountered in a shallow dive when two torpedoes were carried externally; if one torpedo was carried it generated so much drag as to render turns in the opposite direction impossible.

The aircraft completed its trials programme in 1955. All its shortcomings notwithstanding, the Navy expected to modify some of its Il-28s to this standard. However, this conversion programme never materialized because the Il-28 was getting long in the tooth and the Soviet bomber and torpedo-bomber force was re-equipping with the more modern Tu-16. Still, the PTN-55 sight *did* find its way into service.

Il-28N (Il-28A) nuclear-capable bomber

The Soviet military doctrine of the early 1950s demanded that tactical aviation was to possess nuclear capability. Several types of small tactical nuclear weapons, including the RDS-4 Tat'yana bomb, were under development at the time, and the Soviet government issued a directive demanding the development of new tactical bombers capable of delivering them. However, this would clearly be a time-consuming process, so it was decided to modify existing aircraft in service with the VVS, including the Il-28, for the nuclear role.

First, two Il-28s were specially modified by OKB-30 (the design bureau of MMZ No. 30) for testing the RDS-4 according to the specifications passed by OKB-11, which had developed the bomb. Among other things, the modification involved heat insulation and heating of the bomb bay, installation of special equipment to monitor the weapon's systems status, as well as test equipment to measure the parameters of the explosion, including cine-cameras capturing the development of the famous mushroom cloud.

The first drop of an RDS-4 from the Il-28 took place on 23 August 1953. On that occasion the bomb was in the so-called check configuration with data link sensors and a conventional warhead. The aircraft was flown by pilot V. I. Shapovalov, navigator/bomb aimer A. V. Koz'minykh and gunner/radio operator B. S. Soodakov. The weapon was dropped at 11,000 m (36,089 ft), detonating successfully at the preset altitude. Four RDS-4 bombs were

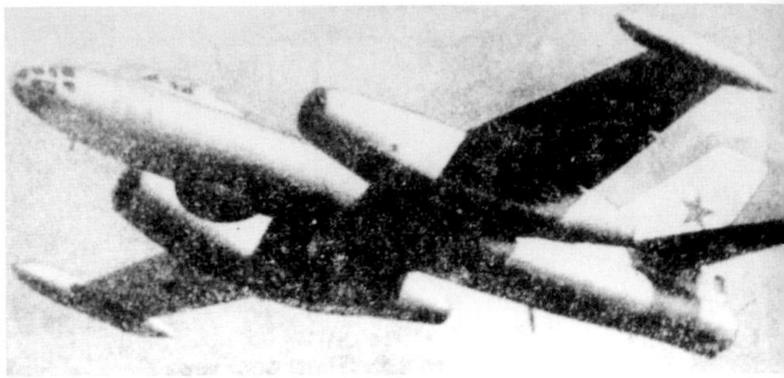

This *Beagle*, with a non-standard deep radome and drop tanks, is probably an Il-28N (Il-28A) nuclear-capable bomber. *(Yefim Gordon archive)*

dropped, with a day's interval in each case, between 29 September and 5 October 1954. All in all the test programme involved more than fifty flights, fifteen of which were weapon drops; the safety of landing with an unused bomb was checked, among other things.

After the successful completion of the trials the RDS-4 entered production; so did the nuclear-capable version of the *Beagle*, which was designated Il-28N (*nosi**tel'*** [***spets**boyepri**pah**sa*] – carrier of special, i.e. nuclear, munitions). Apart from the changes to the bomb bay, the aircraft differed from the standard bomber in having an updated avionics suite. The PSBN-M ground-mapping radar was replaced by an RBP-3 unit (***rah**diolokatsee**o**nnyy bombardi**ro**vochnyy pri**tsel*** – radar bomb sight) in a much deeper radome.[7] It indicated headings, distance to ground waypoints, altitude above such waypoints, ground speed and aircraft position. The bomb bay was provided with a heating system to keep the nuclear bomb's systems from freezing up, and the cockpits featured shutters protecting the crew from the flash of the nuclear explosion. An RSIU-5V UHF communications radio, a US-8 receiver, and RV-18 and RV-2 radio altimeters were fitted. The electrical system was modified to include PO-3000 (main) and PO-3000A (reserve) single-phase AC transformers.

The Il-28N's empty weight was 13,040 kg (28,747 lb) – 150 kg (330 lb) more than the standard bomber's; TOW was 18,550 kg (40,895 lb). The CG had shifted slightly aft, but this had virtually no effect on the aircraft's handling and performance.

Forty-two Il-28Ns were briefly deployed to Cuba in 1962 during the Cuban missile crisis. This version is sometimes referred to as Il-28A (***ah**tomnyy* – atomic, i.e. nuclear-capable).

Il-28S tactical bomber project

In 1949–50 OKB-240 sought ways of further improving the design of the basic Il-28. The main objective was to increase the bomber's speed and range. This was to be achieved by mating the existing fuselage and tail surfaces with all-new wings swept back 35° at quarter-chord and installing more powerful and fuel-efficient Klimov VK-5 centrifugal-flow turbojets. The VK-5 was a derivative of the production VK-1A uprated to 3,100 kgp (6,834 lb st) for take-off and 2,760 kgp (6,084 lb st) for cruise, differing mainly in having a more efficient compressor; the engine's dry weight and external dimensions remained unchanged. This undoubted achievement was made possible by the use of new heat-resistant alloys, a higher turbine temperature and more efficient cooling. Specific fuel consumption (SFC) was 6 per cent lower than that of the production VK-1A.

However, preliminary design studies showed that the swept-wing Il-28S (*strelo**vid**noye krylo* – swept wings) offered no significant advantages over the production *Beagle*. Moreover, the incorporation of new wings would incur major technological problems. Hence development of the Il-28S was abandoned – a decision later proved correct by the chief competitor's negative experience. The Tupolev OKB had achieved scant success with the experimental 'aircraft 82' (Tu-82) swept-wing tactical bomber (which, incidentally, closely resembled the would-be Il-28S).

7 Some sources claim the Il-28N was outwardly identical to the standard bomber.

Il-28RM experimental tactical reconnaissance aircraft

Meanwhile, the Ilyushin OKB attempted to introduce the new VK-5 powerplant on production versions of the straight-wing Il-28. Several government directives and MAP orders were issued, envisaging the installation of VK-5s on all three principal versions of the *Beagle* – conventional bomber, torpedo-bomber and reconnaissance aircraft.

The last version received the highest priority, since the VVS was desperate to extend the reach of its tactical reconnaissance aircraft. The PHOTINT aircraft then under development at the Mikoyan (OKB-155) and Yakovlev (OKB-115) design bureaux were *a priori* handicapped by inadequate range, being derived from tactical fighters; conversely, the Il-28R and 'aircraft 78' (Tu-78, the PHOTINT version of the Tu-14) were based on bombers designed to have much longer range. The 3,000 km (1,863 mile) range target was to be met by installing more fuel-efficient engines.

On 3 August 1951 the Council of Ministers issued directive No. 2817-1388ss, ordering the development of the Il-28RM ([*samo**lyot**-*] *raz**ved**chik, modifi**tsee**rovannyy* – reconnaissance aircraft, modified) powered by VK-5 engines. The deadline for submission for State acceptance trials was set at

The Il-28RM prototype; note the angular cockpit windshield. *(Yefim Gordon archive)*

The same aircraft with the drop tanks removed, revealing the vertically cut-off wingtips with drop tank fittings instead of the usual wingtip fairings. *(Yefim Gordon archive)*

Head-on view of the Il-28RM. *(Yefim Gordon archive)*

Table 11. Il-28RM specifications

	Manufacturer's flight tests	State acceptance trials
Length overall	17.65 m (57 ft 10.88 in.)	
Height on ground	6.0 m (19 ft 8.22 in.)	
Span	21.45 m (70 ft 4.48 in.)	
Wing area	60.8 m² (653.76 sq. ft)	
Wing loading, kg/m² (lb/ft²)	321 (1,560)	n.a.
Power loading at sea level, kg/kgp (lb/lb st)	3.12	n.a.
Operating empty weight, kg (lb)	13,485 (29,728)	13,467 (29,689)
Normal all-up weight, kg (lb)	19,500 (42,989)	20,200 (44,532)
Maximum AUW (with drop tanks), kg (lb)	22,950 (50,595)	22,930 (50,551)
Fuel load, kg (lb):		
internal	5,030 (11,089)	5,030 (11,089)
with drop tanks	8,250 (18,187)	8,200 (18,077)
Payload, kg (lb):		
normal	6,015 (13,260)	6,015 (13,260)
in overload configuration (with drop tanks)	9,467 (20,870)	n.a.
Top speed, km/h (kt):		
at 4,250 m (13,943 ft)	926/n.a.	n.a.
	(500.54/n.a.)*	
at 5,000 m (16,404 ft)	877/851	n.a.
	(474.0/460.0)**	891/863
at 6,600 m (21,653 ft)	n.a.	(481.62/466.48)**
		n.a./863
at 7,000 m (22,965 ft)	n.a.	(n.a./466.48)**
at 10,000 m (32,808 ft)	862/827	n.a./841
	(465.94/447.0)**	(n.a./454.59)**
Rate of climb, m/sec (ft/min):		
at sea level	24.5/17.0 (4,821/3,345)**	n.a.
at 5,000 m (16,404 ft)	15.4/10.3 (3,030/2,027)**	n.a.
at 10,000 m (32,808 ft)	6.6/3.4 (1,299/669)**	n.a.
Climb time, min:		
to 5,000 m (16,404 ft)	4.2/6.15**	6.2/n.a.**
to 10,000 m (32,808 ft)	12.4/9.3**	18.0/n.a.**
Service ceiling, m (ft)	13,050/12,175	12,500/11,500
	(42,814/39,944)**	(41,010/37,729)**
Range without drop tank separation, km (miles)	3,007 (1,867) #	2,090 (1,298) ##
Range with drop tank separation, km (miles)	3,042/3,254	3,250 (2,018) ‡
	(1,889/2,021) †	
Endurance without drop tank separation	4 hr 40 min #	n.a.
Endurance with drop tank separation	4 hr 39.5 min/	n.a.
	4 hr 49.5 min †	
Take-off run, m (ft)	963/1,233	995/1,295
	(3,159/4,045) ††	(3,264/4,248) ††
Take-off distance, m (ft)	1,807/2,477	2,030/2,400
	(5,928/8,126) ††	(6,660/7,874) ††

Notes:

* At take-off power (N = 11,560 rpm); other data for N = 11,200 rpm.

** With normal/maximum AUW – 19,700/22,570 kg (43,430/49,757 lb) respectively during manufacturer's flight tests and 20,200/22,930 kg (44,532/50,551 lb) respectively during State acceptance trials.

TOW 23,000 kg (50,705 lb), cruise altitude 10,000 m (32,808 ft) and cruising speed 670 km/h (362.16 kt).

TOW 22,930 kg (50,551 lb), cruise altitude 5,000 m (16,404 ft) and cruising speed 560 km/h (302.7 kt).

† TOW 23,000 kg (50,705 lb), cruise altitude 10,000/10,500–12,500 m (32,808/34,448–41,010 ft) and cruising speed 682/695 km/h (368.64/375.67 kt) respectively.

†† With normal/maximum TOW respectively.

‡ At optimum cruise altitude and cruising speed 665 km/h (359.45 kt).

Table 12. Il-28 VK-5-powered prototype specifications

	Manufacturer's flight tests		State acceptance trials	
	c/n 52003701	c/n 52003719	c/n 52003701	c/n 52003719
Length overall	17.65 m (57 ft 10.88 in.)			
Span	21.45 m (70 ft 4.48 in.)			
Wing area	60.8 m² (653.76 sq. ft)			
Wing loading, kg/m² (lb/ft²)	308 (1,496)	311 (1,511)	322 (1,565)	326 (1,584)
Power loading at sea level, kg/kgp (lb/lb st)	3.2	3.2	3.16	3.2
Operating empty weight, kg (lb)	13,350 (29,431)	13,560 (29,894)	13,113 (28,908)	13,365 (29,464)
Normal all-up weight, kg (lb)	18,710 (41,247)	18,920 (41,710)	19,600 (43,209)	19,850 (43,761)
Maximum AUW (with drop tanks), kg (lb)	24,090 (53,108)	24,300 (53,571)	24,050 (53,020)	24,220 (53,395)
Fuel load, kg (lb):				
internal	3,800 (8,377)	3,800 (8,377)	3,800 (8,377)	3,800 (8,377)
with drop tanks	8,000 (17,636)	8,000 (17,636)	8,150 (17,967)	8,050 (17,746)
Payload, kg (lb):				
normal	5,360 (11,816)	4,360 (9,612)	6,487 (14,301)	6,485 (14,296)
maximum	10,740 (23,677)	10,740 (23,677)	10,837 (23,891)	10,855 (23,930)
Top speed at 19,300 kg (42,548 lb) AUW and N = 11,560 rpm, km/h (kt):				
at S/L	800 (432.43)*	800 (432.43)*	800 (432.43)*	800 (432.43)*
at 2,850 m (21,653 ft)	917 (495.67)	n.a.	n.a.	n.a.
at 3,000 m (22,965 ft)	n.a.	918 (496.21)	911 (492.43)	900 (486.48)
at 4,000 m (13,943 ft)	n.a.	921 (497.83)	n.a.	n.a.
at 5,000 m (16,404 ft)	900 (486.48)	918 (496.21)	n.a.	n.a.
at 10,000 m (32,808 ft)	828 (447.56)	n.a.	844 (456.21)	844 (456.21)
Landing speed, km/h (kt)	189 (102)	186 (100.5)	n.a.	n.a.
Rate of climb at 19,300 kg (42,548 lb) AUW and N = 11,250 rpm, m/sec (ft/min):				
at sea level	21.5 (4,231)	19.5 (3,837)	n.a.	n.a.
at 5,000 m	13.9 (2,735)	13.1 (2,578)	n.a.	n.a.
at 10,000 m	6.5 (1,279)	6.75 (1,328)	n.a.	n.a.
Climb time at 19,300 kg AUW and N = 11,250 rpm, min:				
to 5,000 m	4.85	5.25	n.a.	n.a.
to 10,000 m	13.3	13.8	14.0	14.0
Effective range with drop tanks and 2,000 kg (4,409 lb) of bombs, km (miles)	3,000 (1,863)	3,000 (1,863)	2,710 (1,683)	2,670 (1,658)
Technical range with drop tanks and 2,000 kg of bombs, km (miles)	3,100 (1,925)*	3,012 (1,870)**	2,820/3,020 # (1,751/1,870)	2,790/2,980 ## (1,733/1,850)
Technical range without drop tanks and with 1,000 kg (2,204 lb) of bombs, km (miles)	1,298 (806)***	1,309 (1,870) ‡	n.a.	n.a.
Endurance with drop tanks and 2,000 kg of bombs	4 hr 51 min*	4 hr 33 min**	n.a.	n.a.
Endurance without drop tanks and with 1,000 kg of bombs	2 hr 07 min ***	2 hr 02 min ‡	n.a.	n.a.
Take-off run, m (ft):				
with normal TOW	920 (3,018)	945 (3,100)	1,000 (3,280)	1,050 (3,444)
with maximum TOW	1,410 (4,626) †	1,430 (4,691) ††	1,370 (4,494)	1,360 (4,462)
Take-off distance, m (ft):				
with normal TOW	1,875 (6,151)	2,000 (6,561)	1,760 (5,774)	1,954 (6,410)
with maximum TOW	2,525 (8,284) †	2,708 (8,884) ††	2,415 (7,923)	2,345 (7,693)
Landing run, m (ft):				
no airbrakes	913 (2,995)	n.a.	660 (2,165)	800 (2,624)
airbrakes deployed	607 (1,991)	524 (1,719)	550 (1,804)	660 (2,165)
Landing distance, m (ft):				
no airbrakes	1,692 (5,551)	n.a.	n.a.	n.a.
airbrakes and brake parachute deployed	1,255 (4,117)	(3,618)	n.a.	n.a.

March 1952 – a tight schedule which proved impossible to maintain. The unserialled Il-28RM prototype (c/n 52003714) first flew on 17 February 1952, but the manufacturer's flight tests were not completed until 12 April (the test report was signed on 29 April); thus the State acceptance trials did not commence until 10 July. The trials were duly completed on 15 January 1953.

The Il-28RM featured the latest version of the intended powerplant – the VK-5E (*ekonomichnyy* – fuel-efficient), incorporating additional measures aimed at reducing the SFC. This engine passed its State acceptance trials concurrently with the aircraft itself. The new engines necessitated a redesign of the engine bearers and engine nacelle structure, the engine control system had to be modified and the lower skins of the outer wings stiffened. No changes were made to the armament and equipment.

Nevertheless, the good performance of the aircraft and its powerplant did not help. Because of the scrapping of the Il-28S and Tu-93 projects for which the new engine was primarily intended (the Tu-93 was a VK-5 powered version of the Tu-14), the VK-5 did not enter production – and hence neither did the Il-28RM. Besides, it was clear by then that axial-flow turbojets were superior to centrifugal-flow engines.

The specifications of the Il-28RM are detailed in Table 11.

Il-28 experimental tactical bomber with VK-5 engines

The next version of the *Beagle* to be powered by VK-5s was the regular bomber. Logically this aircraft should have been designated Il-28M, but no separate designation was allocated for some reason, and the designation Il-28M was eventually used for another version (see below). Development of the re-engined bomber variant was initiated by Council of Ministers (CofM) directive No. 5329-2088ss of 29 December 1952 and MAP order No.1ss of 1 January 1953.

The two prototypes were converted from standard Moscow-built Il-28s (c/ns 52003701 and 52003719). Pursuant to the above-mentioned CofM directive the first prototype was to be transferred to LII for testing, while the other aircraft was to be delivered to NII VVS in April 1953 for State acceptance trials.

Apart from the engines, the bombers had a few other changes. Both aircraft had wings taken from the Il-28R, with wingtip drop tanks to extend their range. The second prototype featured enlarged 1,260 × 390 mm (49.6 × 15.35 in.) mainwheels borrowed from the Il-28R and an automatic wheel-brake system, while the first prototype retained standard 1,150 × 355 mm (45.27 × 13.97 in.) mainwheels. The 12-A-30 DC batteries were replaced by new 12SAM-25 batteries and moved forward to the radar bay to shift the CG forward.

The defensive armament was identical to that of the standard Il-28, comprising two nose-mounted NR-23s with 100 rpg and two NR-23s with 225 rpg in the tail turret. The normal bomb load and the maximum bomb load were 1,000 kg (2,204 lb) and 2,000 kg (4,409 lb) respectively.

Both aircraft were completed within a short timescale and duly tested; the manufacturer's flight tests report was endorsed on 28 April 1953, and the State acceptance trials report exactly three months later. The specifications of the VK-5-powered bomber prototypes are given in Table 12.

On 10 September 1953 NII VVS concluded that it would be advisable to launch series production of the VK-5-powered Il-28. However, the upgraded bomber did not enter production for the reasons stated above.

Notes to Table 12:

* TOW 24,170 kg (53,284 lb), cruising speed 650 km/h (351.3 kt) and cruise altitude 10,500–13,200 m (34,448–43,307 ft).

** TOW 24,330 kg (53,637 lb), cruising speed 680 km/h (367.5 kt) and cruise altitude 10,500–13,100 m (34,448–42,979 ft).

*** TOW 18,710 kg (41,247 lb), cruising speed 650 km/h (351.3 kt) and cruise altitude 10,000 m (32,808 ft).

‡ TOW 18,920 kg (41,710 lb), cruising speed 700 km/h (378.3 kt) and cruise altitude 10,000 m (32,808 ft).

TOW 24,050 kg (53,020 lb), cruising speed 668 km/h (361.0 kt) and cruise altitude 10,000 m/10,000–12,000 m (32,808/32,808–39,370 ft).

TOW 24,220 kg (53,395 lb), cruising speed 668 km/h (361.0 kt)and cruise altitude 10,000 m/10,000–12,000 m (32,808/32,808–39,370 ft).

† TOW 23,800 kg (52,469 lb).

†† TOW 24,000 kg (52,910 lb).

4 Red, the Il-28TM torpedo-bomber prototype, photographed during trials in 1953. *(Yefim Gordon archive)*

Another view of the Il-28TM; the c/n 50301106 reveals the aircraft was converted from the first prototype Il-28T. *(Yefim Gordon archive)*

Il-28TM experimental torpedo-bomber

The Il-28TM torpedo-bomber (*torpedo**nos**ets modif**its**ee**ro**vannyy*) was the last of the three *Beagle* variants modified to take the VK-5 engine. It was developed in accordance with CofM directive No. 7218rs of 22 May 1953 and Ministry of Defence Industry (MOP – *Minis**ter**stvo obo**ron**noy pro**mysh**lennosti*) order No. 295ss of 27 May. The schedule stipulated by the government was extremely tight: the prototype was to be handed over to the Navy's Research Institute No. 15 in just one month.

In those days it was customary in the Soviet Union to strictly comply with government orders and directives concerning the defence industry, whatever the cost. OKB-240 managed to complete the prototype within the stated timescale by converting one of the Il-28T prototypes (c/n 50301106).[8] The installation of VK-5 engines with new extension jetpipes led to several associated changes. The front parts (detachable engine cowlings) and rear parts of the nacelles were modified, the electric wiring inside the nacelles was rerouted and the engine cooling ducts were modified. Changes were also made to the engine controls, a

8 The c/n shows that the aircraft was built in 1950, so this was probably a development aircraft retained by the Ilyushin OKB.

Table 12a. Il-28TM weapon configuration

Normal weapons load	Total weight, kg (lb)	Maximum weapons load	Total weight, kg (lb)
2 × FAB-500M-46 bombs	1,000 (2,204)	12 × OFAB-100 bombs	1,200 (2,645)
1 × 45-36AMV torpedo	1,073 (2,365)	8 × FAB-250M-46 bombs	2,000 (4,409)
1 × 45-36AMN torpedo	1,030 (2,270)	4 × FAB-500M-46 bombs	2,000 (4,409)
1 × RDT torpedo	615 (1,355)	1 × FAB-1500M-46 bomb	1,500 (3,306)
2 × AMD-500 mines	1,018 (2,244)	1 × FAB-3000M-46 bomb	3,000 (6,613)
1 × AMD-1000 mine	1,018 (2,244)	1 × TAS torpedo	1,520 (3,350)
1 × Lira mine	988 (2,178)	1 × TAV torpedo	1,283 (2,828)
1 × Desna mine	768 (1,693)	4 × AMD-500 mines	2,018 (4,448)
		1 × AMD-M mine	1,188 (2,619)
		1 × Serpey mine	1,268 (2,795)
		2 × 45-36AMV torpedoes	2,128 (4,691)
		2 × Lira mines	1,958 (4,316)
		2 × Serpey mines	2,518 (5,551)
		2 × Desna mines	1,518 (3,346)

new fire-extinguishing system was installed and the engines' foreign object damage (FOD) protection screens, made of wire mesh, were provided with a de-icing system.

In addition, a seventh fuel cell (No. 3B) was fitted, drop tanks were installed at the wingtips and the liquid oxygen bottles were relocated. The higher gross weight required the standard mainwheels to be replaced with 1,260 × 390 mm (49.6 × 15.35 in.) mainwheels, as on the Il-28R. Finally, a second nose cannon with 100 rounds was installed on the starboard side (as already mentioned, the production Il-28T had only the portside forward-firing cannon).

Table 12a shows the Il-28TM's weapons configurations.

Serialled 4 Red, the aircraft completed its manufacturer's flight tests by late June 1953 (the test report was signed on 30 June) and passed State acceptance trials in July (the Soviet Navy's Research Institute No. 15 issued its act of acceptance on 1 August). Still, the Il-28TM fared no better that its comrades-in-engines, i.e. the other versions sharing the VK-5 powerplant. The specifications of the Il-28TM prototype are given in Table 13.

Il-28-131 guided bomb carrier

Back in the early 1950s the Soviet Union started experimenting with precision guided munitions (PGMs). An experimental batch of UB-2000F radio-controlled guided bombs (UB = *oopravlyayemaya bomba* – guided bomb) was built

An Il-28-131 with a UB-2F Chaika guided bomb suspended under the fuselage. *(Yefim Gordon archive)*

Table 13. Il-28TM prototype specifications

	Manufacturer's flight tests	State acceptance trials
Length overall	17.65 m (57 ft 10.88 in.)	
Span	21.45 m (70 ft 4.48 in.)	
Wing area	60.8 m² (653.76 sq. ft)	
Wing loading, kg/m² (lb/ft²)	380 (1,846)	366 (1,778)
Power loading at sea level, kg/kgp (lb/lb st)	3.3	3.56
Operating empty weight, kg (lb)	13,395 (29,530)	13,395 (29,530)
Normal all-up weight, kg (lb)	18,790 (41,424)	18,788 (41,419)
Maximum AUW (with drop tanks), kg (lb)	22,070 (48,655)	22,068 (48,650)
Maximum AUW (with drop tanks and PSR-1500-15 JATO bottles), kg (lb)	22,550 (49,713)	n.a.
Fuel load, kg (lb):		
internal	3,800 (8,377)	3,800 (8,377)
with drop tanks	6,880 (15,167)	6,880 (15,167)
Payload, kg (lb):		
normal	5,397 (11,898)	5,383 (11,867)
maximum	8,675 (19,124)	8,663 (19,098)
Top speed at 22,070 kg (48,655 lb) TOW and take-off power rating, km/h (kt):		
at sea level	800 (432.43)*	800 (432.43)*
at 5,000 m (16,404 ft)	901 (487.0)	895 (483.78)
at 10,000 m (32,808 ft)	836 (451.89)	837 (452.43)
Landing speed, km/h (kt)	188.5 (101.9)	178 (96.2)**
Rate of climb at 22,070 kg TOW and cruise power rating, m/sec (ft/min):		
at sea level	15.4 (3,030)	16.3 (3,207)
at 5,000 m (16,404 ft)	11.22 (2,208)	9.3 (1,830)
10,000 m (32,808 ft)	6.85 (1,348)	4.0 (787)
Climb time at 22,070 kg TOW and cruise power rating, min:		
to 5,000 m (16,404 ft)	6.36	6.6
to 10,000 m (32,808 ft)	6.85	19.5
Effective range at 10,000 m with drop tanks and 45-36AMV torpedo, km (miles)	2,172 (1,349)	2,166 (1,345)
Technical range at 10,000 m/600 km/h (324 kt) with drop tanks and 45-36AMV torpedo, km (miles)	2,326 (1,444)	2,315 (1,437)
Technical range at 10,400–12,550 m (34,120–41,174 ft)/585–900 km/h (316–486 kt) with drop tanks and 45-36AMV torpedo, km (miles)	2,499 (1,552)	n.a.
Endurance at 10,000 m with drop tanks and 45-36AMV torpedo	3 hr 48 min	3 hr 41 min
Endurance at 10,400–12,550 m/585–900 km/h with drop tanks and 45-36AMV torpedo	4 hr 20 min	n.a.
Take-off run at maximum TOW, m (ft)	1,090 (3,576)	1,260 (4,133)
Take-off distance at maximum TOW, m (ft)	2,055 (6,742)	2,025 (6,643)
Landing run, m (ft)	890 (2,920)	940 (3,084)***
Landing distance, m (ft)	1,510 (4,954)	2,125 (6,971)***

Notes:

* Speed limited because of dynamic strength limit.

** Data for VK-1-powered Il-28T.

*** Data for VK-1-powered Il-28T with a 15,000 kg (33,068 lb) landing weight.

Above: This head-on view of an Il-28U shows how the trainer provided both pilots with an unrestricted forward view. *(RART)*

Above: Il-28 01 Red (c/n 36603807) is part of the open-air display at Moscow-Khodynka airfield. *(Yefim Gordon)*

Above and Below: Il-28 04 Red (c/n 53005771) is on display at the Russian Air Force Museum in Monino. *(Yefim Gordon)*

Above: Il-28 01 Red (c/n 36603807) is part of the open-air display at Moscow-Khodynka airfield. *(Yefim Gordon)*

Above: This *Beagle*, preserved at the Civil Aviation Museum in Ulyanovsk (c/n 56605702), is supposedly an Il-20, with an appropriate (now faded) Soviet flag and winged Aeroflot logo. However, there are reasons to believe that it was painted like this *after* coming to the museum and is really Soviet Air Force 38 Red! Note the Il-28 nose titles. *(Yefim Gordon)*

Above: This stripped-out hulk of a *Beagle* sat for many years on the far side of the airfield at Kubinka AB. *(Yefim Gordon)*

Left: The rear fuselage and tail unit of East German AF Il-28 208 Red, showing the tail turret; the cannon have been removed, probably to be displayed separately. *(Yefim Gordon)*

Above and Below: Former East German Air Force Il-28 208 Red (c/n 55006448) preserved at Bautzen Museum. This was the only EGAF *Beagle* to wear a camouflage finish. *(Yefim Gordon)*

The *Muzeum Lotnictwa i Astronautyki* boasts an Il-28U serialled S3 Red (c/n 69216). *(Yefim Gordon)*

Above: Polish Air Force Il-28 65 Red (c/n 2212) is preserved on the premises of the Officers' Higher Flying School in Dęblin. *(Yefim Gordon)*

Above: Il-28R 72 Red (c/n 41909) resides at the *Muzeum Lotnictwa i Astronautyki* (Aerospace Museum) in Kraków. *(Yefim Gordon)*

Above: The forward fuselage of Il-28U S3 Red in Kraków. *(Yefim Gordon)*

Above: Albanian Air Force H-5 3608 at Rinas AB, Tirana, with Avia 14 31-61 in the background. *(Key Publishing)*

Above: Work underway on B-5 308 Red, with a hardened aircraft shelter (HAS) – not meant for the bomber – behind it. Note the excellent finish on this aircraft. *(RART)*

Above: Romanian Air Force BT-5 407 Red is non-airworthy and stored at Bacău AB. *(RART)*

Above: Looking somewhat weather-beaten, B-5s 703 Red and 706 Red sit on the grass at Bacău in non-flying condition. *(RART)*

Above: Romanian Air Force B-5s parked at Borcea-Feteşti AB. *(RART)*

Above: The Plexiglass of the canopy yellowed by age, Bulgarian Il-28 43 Red sits at the Bulgarian Air Force Museum in Plovdiv. *(RART)*

Above: NH-2 in full splendour at its home base, Utti. *(RART)*

Above: Finnish Air Force Il-28 NH-1/01 in its original guise with green-painted engine cowlings. *(RART)*

Above: An impressive line-up of H-5s at a PLAAF airbase during a military exercise; both flight and ground crews are gathered near each aircraft. *(China's Aviation Industry)*

Above: This anonymous H-5 is in the open-air display at the PLAAF Museum in Datangshan, keeping company with a Nanchang CJ-5 (licence-built Yak-18 *Max*) basic trainer. *(F. C. W. Käsmann)*

Above: Harbin H-5 bombers in the final assembly shop. *(China's Aviation Industry)*

Above: H-5s cruising over the Tien-Shan. *(China Aircraft)*

Above: This Il-28, which escaped to Taiwan on 11 November 1966, exemplifies the green camouflage worn by some PLAAF *Beagles*. It is now on display at the ROCAF museum at Taoyuan AB. *(RART)*

Above: PLAAF H-5s dropping bombs during an exercise. *(RART)*

Above: This H-5 (44690 Red) preserved in the People's Liberation Army Air Force Museum at Datangshan AB has a non-standard nose glazing with a second optically flat panel in front. *(Helmut Walther)*

Above: The FNAF *Beagles* wore crudely applied green and black camouflage. *(RART)*

Above: A Nigerian Il-28 sharing the ramp at Enugu with MiG-17F NAF-615. *(RART)*

as early as 1953 and tested on specially modified Il-28 and Tu-4 bombers. Designed by a team under A. D. Nadiradze, the UB-2000F bore a certain resemblance to the German *Fritz X* gliding bomb of World War II vintage, with a squashed-X wing arrangement to provide adequate ground clearance. However, the wings were of delta planform with inset rudders, and the casing had a constant diameter (in contrast, the German bomb had trapezoidal wings and a bulged warhead).

Tests showed that two or three smart bombs were enough to destroy a target measuring 30 × 70 m (98 × 229 ft) which would have required the expenditure of 168 FAB-1500 dumb bombs. Hence in 1955 the UB-2000 entered production and was included in the VVS inventory as the UB-2F Chaika (Seagull) or 4A-22. About thirty Il-28s specially equipped to carry these PGMs were built in 1956. This weapon was carried externally under the fuselage. Outwardly the Il-28-131 could be identified by a small angular fairing under the nose, probably housing the guidance antenna for the bomb. The UB-2F was also carried by specially modified Tu-16 *Badger-A* bombers which carried two such bombs on underwing pylons.

Il-28PL anti-submarine warfare aircraft

The late 1950s and early 1960s saw another escalation of the Cold War which nearly turned into a full-blown hot war during the Cuban missile crisis. The deployment of Soviet ballistic missiles to Cuba worried the USA and its NATO allies immensely, causing them to step up their submarine activities. This, in turn, led the Soviet Union to bolster its Navy, including the Naval Air Arm. Not having enough ASW aircraft to monitor the activities of Western navies along the Soviet Union's marine borders and destroy, the AVMF decided to convert some of the bombers it had on its strength.

The aircraft converted for the ASW role were mostly Tu-16 *Badgers* and Il-28s. For instance, the Baltic Fleet's 759th OMTAP[9] (*otdel'nyy* ***min****no-tor****pednyy*** ***avia****polk* – independent minelaying and torpedo-bomber regiment) converted ten Il-28 bombers and torpedo-bombers (Il-28T), which were redesignated Il-28PL (***p****rotivo****l****odochnyy* – anti-submarine). These aircraft were fitted with the SPARU-55 sonobuoy receiver (*sa****mo****lyotnoye pree****yo****mnoye av****to****ma****ti****cheskoye* ***ra****hdious****t****roystvo* – airborne automatic radio receiver device, 1955 model) constituting part of the Baku sonar system recently adopted by the AVMF (the same system was fitted to the Kamov Ka-25PL *Hormone-A* shipboard ASW helicopter). The bomb bay was big enough to carry RGB-N sonobuoys (***r****ahdio****g****hid****r****oakoos****t****i****ch****eskiy* ***b****ooy*) and depth charges without requiring modifications.

The SPARU-55 was a superheterodyne receiver working in the 49.2 to 53.4 MHz waveband. This range was split into eighteen preset frequencies through which the receiver cycled automatically. If a signal from a sonobuoy was detected on one of the frequencies, the receiver locked onto it, enabling the operator to determine if the sonobuoy had really detected a submarine. If that was the case, he activated the SPARU-55's direction-finder mode, and the aircraft homed in on the operating buoy to attack the submarine. A major drawback of the SPARU-55 was its long cycling time (in automatic mode it needed 110 seconds to switch from one buoy to the next!). An outward identification feature of the Il-28PL may have been several additional blade aerials on the aft fuselage underside; these were probably associated with the SPARU-55 receiver.

In 1962 the AT-1 ASW torpedo was included in the AVMF inventory; it could also be carried internally by the Il-28PL, being 3.9 m (12 ft 9.54 in.) long and weighing 530 kg (1,168 lb).

Officially the reason for the Il-28PL's existence was the necessity to quickly receive ASW support once it had been requested by whoever spotted the unfriendly submarine, since the Il-28 was more than twice as fast as the obsolete piston-engined Beriyev Be-6 *Madge* flying boat operated by the Soviet Navy at the time. Besides, the flying boats were difficult to operate in winter when their bases froze up. But perhaps the real reason was the naval command's wish to stop the *Beagle* kennels from being disbanded, as they inevitably would be, and keep the pilots flying.

In 1966 the HQ of the Baltic Fleet's air arm approached the Soviet Navy's GHQ, requesting the formation of two regiments equipped with the Il-28PL, but the request was turned down.

Il-28Sh attack aircraft

In the late 1950s the Ilyushin OKB considered adapting the *Beagle* for the strike role. This involved installation of a battery of twenty unguided rockets in the bomb bay. This would give adequate firepower without spoiling the aircraft's aerodynamics with high-drag external stores. The launch tubes were to be mounted almost vertically, firing down and aft; a salvo of rockets equipped with shaped-charge warheads was expected to be an effective way of destroying armoured vehicles. The crew was

9 Some sources state the unit as the 769th OMTAP.

reduced to two, the navigator/bomb aimer being superfluous. But it was quickly established that the efflux of twenty rockets impinging on the airframe would make the aircraft uncontrollable and the idea was dropped.

However, the limited warload of the fighter-bombers of the period forced the military and the engineers to dust off the idea of an Il-28 attack aircraft. The specification for such an aircraft was drawn up in the spring of 1967 – before the famous Six-Day War, in fact. The aircraft was to have a combat radius identical to that of the Sukhoi Su-7BM *Fitter-A* fighter-bomber but an ordnance load two or three times greater. The result was the Il-28Sh (*shtoormo**v**ik* – attack aircraft). It featured twelve underwing pylons for unguided rockets – five outboard and one inboard of each engine. This was considered a more acceptable approach, even at the expense of the extra drag created by the external stores.

Possible weapons configurations included twelve UB-16-57 rocket pods with sixteen 57 mm (2.24 in.) S-5 folding-fin aircraft rockets (FFARs) each,[10] or six 250 mm (9.84 in.) S-24 rockets, or various gun pods, submunitions containers and free-fall bombs. Depending on the mission, the pilot could select a salvo launch or just two pylons, four pylons, etc. Flight tests which began in 1967 showed that even when all 192 S-5 rockets or all six S-24 rockets were fired at once, the engines showed no inclination to surge or flame out.

The Il-28Sh commenced State acceptance trials in October 1967. The test pilots reported that the aircraft was suitable for low-level and ultra-low-level strike missions. It was established that flying at – and delivering accurate rocket/bomb strikes from – altitudes right down to 60 m (196 ft) could be mastered by service pilots without any trouble; flying still lower, though, demanded a lot of concentration and extra training. The aircraft could be prepared for a sortie within four hours.

Below 200 m (656 ft) the Il-28Sh had a speed limit of 660 km/h (356 kt). Fuel consumption at low altitude increased by 30–50 per cent as compared to the basic bomber because of the external stores and the aircraft's combat radius with a full load of FFAR pods was 295 km (183 miles).

This poor but interesting shot shows the prototype Il-28Sh attack aircraft during trials. The many underwing pylons are clearly visible. *(Yefim Gordon archive)*

Yet, despite all its merits as a strike aircraft, the Il-28Sh had inadequate armour protection and the ejection seats were not yet of the zero-zero type, which meant the crew had no chances of survival if shot down at low altitude. Hence the Ilyushin OKB discontinued development of the Il-28Sh, and though originally 300 Il-28 bombers were slated for conversion for the ground-attack role, only a few were eventually converted at the Soviet Air Force's aircraft overhaul plants and delivered to first-line units.

Il-28ZA weather reconnaissance aircraft

On 23 February 1959 the State Committee on Aircraft (GKAT – *Gosoo**dahr**stvennyy komi**tet** po aviatsee**on**noy **tekh**nike*) issued an order concerning the development of the Il-28ZA (*zondiro**v**schchik atmos**fery*** – lit. atmosphere sampler) weather reconnaissance aircraft for civil aviation needs. A few *Beagle*s were converted to this configuration. Unfortunately almost nothing is known about this version.

Target-towing versions

a) Soviet versions (Il-28BM)

Two versions (the basic bomber and the Il-28R) were widely used as target tugs – both for testing new AA guns and for training fighter pilots. The special equipment for this mission included a BLM-1000 (BLM-1000M) or BLT-5 winch installed in the bomb bay and a 77BM-2 (77BM-2M) or PM-3Zh winged target towed on a cable anywhere between 5 and 2,500 m (16–8,202 ft) long.[11] For take-off and landing the target was connected to the aircraft by a rigid link permitting operation from both paved and unpaved strips. The bomber version used short linkage rods, whereas the Il-28R was fitted with long ones. The installation of target-towing equipment did not seriously affect the aircraft's CG position, which stayed well within the prescribed

10 UB = *oonif**itseer**ovannyy blok* – standardized [FFAR] pod; the UV-16-57 designation sometimes found in Western literature is incorrect. S = *sna**ryad*** – in this case, unguided rocket.

11 BM = *book**sirooy**emaya mi**shen'*** – towed target; PM = ***plah**ner-mi**shen'*** – gliding target. Some sources stated a towing cable length of 20–2,500 m (65–8,202 ft).

An Il-28BM target tug based on a standard bomber with a gliding gunnery target in tow. *(Yefim Gordon archive)*

42 Blue, an Il-28R converted to Il-28BM configuration (note tip tanks), takes off with a target connected by a rigid tow-bar. The aft position of the tactical code is noteworthy. *(Yefim Gordon archive)*

Table 14. Comparison of performance characteristics of Il-28 + 77BM-2M combination and Il-28R + PM-3Zh combination

		Il-28 + 77BM-2M	Il-28R + PM-3Zh
Climb time, min:	to 1,000 m (3,280 ft)	3.5–4.0	4.0
	to 4,000 m (13,123 ft)	9.75–10.25	10.75
	to 8,000 m (26,246 ft)	23.75–24.0	27.25
	to 10,100 m (33,136 ft)	n.a.	55.0
	to 10,900 m (35,761 ft)	57.0	n.a.
Range at 10,000 m (32,808 ft)/620 km/h (335 kt), km (miles)		845 (524)	n.a.
Range at 8,000 m/540 km/h (292 kt), km (miles)		n.a.	1,140 (708)
Maximum range, km (miles)		1,475 (916)	1,555 (965)
Endurance at 8,000 m/540 km/h		n.a.	2 hr 07 min
Maximum endurance		2 hr 44 min	3 hr 11 min
Power loading at sea level, kg/kgp (lb/lb st)		3.3	3.56

limits. The target-towing versions are sometimes referred to as Il-28BM (*booksirovschchik misheney* – target tug).

The field performance of Il-28 bombers with a 20,100 kg (44,312 lb) gross weight and Il-28Rs with a 19,822 kg (43,699 lb) gross weight enabled them to operate with targets from concrete airstrips at least 1,800 m (5,905 ft) long. At a gross weight of 22,207 kg (48,957 lb), the Il-28R could operate with targets from concrete airstrips at least 2,300 m (7,545 ft) long. Endurance with a towed target was 2.5 hours.

Table 14 above gives some performance characteristics of an Il-28/77BM-2M combination (TOW 20,050 kg/44,202 lb, fuel capacity 7,990 lit./1,757.8 imp. gal.) and an Il-28R/PM-3Zh combination (TOW 22,207 kg/48,957 lb, fuel capacity 9,550 lit./2,101 imp. gal.).

When towed targets were supplemented by rocket-powered target drones the Il-28 target tugs were converted into combined tugs/drone launchers. The drones were carried on underwing pylons between the nacelles and fuselage in much the same way as the upgraded Il-28T carried torpedoes. They were launched and flew on towards the shooting range when the aircraft reached an appropriate altitude.

Apart from towed targets, the Il-28BM based on the standard bomber version could carry PM-6R and PM-6G target drones (PM = *pikeeruyuschchaya mishen'* – diving target). These looked rather like bombs with overgrown fins and were equipped with smoke tracers and recovery parachutes. The Il-28R and Il-28T could not be modified to carry these drones because of the reconnaissance and torpedo-bomber versions' increased TOW (which would be excessive if the drones were carried) and some structural details which rendered the conversion impossible.

The PM-6 drones were carried on special underwing pylons attached on two pairs of swept V-struts. The delivery system spun up the drones' stabilizing gyros, using power from the carrier aircraft, and dropped the drones singly or simultaneously at a preset altitude between 2,300 and 8,000 m (7,545–26,246 ft). The drones were aimed using the optical sight or radar; in an emergency they could be dropped by either the pilot or the navigator. With two drones the aircraft's service ceiling was limited to 9,600 m (31,496 ft), and the take-off run increased by 300 m (984 ft).

b) East German version

The East German Il-28s converted into target tugs differed slightly from their Soviet counterparts, as no rigid targets were used. A drum with a 2,000 m (6,560 ft) steel cable was carried in the bomb bay on the standard bomb cradles. To this a fabric 'sock' 8 m (26 ft) long and 1 m (3 ft) in diameter was attached; it was neatly rolled up and suspended from the bomb cradles before flight. A small roller was attached to the lower fuselage to stop the cable from scuffing the fuselage skin as it paid out. Some types of anti-aircraft guns (including the S-60) were radar-directed, so aluminium cones had to be inserted into the sock to provide a radar signature.

Prior to entering the shooting range the pilot lowered the flaps 20° and slowed the aircraft to 280 km/h (155.5 kt) to prevent the target from being ripped apart or torn off by the slipstream as it unfolded. The navigator then dropped the target, which unwound the cable as it deployed; the drum was fitted with a centrifugal brake to make sure the cable unwound smoothly. Two or three minutes later the target was fully deployed, the observer in the gunner's cabin monitoring it. (All armament was usually removed.)

When the sortie was completed the cable and target were jettisoned, usually by means of a pneumatic release mechanism, but the cable could also be cut by a pyrotechnical guillotine in case of malfunction. After landing the cable was rewound and ready for another mission; the target could also be reused, unless it had been shot to shreds.

c) Romanian version

At least one Romanian Air Force Harbin H-5 (Chinese-built Il-28, see below), serialled 307 Red was converted for target-towing duties, using equipment developed by the Air Target Sweden AB company. An MBV7S Mk 3 target-towing winch was installed in the bomb bay, with a faired cable outlet amidships; the cable was 4,500 m (14,765 ft) long. The winch worked with a KR-45-430 sleeve-type target equipped with an AS-131SC acoustic miss distance sensor; the target was hooked up under the fuselage before flight.

Il-28M target drone

Besides towing targets, many *Beagle*s ended up as targets themselves! In the late 1950s many obsolete Il-28 bombers were converted into remote-controlled high-speed target drones designated Il-28M (for ***mishen'*** (target)) and used for testing new anti-aircraft missile systems. To be precise, development of this version was brought about by Semyon A. Lavochkin's OKB-301, which started design work on the Model 400 surface-to-air missile in 1955. This missile was intended for point defence of important targets, such as major industrial cities, and designed to destroy aircraft with a radar cross-section (RCS) similar to that of the Il-28.

The radio control system enabled the Il-28M to take off, climb to cruise altitude, make manoeuvres and land if the drone was lucky enough to stay in one piece. At first this was often the case – the first prototypes of the Model 400 SAM did not score a single hit on the drones! Another anti-aircraft missile developed by the Lavochkin OKB, the 207A, was tested between June 1953 and November 1954; for instance, three test launches against Il-28Ms were made in October 1953, two of the missiles having shaped-charge warheads and the third a directional fragmentation warhead. State acceptance trials of the 207A began in September 1953, using Il-28Ms and Tu-4s as targets. The target drones flew at 9,500–20,000 m (31,168–65,616 ft) and up to 35 km (21.7 miles) from the launch site. All the targets were either destroyed or substantially damaged, the missiles' accuracy being within 7–58 m (23–190 ft).

Not all Il-28Ms were radio-controlled, however. Some *Beagle*s phased out by the VVS were given a brush-up by the manufacturer to make sure mechanical failure would not prevent the aircraft from fulfilling its final mission. Then a pilot would take the doomed bomber into the air, climb to a predetermined altitude, engage the autopilot and eject when told to do so by ground control. Test pilot Fyodor D. Bogdanov made 31 such flights in 1952–7, ejecting at 12,500 m (41,010 ft).

Il-28BMs were also supplied to foreign customers; this is Finnish Air Force NH-3, another converted Il-28R. *(Yefim Gordon archive)*

An Il-28M target drone seen through the gunsight of an attacking fighter. *(Yefim Gordon archive)*

Test and development aircraft

I. Avionics testbeds

a) Il-28LL radar testbed

One Il-28 (identity unknown) was converted in 1952 for testing the RP-6 Sokol (Falcon) radar[12] and designated Il-28LL (*le**ta**yuschchaya labora**to**riya* – lit. flying laboratory).[13] This radar with a 30 km (16.2 nm) detection range had been developed by OKB-339 under G. M. Koonyavskiy for two interceptors – the Yakovlev Yak-120, which entered production and service as the Yak-25 *Flashlight-A*, and the Lavochkin La-200B. Initial tests were performed on a converted Boeing B-17G Flying Fortress. (While this type was not officially supplied under the Lend-Lease programme, a number of B-17s which had crash-landed on Soviet-held bases after raids on Germany were repaired and used by the Soviet Air Force.) When it transpired that development of the Yakovlev fighter was taking longer than predicted and that the La-200 would be the first to receive the new radar, Semyon A. Lavochkin suggested that a heavy aircraft but a faster one than the B-17 be used to bring the radar up to scratch. The Il-28 was the obvious choice.

To accommodate the radar the bomber's nose glazing was cut away at fuselage frame 2 and replaced by a cylindrical metal structure (part of the Yak-120's nose incorporating the avionics bay). The huge dish of the RP-6 was enclosed by a large glassfibre radome which had an almost hemispherical front end instead of the usual pointed or ogival shape. The conversion work was done by Lavochkin OKB specialists under the supervision of the Ilyushin OKB (which was not directly interested in the project but held responsibility for the Il-28 anyway).

The famous test pilot Mark L. Gallai flew the Il-28LL, with R. A. Razumov as test engineer; the latter was the worse off, sitting in a dark and

12 RP = ***rah**diopree**tsel*** – radio sight; this was the Soviet term for fire control radars at the time.

13 This Russian term is used indiscriminately and can denote any kind of testbed (avionics, engine, equipment, weapons, etc.), an aerodynamics research aircraft or control configured vehicle (CCV), a weather research aircraft, a geophysical survey aircraft, etc.

extremely cramped bay aft of the radar set – all that remained of the navigator's station. A total of 33 flights was made without any problems; the test programme, which ended in December 1952, included simulated interception of real aircraft. Later, tests of the Sokol radar continued on the La-200B interceptor prototype which, after being rejected by the VVS, found use as a testbed. By the end of 1953 the radar had been perfected and was fitted to the late-production Yak-25M from 1954 onwards, replacing the RP-1D Izumrood (Emerald) radar fitted to early Yak-25s as a stopgap measure.

b) missile targeting systems research aircraft

In 1960 the Ministry of Defence's Central Research Institute No. 30 (TsNII-30 – *Tsen**trahl'**nyy naoo**chno**-iss**led**ovatel'skiy insti**toot***) joined forces with NII-2 and the Research Institute of the State Committee for Electronics (NII GKRE – *naoo**chno**-iss**led**ovatel'skiy insti**toot** Gosoo**dahr**stvennovo komi**teta** po **rah**dioelek**troni**ke*) to develop active radar homing systems for anti-shipping missiles. To this end it was necessary to analyse the characteristics of the radar pulse reflected from surface ships. Thus an Il-28 and a Lisunov Li-2 *Cab* transport (a licence-built Douglas DC-3 derivative) were converted into avionics testbeds equipped with two experimental radars and special recording equipment.

The measurement and recording system (MRS) developed by NII-2 was housed in the *Beagle*'s bomb bay. It included a high-speed cine-camera capturing the radar pulses reflected from the ship and appearing as lines on the radar display. The two testbeds made more than fifty flights from Kirovskoye airbase on the Crimean Peninsula, using Black Sea Fleet cruisers, destroyers and minesweepers as targets. The ships were either anchored on the roadstead at Feodosiya or moved on predetermined headings. Measurements were made in 38 flights at 2,000–5,000 m (6,651–16,404 ft) and 110–167 m/sec (360–547 ft/sec) at 10–50 km (5.4–27 nm) range.

Forty-three measurements were made with the cruisers, 64 with destroyers and 40 with minesweepers at various sighting angles in various sea state conditions. The results were analysed by a computer, which made it possible to develop algorithms for determining the class of a ship in a group; this helped to develop guidance systems for stand-off anti-shipping missiles.

c)

An Il-28U coded 18 Blue was apparently converted into an avionics testbed of some sort, sporting several non-standard aerials under the forward and rear fuselage. Unfortunately no details are known of this aircraft; it may have been a navaids calibration (flight checker) aircraft.

This Il-28U, coded 18 Blue, appears to have been converted to an avionics testbed of some kind; note the many non-standard aerials under the fuselage. *(Sergey and Dmitriy Komissarov archive)*

II. Il-28LL ejection seat testbed

The Il-28 was extensively used for research and development work. In the early 1960s several aircraft were converted into testbeds for various systems of the *Vostok* (East) manned spacecraft under development by Sergey P. Korolyov's team. One of these was 10 Blue (c/n 53005710), an ejection seat testbed used to test, among other things, the ejection seat of the Vostok's re-entry vehicle. Interestingly, this aircraft has likewise been referred to as Il-28LL.

The bulky Vostok ejection seat was installed in

10 Blue, the Il-28LL ejection seat testbed, firing the seat for the Vostok spacecraft's re-entry vehicle. Note the photo calibration markings on the fuselage and tail and the dual cine-camera fairings on each wingtip. *(Yefim Gordon archive)*

Close-up of the Vostok ejection seat as it clears the superstructure above the modified bomb bay. *(Yefim Gordon archive)*

Another view of the Vostok ejection seat as it separates from the Il-28, spouting terrific flames. Note the SM-50 chase plane in the background. *(Sergey and Dmitriy Komissarov archive)*

The same aircraft as it fires another ejection seat from the heavily modified gunner's station. *(Yefim Gordon archive)*

An experimental seat is ejected from the rear station of 10 Blue. It appears that the seat fires through a simulated cockpit canopy, shattering the glazing which is painted in stripes for better visualization. Note the stabilizing booms tipped with drogue parachutes extending aft from the headrest; this may be an early version of the famous Zvezda K-36 seat. *(Yefim Gordon archive)*

the faired-over bomb bay immediately ahead of the wing torsion box and protruded above the upper fuselage; hence a large teardrop fairing with flattened sides had to be installed aft of the pilot's cockpit to protect the test pilot sitting in the seat from the slipstream. Additionally, the tail gunner's compartment was replaced by a large slab-sided fairing extending much further aft, from which another ejection seat could be fired both upwards and downwards. Cine-cameras were mounted in teardrop fairings above and below the wingtips to capture the ejection sequence.

The Vostok ejection seat was tested successfully by future cosmonaut Gherman Titov. The Mikoyan SM-50 fighter (aka MiG-19SU, an experimental version of the MiG-19SF *Farmer-C* with a ventral U-19 liquid-propellant rocket booster) acted as chase plane and camera ship.

III. In-flight refuelling system testbeds

a) fighter IFR system integration

A Voronezh-built Il-28 (01 Red, c/n 2402101) was converted into a makeshift tanker trainer used for testing the hose-and-drogue flight refuelling system developed by OKB-918 led by Guy Ilyich Severin.[14] The aircraft worked with the the tenth production Gor'kiy-built MiG-19 *Farmer-A* coded 10 Red (c/n 59210110), converted at LII in late 1957. This fighter had no fewer than four dummy refuelling probes (one ahead of the windshield and three on

14 Now the Zvezda (Star) Joint-Stock Company. The company later developed the UPAZ-1A Sakhalin podded HDU (UPAZ = *oonifitseerovannyy podvesnoy agregaht zaprahvki* – standardized suspended, i.e. external refuelling unit) used on the Il-78/Il-78M *Midas* tanker, but is best known for its K-36 ejection seat.

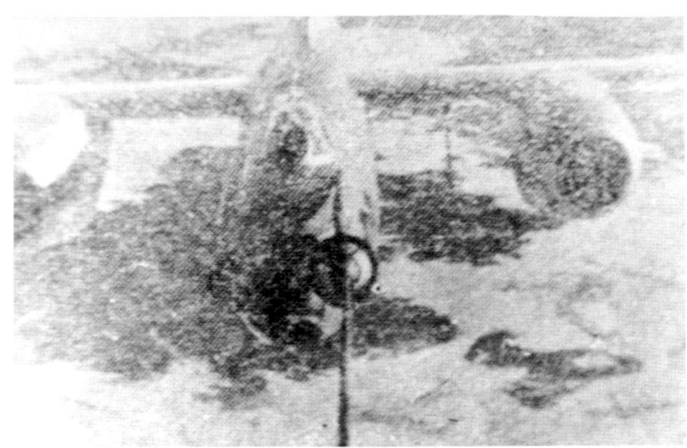

Though of poor quality, these shots are extremely interesting, showing an Il-28 refuelling tanker trailing a hose from the bomb bay, and another *Beagle* equipped with a nose-mounted refuelling probe taking on fuel from this aircraft. *(Yefim Gordon archive)*

the port wing) because the best location had to be determined experimentally.

An experimental winch emulating a hose drum unit (HDU) was installed in the Il-28's bomb bay, paying out a 5 mm (0.19 in.) steel cable with a drogue of 640 mm (2 ft 1.19 in.) diameter to a point 42 m (137 ft) beyond the bomber's tail. Initially a 36 kg (79 lb) unstabilized drogue was used. After the first four flights, however, it was replaced with a drogue incorporating a stabilizing device 100 mm (3.93 in.) wide mounted 60 mm (2.36 in.) from the base. Both models had a lock for engaging the probe.

The MiG-19 would make contact with the tanker at 7,000 m (22,965 ft) and 450–470 km/h (250–261 kt) IAS, approaching from a stand-by position 10–20 m (32–65 ft) behind the drogue. Contact was usually made in a climb, with or without side slip. Approach speed varied from 0.3 to 12 m/sec (1–39 ft/sec) or 1–30 km/h (0.54–16.2 kt) IAS. After making contact the MiG-19 stayed locked into the drogue for 3–5 seconds, then slowed down and broke away. For safety's sake the drogue lock was set at an unlocking force of 60–80 kg (132–176 lb). Usually the fighter carried drop tanks to increase mission time.

Test pilot Nikolai O. Goryaynov (who has the distinction of being the first Soviet pilot to successfully refuel a heavy bomber in flight) was assigned project test pilot for the tanker trainer. On 28 August 1957 he made a flight to check the operation of the winch. The drogue was deployed at 7,000 m (22,965 ft) and 400, 450, 500 and 550 km/h (216, 243, 270 and 297 kt) IAS. After that, test pilots S. F. Mashkovskiy, Pyotr I. Kaz'min and Sergey N. Anokhin made ten refuelling flights, as detailed in the table below.

The tenth flight had to be cut short when the drogue entered the fighter's air intake and collapsed, the debris damaging one of the engines. The trials showed that the chances of making contact with the tanker depended mainly on the drogue's stability, which left much to be desired, as the drogue twisted violently in the slipstream.

Table 15. In-flight refuelling test results

Flight	Date	MiG-19 pilot	Successful attempts
No. 1	18 September	Mashkovskiy	2 of 4 (nose probe)
No. 2	20 September	Mashkovskiy	2 of 7 (nose probe)
No. 3	24 September	Mashkovskiy	2 of 5 (nose probe)
No. 4	27 September	Mashkovskiy	No contact
No. 5	3 October	Mashkovskiy	1 of 33
No. 6	16 October	Anokhin	2 of 41
No. 7	30 October	Mashkovskiy	1 of 12
No. 8	1 November	Mashkovskiy	2 of 34
No. 9	7 December	Kaz'min	9 of 30
No. 10	27 December	Kaz'min	No contact

The Il-28LSh testbed was developed to investigate the possibility of using skis on tactical aircraft. This view shows the experimental skid, and the ballast container to which it is attached, in the fully raised position. *(Yefim Gordon archive)*

The Il-28LSh (12 Red, c/n 53005112) with the skid fully lowered. Note the non-retractable twin mainwheels. *(Yefim Gordon archive)*

b) bomber IFR system tests

In due course the Soviet military put forward more stringent requirements, which the Il-28 could no longer meet. One of the greatest deficiencies was the *Beagle*'s inadequate range. However, at that stage it was deemed inadvisable to retire the many Il-28s in VVS service, so someone suggested retrofitting the bombers with the probe-and-drogue refuelling system. To this end two more Il-28s were converted for real-life IFR system tests. One of them was a tanker with a real HDU in the bomb bay, while the other *Beagle* featured a fixed refuelling probe offset to port above the navigator's station. The two aircraft made successful contacts but the system was not fitted to Soviet Air Force Il-28s because Aleksandr S. Yakovlev's OKB-115 brought out the more promising Yak-129 supersonic tactical bomber which eventually entered production and service as the Yak-28 *Brewer*.

IV. Landing gear testbeds

a) Il-28LSh

In 1958 a Moscow-built Il-28 coded 12 Red (c/n 53005112) was converted into the Il-28LSh testbed (LSh = ***lyzh****noye* ***sh****assee* – ski landing gear) for testing the efficiency and durability of aircraft skis designed for dirt strips. The aircraft was fitted with a semi-retractable sprung skid under the centre fuselage. The skid was equipped with pressure sensors and mounted on a hollow box which could be filled with ballast to test it for various loads; the whole assembly could be raised and lowered by hydraulic rams. The nose gear unit was fitted with larger wheels and the the main units had widely spaced twin wheels rather than the usual single ones. This modified undercarriage could not be retracted, so the mainwheel well doors were deleted to avoid making contact with the wheels. The skid was tested on airstrips with various soil densities; the aircraft made high-speed runs but did not become airborne.

b) tracked landing gear testbed

To enhance the *Beagle*'s ability to operate from tactical airfields a special tracked landing gear was designed, built and tested on an Il-28 pursuant to a Council of Ministers directive of 11 January 1951. It allowed the bomber to operate from soft, wet, soggy or snow-covered airfields which rendered take-off with a conventional wheeled landing gear very difficult or utterly impossible. The tests were considered successful, but owing to the extra weight and complexity of the experimental landing gear, it was not retrofitted to production aircraft.

V. Engine testbeds

a) Soviet testbed

One Il-28R (identity unknown) was modified to test a liquid-propellant rocket motor developed by L. S. Dooshkin. The experimental powerplant was

The Il-28LSh runs along a dirt strip. *(Yefim Gordon archive)*

This Il-28R served as a testbed for a liquid-propellant rocket motor developed by L. S. Dooshkin. *(Yefim Gordon archive)*

installed in a short fairing shaped like a cropped cone supplanting the gunner's station. The tests took place in 1953–7.

b) East German engine testbeds

Few remember nowadays that East Germany had an aircraft industry of its own. Besides building the Il-14P airliner under licence in Dresden, the Germans designed their own aircraft as well. In the early 1950s Brunolf Baade started work on the 152 – a 72-seat medium-haul airliner powered by four indigenous Pirna 014 turbojets rated at 3,150 kgp (6,944 lb st).[15]

Design work on the engine began in 1955, and the prototype was bench-run a year later. As the flight test stage approached, VEB Entwicklungsbau Pirna (Pirna Development & Manufacturing) at Pirna-Sonnenstein bought an Il-28R (c/n 1418) and converted it into an engine testbed. The reconnaissance version was chosen because of the stronger landing gear – a useful feature, since the engine alone, not including the test instrumentation, weighed 1,060 kg (2,336 lb). The aircraft was delivered *sans* radar and armament and registered DM-ZZI. Curiously, it carried the **West** German flag on the fin – for some obscure reason the elaborate coat of arms placed in the centre of the otherwise identical East German flag had been omitted.

The experimental engine was housed in a large nacelle under the centre fuselage (called *Tropfen*, drop [of water], in local slang); the bomb bay doors were faired over. To prevent FOD on take-off/landing and windmilling during cruise, the air intake was closed by a hydraulically actuated shutter which the test engineer could open or close by means of a hand-driven pump at up to 350 km/h (194 kt). The lower lip of the intake was flattened, resulting in a shape not unlike that of the Boeing 737-300/400/500; this was probably owing to the shape of the shutter rather than to inlet aerodynamics. The lower aft fuselage was covered

15 In Western publications the aircraft is often called BB 152 or VEB-152; however, (former) East German sources invariably refer to the aircraft simply as the 152. In fact, the prototypes should have been designated EF 152 (for *Entwicklungsflugzeug* – development aircraft), in keeping with the traditions of Junkers AG where Baade had once worked, but this designation was not taken up.

Avia B-228 6915 (c/n 56915) was used to test two jet engines. Here it is shown with a Walter M-701 turbojet installed in place of the tail turret; note the ventral air intake. *(Yefim Gordon archive)*

The same aircraft in its latter days. The recontoured tail fairing once housed an Ivchenko AI-25TL turbofan but the engine is removed here and the ventral intake and jetpipe faired over. In this guise 56915 was used for testing rescue parachutes by dropping dummies. *(Yefim Gordon archive)*

by some kind of heat-resistant gunk to protect it from the jet blast.

The bomb bay housed test instrumentation – a priming tank, a data recorder, an instrument panel and an AK 8 or AK 16 remote-controlled cine-camera (or a still camera) with appropriate lighting to film the instrument readings. The navigator was exiled to the gunner's cabin from which he kept an eye on the test engine via forward-view mirrors under the tailplanes, watching out for a possible fire, fuel leaks, etc. The regular navigator's compartment housed the test engineer, the Pirna 014's controls and more instruments. One of the fuel cells had to be removed, but the wingtip fuel tanks made up for this.

The first flight-cleared engine (the Pirna 014 V-9)[16] was fitted to DM-ZZI in 1959. For ground runs, the aircraft was wheeled onto special elevated supports to minimize FOD risk. Finally, on 11 September the aircraft made its first test flight from Dresden-Klotzsche airport (which was also the seat of VEB Flugzeugbau Dresden and a major air force base).

The test programme included performance testing at altitudes up to 12,500 m (41,010 ft) in 500 m (1,640 ft) increments and speeds up to Mach 0.78. Flight idling rpm and windmilling rpm at various speeds and altitudes were determined, relight possibilities at up to 12,000 m (39,370 ft) and the inclination to surge in different flight conditions were checked, icing tests and ground noise level measurements were made. For safety reasons the development engine was always started at altitudes in excess of 600 m (1,968 ft).

Flights were typically made in a racetrack pattern between the towns of Pulsnitz and Stolpen in the north-east (near the outer marker beacon of Dresden-Klotzsche) and the towns of Flöha and Zschopau to the south-west (near Karl-Marx-Stadt – now Chemnitz). Performance and handling differed little from that of a standard Il-28, except that with the test engine running at full power the aircraft's rate of climb increased to 35 m/sec (6,888 ft/min). In level flight at 10,000 m (32,808 ft) the testbed reached speeds of nearly 900 km/h (486 kt), so the main engines had to be throttled back so as not to exceed the Il-28's design limit of Mach 0.7.

DM-ZZI made a total of 109 test flights; the last flight took place on 22 February 1961 with a

Aeroflot personnel carry sacks of mail from an Il-20 mailplane (c/n 54005777). *(Yefim Gordon archive)*

production-standard Pirna 014A-1 built at Ludwigsfelde. However, the test programme was taking rather longer than anticipated, so another Il-28R (c/n 5901207) was converted into an identical testbed, registered DM-ZZK, to speed up the tests. This aircraft made 102 flights between 26 February 1960 and 12 June 1961 (the last flight was with Pirna 014 V-28). Other examples of the engine installed on the two aircraft included Pirna 014 V-20 (the first Pirna 014A-1) and Pirna 014 V-22.

Technically the tests went well – in fact, the engine performed rather better than expected. However, there were incidents of a different nature. On one occasion (28 March 1960) DM-ZZK, crewed by pilot Gerhard Puhlmann, navigator/radio operator Helmut Krautz and test engineer Klaus-Hermann Mewes, was intercepted by three Soviet Air Force (296th APIB)[17] MiG-17Fs. An aircraft had left the international air route near Magdeburg; hence the airspace had been closed, and Dresden ATC had neglected to call the Il-28 back promptly. The MiGs had scrambled from the nearby airbase at Grossenhain, expecting to find a Western spyplane – and the West German flag on the tail certainly did not help! One of the fighters lined up in front, with the others on the flanks, and unambiguously signalled the crew to follow them to Grossenhain. Luckily the situation was quickly clarified when the justifiably alarmed pilot called Dresden ATC, which promptly contacted the Soviet airbase and straightened things out. Even so, it was a nasty experience for the crew!

That was not the end of it. After landing at Dresden the cine-camera was reloaded, fresh chart paper was loaded into the test equipment recorders and the aircraft took off again to complete the day's test programme which had been so rudely interrupted. As it did so, a freak gust of wind caught it from behind, causing the aircraft to bounce twice before leaving the ground – just missing the localizer at the far end of the runway! Fearing that the mainwheel tyres were damaged and might explode at high altitude, the crew chose to terminate the assignment and land. It was just as well that they did: the tyres were indeed ruined and needed replacement. The day's programme had gone down the drain.

Meanwhile, the 152 V-1 (DM-ZYA) was rolled out in Dresden on 30 April 1958. On 4 December the aircraft made its first flight, powered by Mikulin RD-9B turbojets since no flight-cleared Pirna 014 engines were available yet. Three months later, on 4 March 1959, the prototype crashed owing to a fuel system defect, killing the crew. The much-modified second prototype (152 V-4, DM-ZYB), powered by Pirna 014A-1 engines, flew on 26 August 1960; the defect was soon discovered during defuelling tests and could be easily rectified. The third prototype (DM-ZYC) was completed in due course and the first 28 production aircraft were in various stages of completion.

Then the East German government lowered the boom. It had long considered the local aircraft industry unprofitable, and in late November 1960 it was decided to eliminate the industry altogether. Big Brother would supply East Germany with all the aircraft she needed anyway. And by mid-1961 the BB 152 (and hence the Pirna 014) was abandoned. DM-ZZI and DM-ZZK were reconverted to Il-28R standard and delivered to the East German Air Force as 180 Black and 184 Black respectively on 1 November 1961 for use as target tugs. The navigator's station was reinstated, but the armament and radar were still missing.

(As a point of interest, the Germans were vindicated before long. The Soviet Yakovlev Yak-30/Yak-32 advanced trainers and Beriyev Be-30/Be-32 feederliner were similarly victimized by the COMECON strategists in the mid-1960s, even though they were at least as good as the Aero L-29 Delfin and Let L-410 Turbolet pressed into Soviet service.)

c) Czech engine/parachute testbed

A Czech Air Force Il-28 (Avia B-228) serialled 6915 (c/n 56915) was converted into an engine testbed by Walter (currently named Motorlet) in June 1960. Originally it served to test the indigenous 890 kgp (1,960 lb st) Walter M-701 turbojet developed for the Aero L-29 Delfin advanced trainer. The centrifugal-flow turbojet was rather too portly to fit under the *Beagle*'s fuselage, so a rather unorthodox installation was chosen – the engine was mounted in an ogival fairing instead of the tail turret, breathing through a ventral 'elephant's-ear' air intake. The bomb bay was occupied by test instrumentation.

Later the same machine was used to test the 1,500 kgp (3,306 lb st) AI-25TL turbofan in a recontoured and more elongated fairing. This Soviet engine, designed by OKB-478 under Aleksey G. Ivchenko, powered the Aero L-39 Albatros advanced trainer (the licence-built version was sometimes referred to as the Walter Titan). The engine and associated equipment were subsequently removed but for some obscure reason the long fairing was retained, though the air intake and nozzle

16 V = *Versuchsmuster* – test article or development aircraft.

17 APIB = ***avia**polk* *istre**bit**eley-bombardi**rov**schchikov* – fighter-bomber regiment (≅ fighter-bomber wing).

were faired over. In this configuration the aircraft was used to test new models of parachutes by dropping dummies filled with sand.

d) Il-28H

The type did some development work in Poland as well. One Il-28, serialled 119 Blue, was transferred to the *Instytut Lotnictwa* (Institute of Aviation) in Warsaw and converted into an engine testbed designated Il-28H (*hamownia* – test rig or, in this case, testbed). It was used to test the indigenous 1,000 kgp (2,204 lb st) PZL-Rzeszów SO-1 turbojet[18] developed for the PZL TS-11 Iskra (Spark) advanced trainer.

The engine was installed on a special mount and was semi-recessed in the open bomb bay when on the ground. It was lowered clear of the fuselage by hydraulic rams before startup; for ground runs the aircraft was parked over a special trench. The experimental engine's controls were installed in the navigator's compartment where the test engineer sat. The test programme was successfully completed in the spring of 1964. Later the Il-28H was used as a carrier/launcher for the indigenous Mak-30 remotely piloted vehicle (RPV).

VI. Parachute testbed

Two Polish Air Force Il-28s, 001 Red and 2 Red, were used by the Polish Air Force's Technical Institute (ITWL – *Instytut Techniczny Wojsk Lotniczych*) to test the PB-28 brake parachute with a 7 m (23 ft) diameter.

Il-20 (Il-28P) mailplane

The *Beagle* had a paw in the development of civil jet aviation in the Soviet Union as well. In order to familiarize pilots and ground personnel of Aeroflot (the sole Soviet airline) with jets and help Aeroflot to gain practical experience operating them, a few demilitarized Il-28 bombers were transferred to the airline. These aircraft were designated Il-20[19] or Il-28P (*poch**t**ovyy* [*samo**lyot***] – mailplane). The type was chosen carefully, as the Il-28 was easy to fly and service and posed no problems for Aeroflot crews

Another Il-20, SSSR-L ...538 (the first digit is illegible; c/n 54006104). Unlike c/n 54005777, this example has a civil-style colour scheme with a red cheatline and blue pinstripe, not just Aeroflot titles and logo. *(Yefim Gordon archive)*

Aeroflot pilots read a fresh newspaper which has just been delivered by an Il-20. This was one of the perks of the job! *(Sergey and Dmitriy Komissarov archive)*

flying Il-12 and Lisunov Li-2P (or Douglas C-47 Dakota) airliners. The Il-28's high speed, long-range and modern (in its day) avionics allowed the crews to quickly master jet aircraft flying techniques, and eased the subsequent transition to the big jets considerably. The aircraft's good field performance enabled it to use most civilian airports of the time.

The first group of Aeroflot flight crews started conversion training for the Il-20 in October 1953, and the type began carrying freight and mail in late 1954. The Il-20 was much used to deliver matrices of the *Pravda* and *Izvestiya* central newspapers from Moscow to Irkutsk, where both papers had additional print shops. If the papers were delivered all the way from Moscow they would be one day old by the time they reached the Far Eastern regions of the Soviet Union, and who wants yesterday's news? Together with the so-called Tu-104G (*groozo**voy*** – cargo, used attributively), which was really a demilitarized Tu-16 *Badger-A* bomber, the Il-20 enabled Aeroflot to develop a training programme which speeded up the introduction of the first Soviet jet airliner, the Tu-104 *Camel.*

Foreign production

a) Chinese production

As it did with many Soviet types, China built the Il-28 – *without* the benefit of a licence. This piracy began after the rift in Sino-Soviet relations over ideological differences in the mid-1960s put an end to new aircraft deliveries from the USSR. Since China had no indigenous tactical bomber, there was no option but to copy a Soviet design.

In 1964 the aircraft factory in Harbin started manufacturing spare parts for the Soviet-built Il-28s operated by the Chinese air arm. This logically led to the production of complete aircraft; construction of the first two airframes – the prototype and a static test airframe – also began in 1964, and the first locally manufactured Il-28 took to the air on 25

18 SO = *silnik odrzutowy* – jet engine.

19 The designation was reused, initially being used for the experimental ground attack aircraft of 1948. It was subsequently re-reused for yet another spin-off of the Il-18D – an ELINT aircraft (NATO *Coot-B*).

Large numbers of H-5s were built both for domestic use and for export. Outwardly the Chinese version was almost identical to the genuine Soviet-built Il-28. *(China Aircraft)*

September 1966, flown by pilot Wang Wenying, navigator Zhang Huichang and radio operator Zeng Fannan. Full-scale production at Harbin commenced the following year. Chinese-built *Beagle*s were designated **H-5** (*hongzhaji* – bomber) or **B-5** (B = bomber) for export.

To be perfectly honest, the Chinese did not adopt a simple copycat approach, but altered the *Beagle* considerably, changing up to 40 per cent of the design. In particular, the H-5 had a different (conventional) wing design without the Il-28's trademark feature (the technological break along the chord line); this saved some 110 kg (242 lb) of weight, although the manufacturing process became more diffficult.

Outwardly the Chinese reverse-engineered *Chowchow* can be distinguished from the genuine Soviet-built *Beagle* mainly by the shape of the rear extremity of the fuselage. The original Il-K6 ball-turret is replaced by the DK-7 turret mounting two Afanas'yev/Makarov AM-23 cannon with 500 rpg. This turret is borrowed from the Tupolev Tu-16 *Badger* medium bomber; it is of basically cylindrical shape, not spherical. Also, the cockpit canopy has a one-piece blown transparency (without the lengthwise frame member), a taxiing light is built into the forward door of the nosewheel well (a feature not found on most Soviet-built *Beagle*s) and the starboard forward-firing cannon is deleted.

A tactical nuclear strike version similar to the Soviet Il-28A was developed in September 1967; the first test drop of a nuclear bomb from such an aircraft took place on 25 (some sources say 27) December 1968.

The Il-28U was also manufactured in Harbin as the **HJ-5** (*hongzhaji jiaolianji* – bomber trainer) or **BT-5** (bomber trainer), making its second first flight on 12 December 1970. It was officially phased in by the People's Liberation Army Air Force (PLAAF) in 1972, and a total of 187 were built.

The Chinese also brought out torpedo bomber and PHOTINT versions of the H-5; the Chinese equivalent of the Il-28R was developed in 1970, bearing the designation **HZ-5** (*hongzhaji zhenchaji* – bomber/reconnaissance aircraft) for the home market or **B-5R** for export. The aircraft was equipped with two cameras for day/night high-altitude photography. Unlike the Soviet reconnaissance version,

Wearing leather helmets, a Chinese pilot and navigator/bomb aimer take their seats in H-5 0986 Red. This view clearly shows the nose cannon. *(China Aircraft)*

10692 Red, a Harbin HJ-5 (the Chinese version of the Il-28U), in the PLAAF Museum at Datangshan AB. *(F. C. W. Käsmann)*

the HZ-5 had underwing drop tanks instead of tip tanks; these extended the range by 47 per cent, the combat radius by 50 per cent and endurance by 1 hour 23 minutes. Development of the PHOTINT version was rather protracted, and the aircraft was not officially included into the PLAAF inventory until 1977.

b) Czech production

Czechoslovakia, too, built the Il-28, but in this case everything was legitimate, as a licence had been obtained. In the 1950s the Czech Air Force had a habit of giving indigenous designations to foreign military aircraft operated or built in Czechoslovakia. For example, the MiG-15 fighter and UTI-MiG-15 trainer were manufactured by the Aero enterprise as the S-102 (S = *stíhací* [*letoun*] – fighter) and CS-102 (CS = *cvičný stíhací* [*letoun*] – fighter trainer) respectively. Thus the *Beagle* was built locally as the **Avia B-228** (for *bombardovací* [*letoun*] – bomber), while the licence-built version of the Il-28U trainer was designated **CB-228** (for *cvičný bombardovací* [*letoun*] – bomber trainer).

***

By the mid-1950s, the general operational requirements of tactical bombers had become much more stringent, rendering the subsonic Il-28 obsolete. Therefore, on 3 February 1956 the USSR Council of Ministers issued a directive to the effect that production of the Il-28 be stopped. By then, as already mentioned, 6,316 aircraft had rolled off the assembly lines in the USSR; the Il-28 surpassed all other Soviet jet bombers in terms of production.

The importance of the Il-28 in the development of the Soviet Air Force can hardly be played down. To the VVS and other friendly air forces it was what the English Electric Canberra was to the West, which gave rise to the nickname 'Soviet Canberra' – albeit much later when the Il-28 was dead and buried. The Canberra, however, was clearly luckier

Avia B-228s (Czech-built Il-28s) taxi out for a training sortie. Note the stained forward fuselage of AD-31 (probably a result of firing the nose cannon); the soot has been scrubbed away, but only just enough to make the serial readable. *(RART)*

The Il-46 was a scaled-up version of the *Beagle*. Note the unusual side-by-side twin main landing gear units. *(Yefim Gordon archive)*

This view of the sole Il-46 prototype clearly shows its Il-28 lineage. The envisaged swept-wing version was never built. *(Yefim Gordon archive)*

than its Soviet counterpart, soldiering on well into the 1980s (mostly in the reconnaissance and target tug roles), and the last survivors remain operational at the time of writing.

The Il-28 had a follow-on in the shape of the Il-46 medium bomber developed pursuant to a Council of Ministers directive of 24 March 1951. It looked like a scaled-up Il-28 powered by two Lyulka AL-5 axial-flow turbojets (also called TR-3A) rated at 5,000 kgp (11,022 lb st). The defensive armament arrangement was the same but the Il-K8 tail turret was new, featuring a much bigger field of fire and a bigger ammunition supply (320 rpg). The main landing gear design was also similar, except that there were two independent shock struts each side, the outboard units retracting forward and the inboard units aft; this unusual arrangement was used to keep the nacelle cross-section to a minimum. The aircraft had an overall length of 25.325 m (83 ft 1 in.), a wingspan of 29.0 m (95 ft 1.73 in.), a wing area of 105 m^2 (1,129 sq. ft), an empty operating weight of 26,300 kg (57,980 lb) and a normal TOW of 41,840 kg (92,240 lb). The normal bomb load was 3,000 kg (6,613 lb) and the maximum bomb load 6,000 kg (13,227 lb). If the Il-28 was a Beagle, then the Il-46 was surely a Borzoi – a Russian wolfhound. (Or, more likely from a Western viewpoint, a Big Bad Wolf.)

The ADP design stage was completed on 4 December 1951 and the prototype was rolled out on 29 December (!). On 3 March 1952 the Il-46 made its first flight with Vladimir K. Kokkinaki at the controls. Manufacturer's flight tests showed a top speed of 928 km/h (501 kt) at 5,000 m (16,404 ft) and a range of 4,845 km (3,009 miles). The State acceptance trials were completed on 15 October, showing that the bomber fully met the Air Force's operational requirement. The second prototype designated Il-46S, representing the envisaged production version, was to have wings swept back 35°. However, the swept-wing Il-46 was never completed, losing out to the more promising and modern Tu-16.

•3

THE *BEAGLE* IN SERVICE

The advent of the Il-28 signified the beginning of the jet age for the Soviet tactical bomber force. As already mentioned, a bomber unit of the Moscow Defence District commanded by Lt-Col A. A. Anpilov was the first to take delivery of the new bomber in 1950. The availability of the Il-28U prototype facilitated conversion training no end; 27 service pilots transitioned from the Tu-2 to the Il-28 in just ten days, during which 112 training flights were made. In contrast, conversion of the same pilots to the Tu-2 had taken more than two months and a good deal more flying.

The VVS bomber units re-equipped with the *Beagle* by the mid-1950s. Of course, the units and formations stationed in the western defence districts of the USSR which were closest to the potential adversary enjoyed priority in this respect. These included the bomber divisions based at Chernyakhovsk (Lithuania, Baltic Defence District), Starokonstantinov and Stryy (the Ukrainian part of the Carpathian DD),[1] Limanskoye (Odessa DD), etc. Each bomber division (≅ bomber group, in US terms) included two or three bomber regiments (≅ bomber wings) consisting of three squadrons; each squadron had ten *Beagle*s (three flights of three plus a reserve aircraft in case one went unserviceable) and one or two Il-28U trainers. For instance, the 63rd BAD of the 57th VA included the 7th FBAP at Starokonstantinov and the 408th FBAP at Stryy;[2] other units operating the Il-28 included the 230th FBAP at Cherlyany AB.

The Il-28 introduced radar and gave nuclear capability to the tactical bomber force – a feature which was particularly welcome during the Cold War years. Once it had become fully operational – i.e. the crews learned to fly in poor weather conditions and at extreme altitudes (breaking through cloud cover during climb and descent), use radar and synchronised optical sights for bomb-aiming and use the defensive armament effectively – Soviet tactical air power received a major boost. Service introduction was speeded up by holding workshops in which the Air Force C-in-C and other top brass, as well as ordinary service pilots, Ilyushin OKB engineers and representatives from the factories building the bomber took part.

The Il-28 contributed a lot to the development of Soviet free-fall nuclear weapons. As already mentioned, the *Beagle* was used to test the RDS-4 nuclear bomb, which then became the standard weapon of the Il-28N and Yak-28 *Brewer*. On

1 Besides the western part of the Ukraine, the Carpathian DD included Moldavia.

2 BAD = *bombardee**ro**vochnaya* ***a**viadiveeziya* – bomber division; VA = *voz**doosh**naya* ***ar**miya* – air army (≅ air force); FBAP = ***f**rontovoy* ***b**ombardee**ro**vochnyy* ***a**via**polk*** – tactical bomber regiment. Some sources claim the 408th FBAP was based at Cherlyany AB.

Sporting an unusually large Soviet Air Force star on the tail, an Il-28 taxies out past a sister ship. *(Yefim Gordon archive)*

A curious picture showing Soviet Army motorcyclists rolling *en masse* along the flight line of an airbase with a resident *Beagle* unit, most probably on the occasion of a parade for a visiting high-ranking commander. *(Yefim Gordon archive)*

3 August 1953 a specially modified Il-28 dropped the first Soviet hydrogen bomb at the Semipalatinsk proving ground. On 12 August in the same year two Il-28s operating from Zhana-Semey AB monitored the test of the first Soviet neutron bomb performed under the guidance of Igor' V. Kurchatov, the Soviet counterpart of Samuel Cohen.

A case is on record when the *Beagle* actually operated in a nuclear environment. On 14 September 1954 three regiments of Il-28s (the entire 140th BAD) took off and headed for the Totskoye training range in groups of nine aircraft to take part in a tactical nuclear exercise. Each bomber squadron was escorted by two flights of MiG-17s. The

Flaps fully extended, Il-28 23 Red is caught by the camera seconds before touchdown. *(Yefim Gordon archive)*

A formation of *Beagle*s cruises over typically flat east European countryside during a military exercise. *(Yefim Gordon archive)*

Soviet Air Force Il-28s often operated in close formations, as illustrated by this shot taken by the gunner of a sister ship. *(Sergey and Dmitriy Komissarov archive)*

Although of poor quality, this picture is nevertheless interesting, showing an Il-28 dropping a stick of bombs. One can only guess what aircraft served as the camera ship but it was definitely not another *Beagle*. *(Yefim Gordon archive)*

exercise was commanded by Marshal Gheorgiy Konstantinovich Zhukov of Great Patriotic War fame.

The pilots were issued with special goggles to protect their eyes from the flash of the nuclear explosion. When the bomb went off, creating the tell-tale mushroom cloud, the incoming armada started to take evasive action, but suddenly a freak wind blew the cloud straight into its path. The jets were flying in close formation and there was not much room for manoeuvres because of the danger of collision; most aircraft managed to steer clear, but some went smack into the cloud. It is not known what the consequences were for the pilots or their jets.

The AVMF started receiving the *Beagle* in the summer of 1951, initially in basic bomber configuration. The Black Sea Fleet's 943rd MTAP and the Red Banner Baltic Fleet's 1531st MTAP were the first naval units to receive the type; the North Fleet did not follow suit until 1953, the 574th MTAP being the first Il-28 operator there. The introduction of combat jets coincided with a severe escalation of international tension ignited by the Korean War. The outbreak of the war put an end to post-Second World War arms reductions. The Soviet anti-shipping force started growing rapidly owing to both the formation of new units and the transfer of complete bomber regiments from the Air Force to the Navy; soon the AVMF had up to twenty torpedo-bomber units.

Later, as already mentioned, the naval bombers were converted to carry one RAT-52 torpedo; this version was phased in by the AVMF in early 1953. Also, the *Beagle*s of the Red Banner Baltic Fleet's 769th OMTAP were converted to Il-28PL 'quick-fix' ASW aircraft. Two more Baltic Fleet Il-28 units were to undertake a similar conversion, but these plans were rendered void by the advent of the more capable Tu-16.

Interestingly, the Il-28 was the downfall of the Soviet leader's son, Vasiliy I. Stalin, who commanded the air force of the Moscow Defence District. During the May Day parade of 1952, numerous fighters and bombers were to pass over

Soviet Naval Aviation airmen wearing leather jackets and 1950s-style white-topped Navy caps pose beside an Il-28. *(Yefim Gordon archive)*

Red Square in Moscow to emphasize the might of the Soviet air arm. However, the weather forecast said the weather would be beastly, with low clouds and rain all over the place. Hence the VVS C-in-C cancelled the flypast; still, V. Stalin called him on the phone, requesting permission to go ahead if the weather improved. The C-in-C gave the go-ahead, warning that Stalin would bear the full responsibility if anything went wrong. In the end V. Stalin got tired of waiting and ordered the bombers to take off and head for Moscow as planned, even though the visibility was close to nil – an unprecedented decision in peacetime.

The result was deplorable. Some bomber units missed Red Square altogether, others passed across it at right angles to the planned heading, still others were ordered to return to base before reaching Moscow. Even so, the spectators at Red Square could not see the aircraft because of the low clouds, hearing only the jet thunder overhead. But the worst was yet to come: two Il-28s collided near Migalovo AB, Kalinin (now Tver'), and crashed, killing the crews. For this outstanding performance Vasiliy Stalin was promptly removed from office.

On 9 March 1953 a group of Il-28s overflew the Red Square in Moscow during Josef Stalin's funeral in a farewell salute to the deceased leader. The weather that day was bad, with extreme icing conditions, and the *Beagle* was the only aircraft which could accomplish this mission, being, as it were, the only Soviet aircraft at the time to feature a de-icing system.

Soon after the Il-28 had become operational with first-line bomber units, the Soviet Air Force's flying schools also started taking delivery of the type. These included the Tambov Higher Military Pilot School named after the famous record-setting female pilot Marina Raskova (TVVAUL – *Tam**bov**skoye **v**yssheye **v**oyennoye **a**viatsee**onn**oye **oochil**ischche **l**yotchikov*), the Slavgorod branch of the Omsk Military Pilot School and the Nikolayev Minelayer and Torpedo-Bomber Flying School.

The Il-28 was very popular with its crews and technical staff, and with good reason. The aircraft was easy to fly and operate, adequately armed and had a good safety and reliability record, once the learning curve had been overcome. Pilots accustomed to the spartan conditions of the Tu-2 with its cold and noisy cockpits were amazed by the comfortable and well-equipped cockpits of the *Beagle*. They were also quick to appreciate the Il-28's speed, rate of climb and good manoeuvrability. The technical staff, too, liked the Il-28 for its ease of access to the engines and all equipment items requiring maintenance in day-to-day service.

Of course, like any new type, the Il-28 had its share of teething troubles. Typical defects included asymmetric flap deployment (caused by air locks in the hydraulic lines feeding the flap drive jacks), radar and autopilot failures. These were dealt with as they came. The radar was a royal pain in the neck at first, since it used vacuum tubes which are sensitive to vibration and G loads (to say nothing of Soviet electronics, which were notoriously unreliable). Luckily the engineers who had created the PSBN-M had foreseen this and designed the radar as a modular system with line-replaceable units (LRUs), which eliminated the need to keep the aircraft grounded for radar repairs and ultimately was one of the factors of the *Beagle*'s high combat readiness.

Airmen love to tell tall tales, and one of them (concerning the Il-28) is this. After the Ilyushin OKB had made some updates, a bomber unit equipped with *Beagle*s received orders that all the aircraft be urgently upgraded to the new standard. The work had to be done in a hangar, and the local hangar was too small to accommodate all the aircraft present at the base. On the other hand, failure to comply with the orders would result in disciplinary action.

Everybody racked their brains in search of a solution until, with a sly twinkle in his eye, one crew chief said he knew the answer. He would not tell it until he was assured of a reward in the form of a bottle of vodka. His method was simple: the technicians deflated the port mainwheel of each bomber, causing the bomber to bank a few degrees – just enough to allow the port wing of one aircraft *to fit under the starboard wing of another aircraft*! This allowed all the bombers to fit into the hangar and the updates to be made on schedule. Bless the technician, the Man of Infinite Resource and Sagacity!

The *Beagle*'s sturdiness and reliability soon became legendary. On one occasion an Il-28 from Chernyakhovsk ditched in the Baltic Sea after an unspecified malfunction; the aircraft remained afloat for more than two hours before being towed to the shore and was eventually returned to service. On another occasion a 408th FBAP Il-28U hit a storm cloud at 6,000 m (19,685 ft) and emerged from it at 1,800 m (5,905 ft) with several holes burned by lightning strikes and the paint on all leading edges sandpapered away by hail. The VK-1 engine earned particularly high praise. Low-level missions were the order of the day, and quite often Il-28s ingested birds or clipped treetops during such missions, eating branches; but, the engines usually kept running as if nothing had happened!

In defence of peace and socialism, or Cold War warriors

New efficient combat tactics were developed for the type, since the Il-28 was introduced when the Cold War was at its peak and was expected to turn hot any moment. *Beagle* crews practised night-flying and close-formation flying in flights, squadrons and regiments; the distance between aircraft in a flight did not exceed 40 m (131 ft) and the distance between flights in a regiment did not exceed 80 m (262 ft). As the VVS built up experience with the Il-28, pilots started making formation take-offs from dirt strips in groups of three to nine aircraft. From time to time the units flying the Il-28 deployed to remote bases for training purposes; e.g. the *Beagle*s of the 63rd BAD would fly as far as the

The Il-28U was delivered to the Soviet Air Force's flying schools along with the combat version. *(Yefim Gordon archive)*

An Air Force instructor shows the Il-28U's rear cockpit layout to a cadet. *(Yefim Gordon archive)*

Flight training sometimes led to spills. This *Mascot*, 79 Red, made a belly-landing in a field, fortunately suffering almost no damage. *(Yefim Gordon archive)*

Central Asian DD, deploying to Karshi in south-eastern Uzbekistan and Maryy (pronounced like the French name Marie) in Turkmenistan.

During such raids the crews would practise bombing attacks at unfamiliar target ranges. Bombs were dropped from altitudes ranging from 100 to 10,000 m (328–32,808 ft), both by single aircraft and in formations of varying size as commanded by the leader. Special targets with a high radar signature were built at such ranges. Occasionally, however, bomber crews would lose their way *en route*; as a result, grain processing units and vehicle depots of nearby collective farms could get bombed, since their image on the PSBN-M's radar display was very similar to the practice targets. Fortunately the damage was usually minimal because practice bomblets filled mainly with soot were normally used. But one night a disaster was averted at the last moment. An Il-28 carrying a live 1,000 kg (2,204 lb) FAB-1000 high-explosive bomb took off from an airbase near Stanislav (now Ivano-Frankovsk), heading for a target range at Kamenka-Boogskaya, but strayed off course and overflew the city of L'vov instead. It was sheer luck that the bomb aimer happened to look away from the radar display a few seconds before the drop and saw the city lights below.

Combat training in the Soviet Air Force's Il-28 units included operations from unpaved airstrips. *(Sergey and Dmitriy Komissarov archive)*

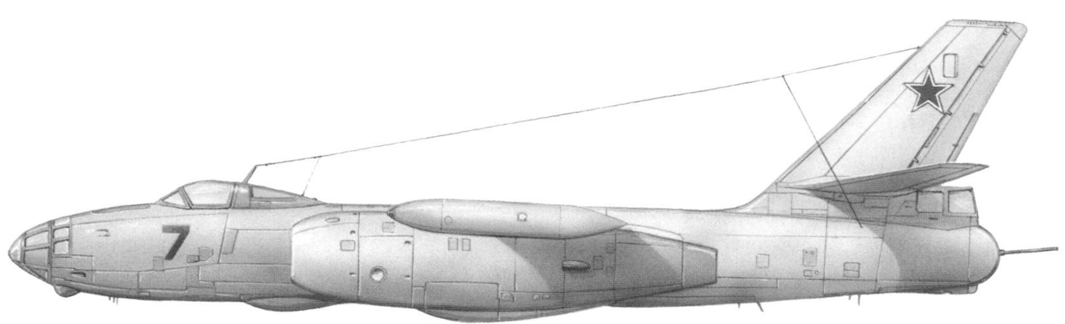

This Soviet Navy Il-28T torpedo-bomber was operated by the Pacific Fleet's 567th MTAP (Minelayer and Torpedo-Bomber Regiment).

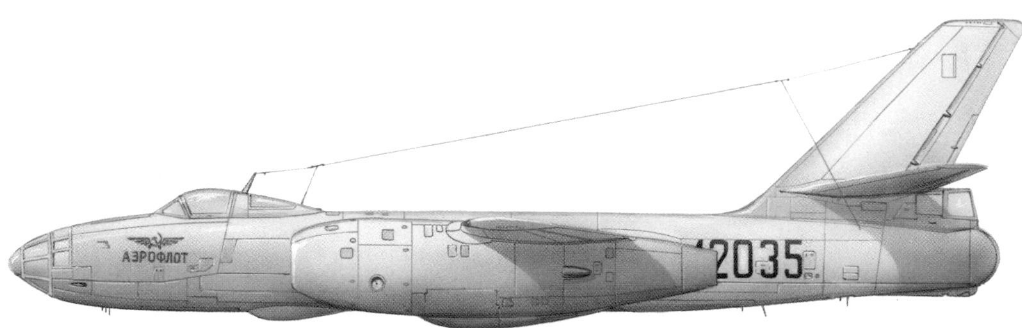

SSSR-L2035, an Aeroflot Il-20 mailplane.

Albanian Air Force Harbin H-5 3608.

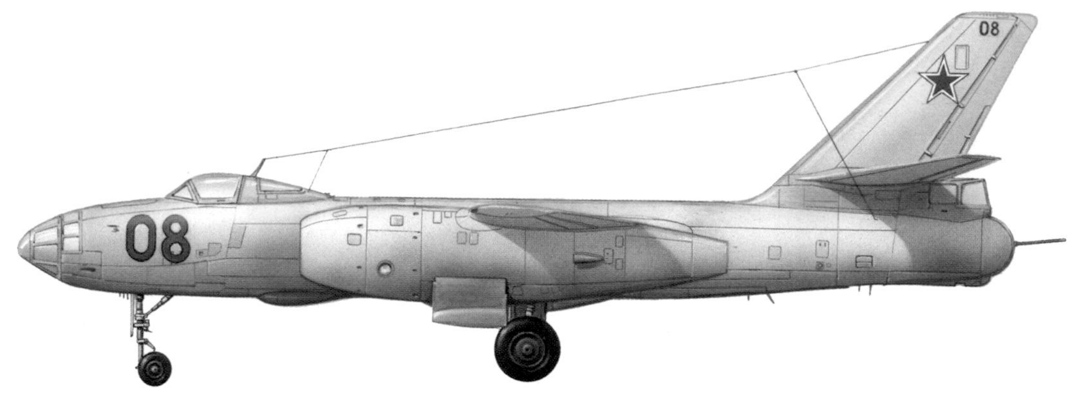
08
08

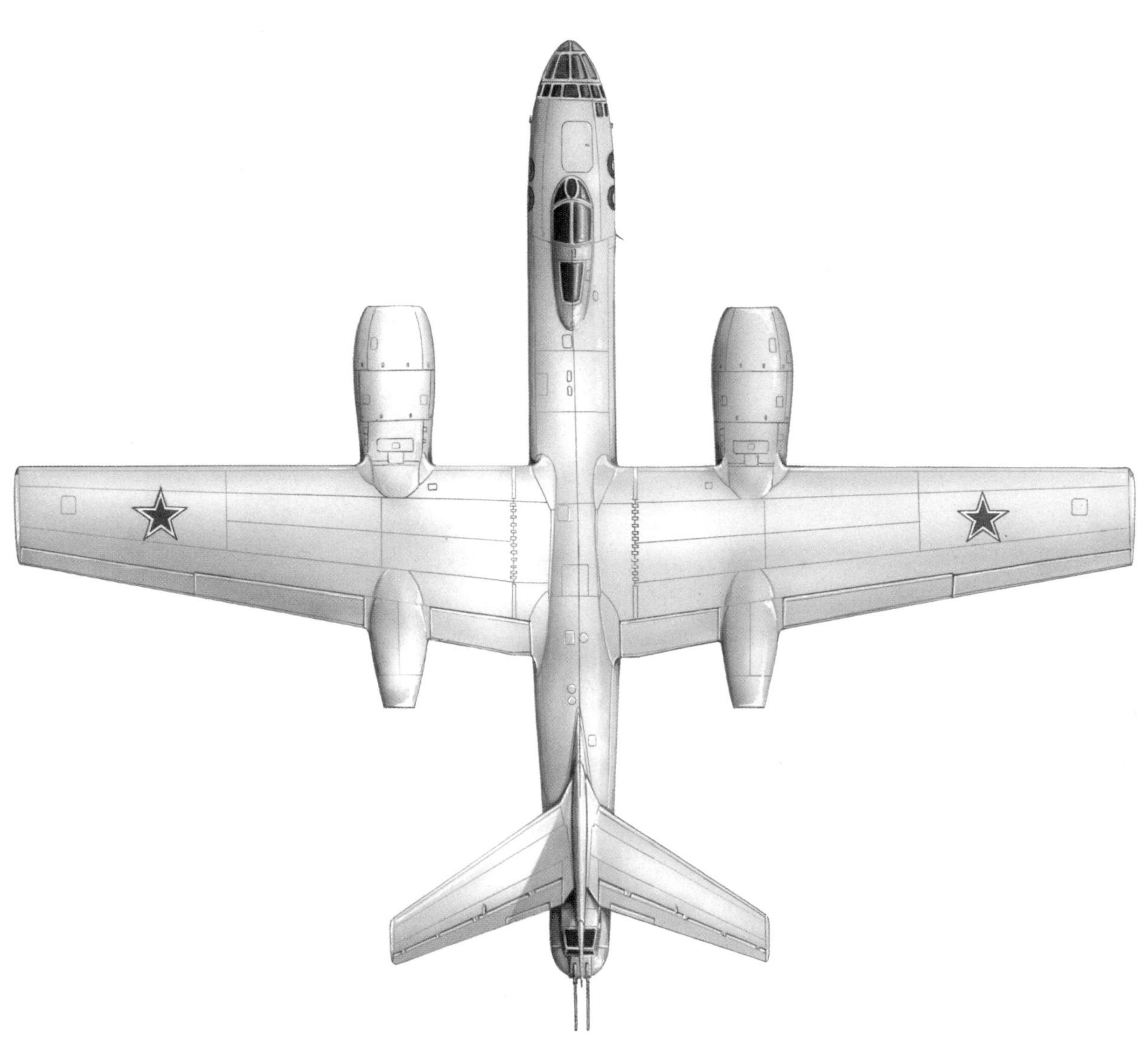

Above and opposite: A three-view illustration of Il-28 08 Blue operated by the 57th VA (Air Army)/63rd BAD (Bomber Division)/409th FBAP (Tactical Bomber Regiment), Cherlyany AB, Carpathian Defence District.

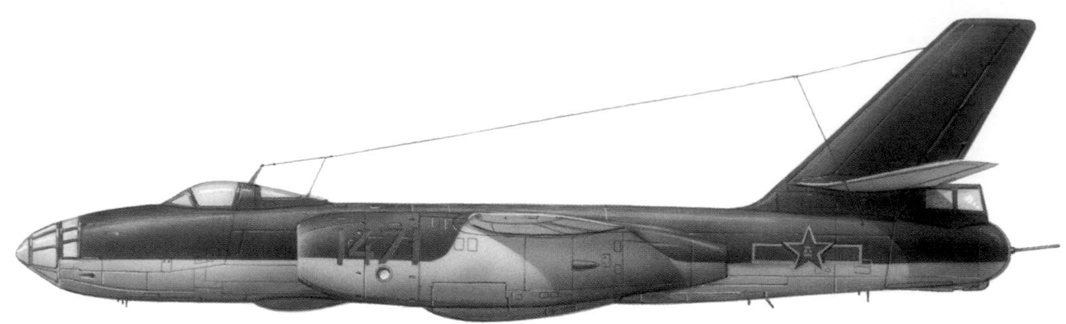

1471 Red, a Soviet-built Chinese People's Liberation Army Air Force Il-28.

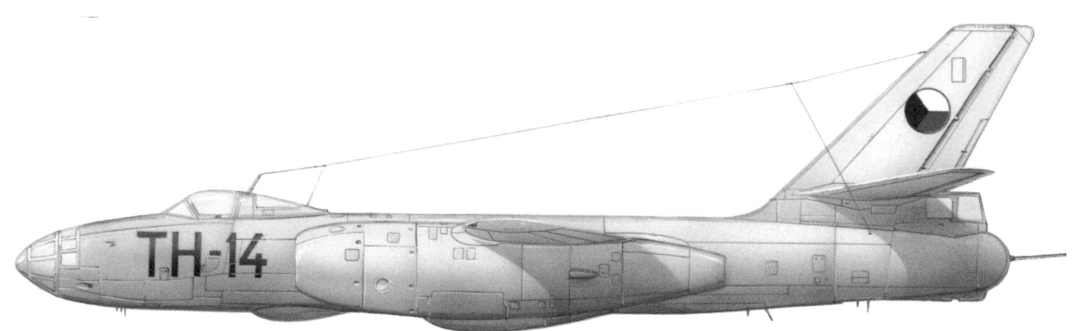

A Czech Air Force Avia B-228 in pre-1957 markings. This particular aircraft was used by the skydivers Jaroslav Jehlička, Zdeněk Kaplan and Gustav Koubek to set a world record on 20 March 1957.

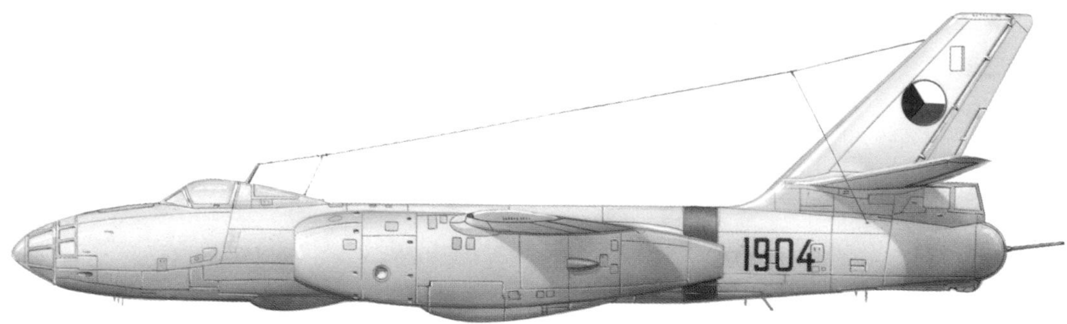

Czech Air Force Il-29 1904 with a post-1957 serial and a red identification band applied for a war game.

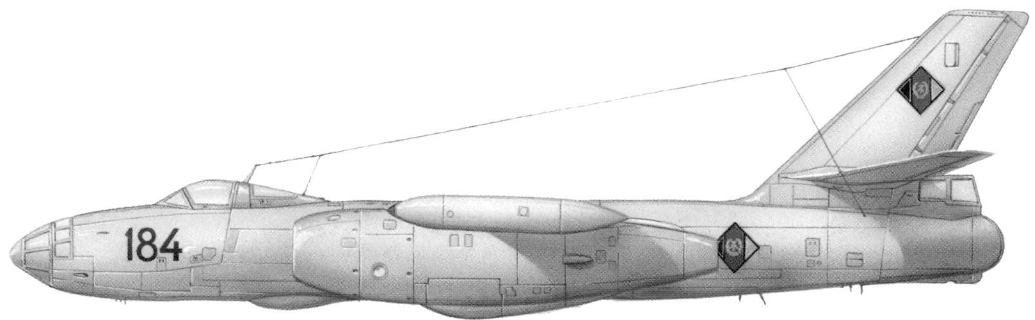

East German Air Force (ZDS 21) Il-28R 184 Black (c/n 5901207). Earlier in its career this aircraft had been registered DM-ZZK and used as a testbed for the Pirna 014A turbojet.

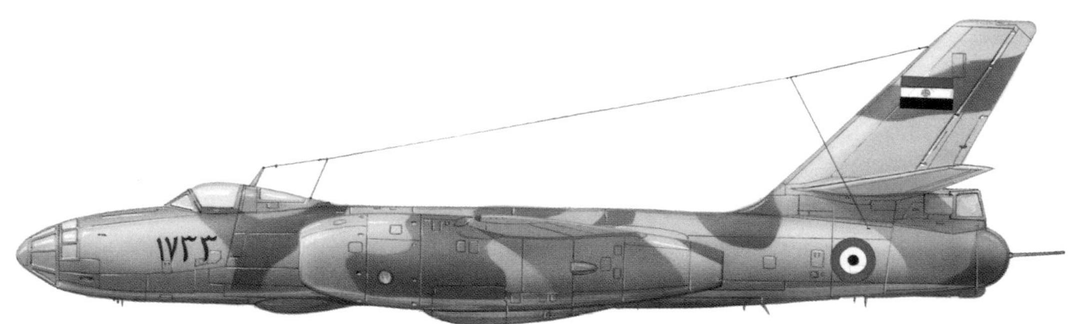

Egyptian Air Force Il-28 1733 in post-1967 camouflage.

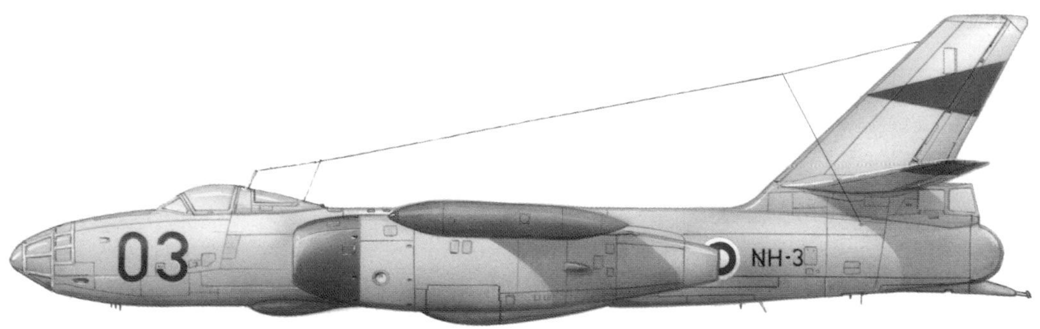

Finnish Air Force Il-28R (Il-28BM) target tug NH-3 (c/n 1713). The zero on the nose was later removed.

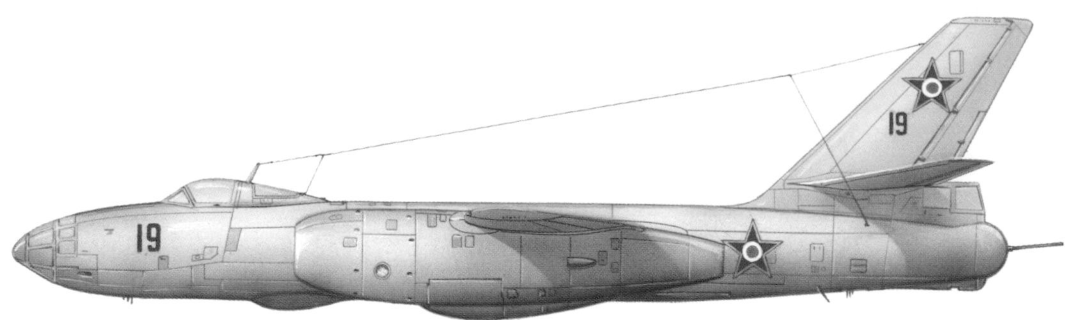

Hungarian Air Force Il-28RTR 19 Red.

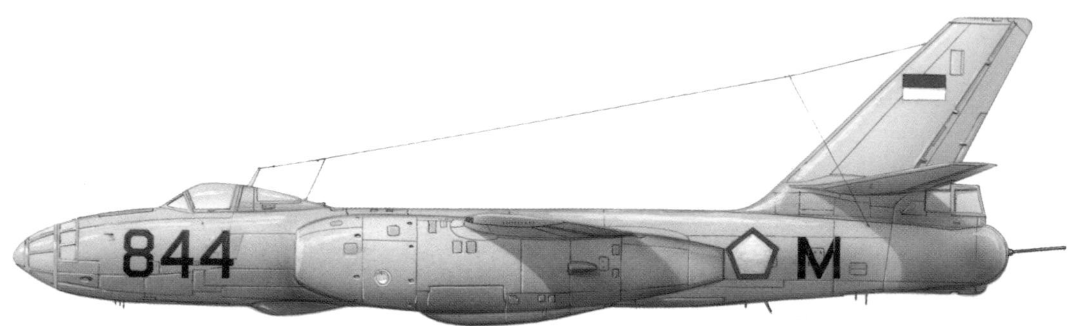

Indonesian Navy Il-28T M844 in early-style markings.

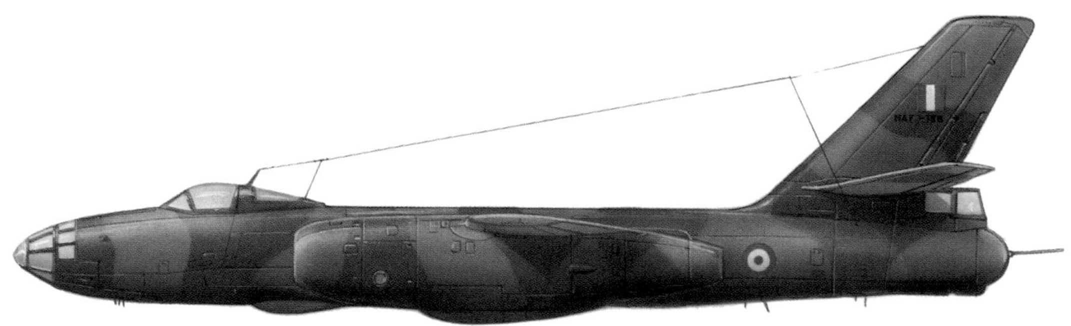

Federal Nigerian Air Force Il-28 NAF-158.

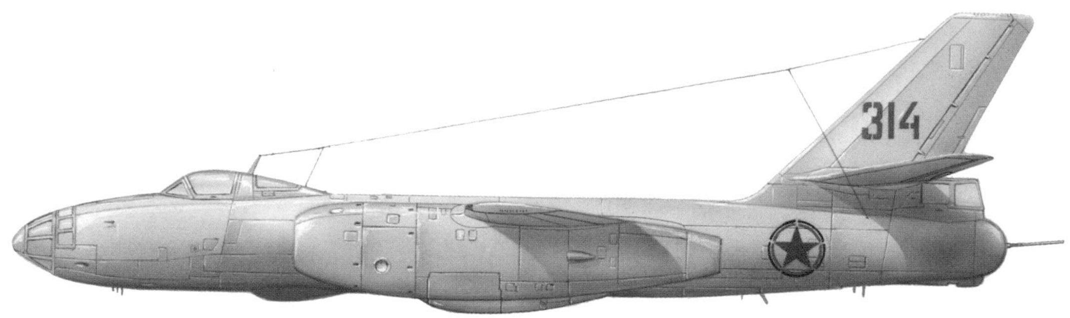

North Korean Air Force Il-28 314 Red.

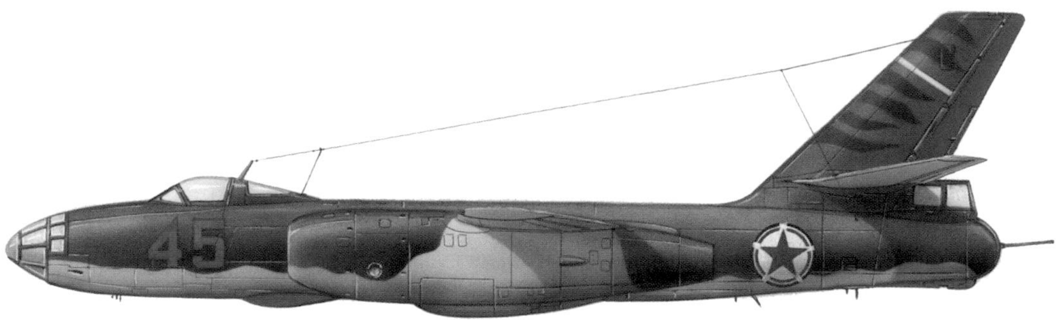

Some North Korean *Beagle*s, like 45 Blue, had a green and blue colour scheme. The tail shows what looks like the beginnings of hastily applied camouflage.

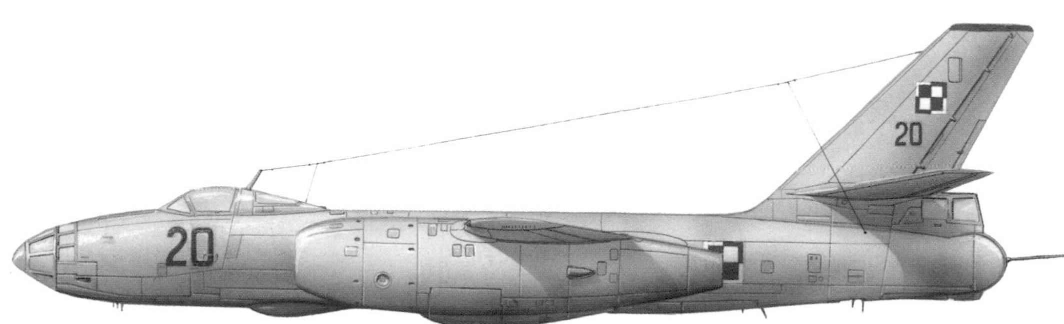

Polish Air Force Il-28 20 Red.

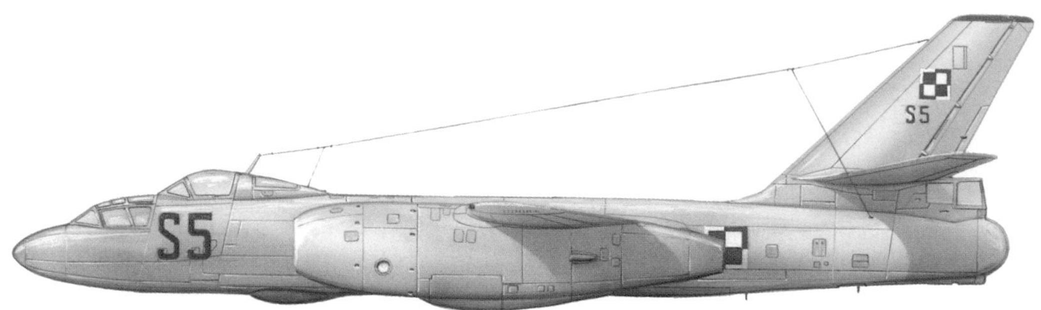

S5 Red was one of several Il-28Us delivered to the Polish Air Force.

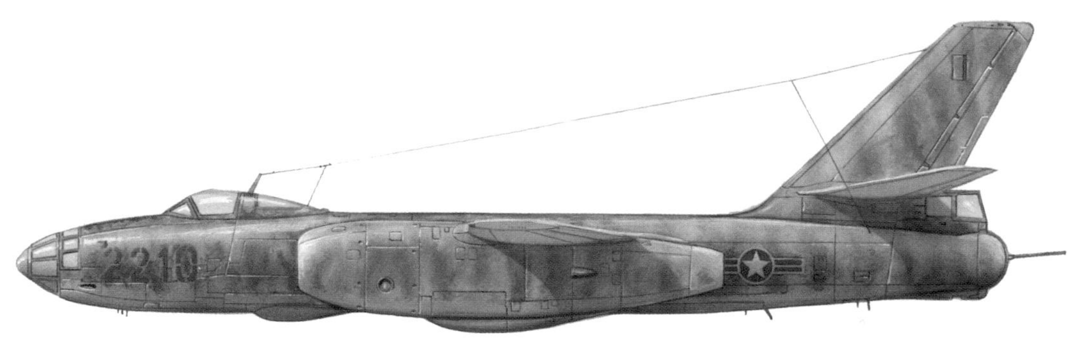

Vietnamese People's Air Force Il-28 2210 Red.

Penetrating enemy air defences was an important aspect of the Il-28 crews' combat training programme. Mock combat with Mikoyan/Gurevich MiG-15 *Fagot*s and MiG-17 *Fresco*s impersonating enemy fighters showed that a fighter armed solely with cannon had no chance against the *Beagle*. In a head-on attack the bomber's high speed caused the fighter to close on the target at an enormous rate, leaving the fighter pilot little time to take aim (quite apart from the fact that the Il-28 had a pair of forward-firing cannon with which to discourage such attacks). In the rear hemisphere the bomber's effective tail turret and high manoeuvrability enabled the crew to successfully repel the fighters.

The advent of the supersonic MiG-19 *Farmer-A/C* did not make things easier for the adversaries – in fact, it made things harder because the closing speed was now greater, and in a stern attack the bomber pilots would reduce speed, causing the fighter to overshoot. It was not until the all-weather MiG-19PM *Farmer-D* armed with RS-2-US (K-5MS; NATO code name AA-1 *Alkali*) air-to-air missiles came on the scene that the tables were turned. In the West, fighter development went along much the same lines; thus, even when NATO had sufficient numbers of North American F-100 Super Sabres, Republic F-105 Thunderchiefs and SAAB J-35 Drakens based in Europe, the Il-28 stood a fair chance of getting away from them, especially when flying at ultra-low level.

For the Western world (the 'free world', in the terminology of the Cold War era) the hundreds of nuclear-capable bombers were one of the personifications of the tell-tale Soviet Threat – and with good reason. The crews of these aircraft were carefully chosen and received especially rigorous training. Each crew was allocated a main target and several alternative targets in Western Europe: nuclear weapons depots, airbases, etc. For instance, the already mentioned 63rd BAD of the 57th VA (Carpathian DD) was to attack targets in West Germany.

In the event of war the tactical scenario for the *Beagle* units was approximately as follows. Each Il-28 carrying a nuclear bomb would be accompanied by at least a squadron of sister aircraft tasked with the electronic countermeasures (ECM) and air defence distraction role. After taking off from

Maintenance work on an Il-28R at a wintry airfield; the aircraft is jacked up for landing gear operation tests. *(Yefim Gordon archive)*

This is how the *Beagle*'s tail cannon were cleaned. *(Yefim Gordon archive)*

Soviet territory the bomber formation would climb to 10,000 m (32,808 ft) in order to save fuel. Then, setting up an ECM barrier, the bombers would descend to low altitude over Poland to avoid detection by the powerful surveillance radar in West Berlin – NATO's first line of defence; some of the aircraft would leave the formation, making deceptive manoeuvres to confuse the AD radar operators. The same tactic would be used to get past the numerous HAWK, Nike Hercules and Nike Ajax anti-aircraft missile systems. Eventually the bomb-toting *Beagle* would be left all alone, pressing on towards the target at treetop level. Then it would climb sharply to 1,000 m (3,280 ft), allowing the navigator to make sure they were in the right place, whereupon the bomb would be dropped and the aircraft would head back, descending to ultra-low level again as it did. The idea was that the Il-28's high speed would enable it to outrun the shock wave and the crew would be protected from the flash by special blinds.

Even if the bomber managed to get that far and deliver the bomb, it had virtually no chance of returning to base because, with all the evasive manoeuvres, it was sure to run out of fuel on the way home. To remedy this, auxiliary airfields were initially built in Poland and East Germany, where the bombers were to make refuelling stops. Later, bomber units operating the Il-28 (including the nuclear-capable version) were stationed in some of the Warsaw Pact nations, which placed them within range of the south coast of England.

The Soviet Union's Central Group of Forces (TsGV – *Tsen**trahl'**naya **groop**pa voysk*) stationed in Czechoslovakia had a number of Il-28BM target tugs based at Zvolen AB. In East Germany the GSVG (***Groop**pa sovet**skikh voysk v Gher**mah**nii* – Group of Soviet Forces in Germany)[3] operated the Il-28 in the basic bomber, reconnaissance and target tug versions. East German bases used by Soviet Air Force *Beagle*s were Allstedt (Il-28Rs, 1968–70), Berlin-Schönefeld (a target-towing flight equipped with Il-28BMs and Il-28Us), Brand (668th FBAP, 35 aircraft since the 1950s; re-equipped with Yak-28 *Brewer* tactical bombers in 1965), Brandis (only occasionally), Finow (207th FBAP, Il-28s since 1956; re-equipped with Yak-28s in 1965), Damgarten (until 1979), Finsterwalde (briefly, early 1950s), Jüterbog-Altes Lager (Il-28Rs, early 1950s), Lärz (1950s), Neu-Welzow (20 bombers first seen in 1953), Oranienburg (Il-28s and Il-28Us, probably 200th FBAD/221st FBAP,

3 Renamed ZGV (***Zah**padnaya **groop**pa voysk* – Western Group of Forces) in 1989.

Maintenance day at a bomber unit, with a line-up of Il-28s unbuttoned for servicing. The nearest aircraft, 12 Blue, is c/n 3402209. Note the open avionics bay cover on 08 Blue; the 8 is applied in a heavier type than the zero, suggesting the aircraft has been re-coded. *(Yefim Gordon archive)*

April–December 1951 and August 1954–August 1956), and Werneuchen.

The target-towing flight at Berlin-Schönefeld airport moved to Brand AB in 1954. It was later upgraded to independent target-towing squadron status (OBMAE – ***o**tdel'naya **b**ooksirovochno-**mish**ennaya **a**viaeskadril'ya*, number unknown), moving to Oranienburg in the autumn of 1971 and thence to Damgarten in 1977. Oranienburg also served as the maintenance base for the GSVG's Il-28s.

An Il-28 based at Oranienburg (221st FBAP?) crashed near the village of Teschendorf 13 km (8 miles) north of the base in February 1956; another one was lost in August same year, just 2 km (1.24 miles) from the site of the previous crash. Shortly afterwards, on 26 August 1956, the regiment was withdrawn from Oranienburg. Military observers from the Allied nations and the local population were invited to see the bombers' departure on 26 August 1956 as a goodwill gesture, and a small air fest was held.

While we are on the subject of Cold War warriors, the *Beagle* actually played an important part in Operation *Mangoosta* (Mongoose) – an event which nearly started the Third World War. Forty-two nuclear-capable Il-28Ns were deployed to Cuba by sea in September 1962 together with a number of ballistic missiles. This was one of the reasons for the famous Cuban Missile Crisis of September–November 1962 when the USA enforced a naval blockade of Cuba, causing the Soviet Union in turn to dispatch a naval task force to the Caribbean.

However, faced with the increasing probability of an all-out armed conflict with the USA which would be a war of destruction, the Soviet leaders had the common sense to back down and withdraw the missiles from Cuba in an effort to ease the situation. Addressing the nation on 20 November, US President John F. Kennedy said that the Soviet leader Nikita S. Khruschev had pledged to withdraw the nuclear-capable Il-28s within 30 days and agreed to let the Americans monitor this process; consequently, JFK had instructed the Secretary of Defense to remove the naval blockade.

The bombers left in early December aboard the freighters S/S *Kasimov* (15 aircraft), S/S *Krasnograd* (15) and S/S *Okhotsk* (12). In order to make it patently clear to the US government that the Soviet Union was honouring its commitments and the *Beagle*s were being withdrawn, the crated aircraft were placed on the ships' upper decks, suffering heavy corrosion damage because next to nothing had been done to protect them from the salty ocean environment. As a result, many of the 42 aircraft had to be written off.

After this, the Cuban leader Fidel Castro Ruz called the Il-28 an obsolete aircraft with limited speed and inadequate range when speaking at a public rally. Obsolete they may have been, but Castro was clearly annoyed at letting go the missiles and bombers and having nothing to threaten *los gringos* with!

As already mentioned, the *Beagle* made its mark in naval aviation in the early 1950s; however, it was there that its obsolescence was most noticeable. By the mid-1950s the Il-28T did not meet the Soviet Navy's requirements any longer. Besides, the weapons cuts initiated by Khruschev in 1960 and his general bias towards missiles dealt a severe blow to bomber aviation in general and naval bomber aviation in particular. All AVMF minelaying and torpedo-bomber units were disbanded, as were many tactical bomber units in the VVS, and many Il-28s were scrapped, even though some aircraft had only

Soviet Air Force Il-28s were stationed outside the USSR as well. Here, several red-coded *Beagle*s wrapped in tarpaulins are pictured at an East German airbase on a foggy morning. *(Yefim Gordon archive)*

60–100 hours' total time. This barbaric process took place at an amazing rate, the work proceeding in three shifts. In the Pacific Fleet alone, about 400 aircraft were demolished within a very short period. Many airmen suddenly found themselves surplus and unwanted; they were dismissed from the Armed Forces without any social security.

Fortunately the VVS command was not enthusiastic about this mayhem, and many Il-28s were simply placed in storage. Numerous *Beagle*s were transferred to flying schools where they served alongside the Il-28U *Mascot* dedicated trainers until the mid-1980s. Others soldiered on as target tugs, also until the mid-1980s. Nearly all of the Soviet Union's defence districts had independent target-towing flights or squadrons operating four to ten, and sometimes more, Il-28BMs. These were based at Novorossiya AB (Far East DD), Berdyansk (Red Banner Odessa DD), Starokonstantinov (Carpathian DD), Tokmak (Central Asian DD, 10th OBAZ),[4] Zvolen (Czechoslovakia), etc.

Moreover, the Il-28 got a new lease of life (if only briefly) in the late 1960s and early 1970s when the post-Khruschev Soviet government headed by Leonid I. Brezhnev decided to revive the ground attack arm of the VVS (which was one of the hardest-hit by Khruschev's reforms). A number of *Beagle*s were converted to Il-28Sh ground attack aircraft. Up to a full regiment of these aircraft was based at Domna AB (Transbaikalian DD) and Khoorba AB near Komsomol'sk-on-Amur (Far East DD).

The Il-28 at war

The Il-28 had its fair share of 'hot' wars, the first of which was the Korean War of 1950–3. China supported North Korea actively during the war, sending the tell-tale one million volunteers (actually regular People's Liberation Army troops) to the battlefields. This angered the USA badly enough to make it promise strikes against China, including nuclear strikes if necessary, if Chinese forces crossed the 38th parallel at which the frontline had stabilized (this was eventually to become the demarcation line between North and South Korea).

Not to be outdone, China threatened to hit both South Korea and US bases in Japan if USAF aircraft as much as overflew Chinese territory. To add weight to these words, 70 Il-28s were deployed on People's Liberation Army Air Force (PLAAF) air bases in Manchuria. The aircraft wore PLAAF insignia but were flown by Soviet crews.

A second major batch of Soviet-built Il-28s was delivered in 1953. It is not known if the *Beagle*s actually saw action in the war, but they *did* put in an appearance in North Korea. UN envoys monitoring prisoner-of-war exchanges reported Chinese bombers, including Il-28s, landing illegally on air bases near Pyongyang in direct violation of the truce agreement.

A short while later, however, the *Beagle* did see action during China's last civil war when the Chinese Nationalists led by Chiang Kai-shek claimed independence for Taiwan. In early January 1956 PLAAF Il-28s bombed the Tachen islands 360 km (200 nm) north of Taiwan which the Nationalists were forced to abandon in February. However, the high accident rate and the danger of being shot town by Republic of China Air Force (ROCAF) Republic F-84 Thunderjets and North American F-86 Sabres forced an end to these attacks.

In the autumn of 1956 a large group of Soviet forces was deployed to Hungary to quash the anti-communist uprising in that country. More than 120 *Beagle*s based in the Carpathian DD were placed on maximum alert duty, ready to launch strikes against the insurgents. Fortunately this never happened, but Soviet Air Force Il-28Rs seconded to the Special Corps tasked with quelling the mutiny did fly reconnaissance missions over Hungary. One of them was shot down by the rebels over Csepel Island on the Danube on 8 November 1956, killing the crew. On 18 December the Supreme Soviet of the USSR (the nation's top governing body) issued a decree granting the Hero of the Soviet Union title posthumously to an Il-28 crew consisting of squadron commander Capt. A. A. Bobrovskiy (pilot), Capt. D. D. Karmishin (navigator) and the squadron's chief of communications Lt. (sg) V. Ye. Yartsev (gunner/radio operator). It seems very probable that it was the same crew.

On the other side, it is reported that a handful of Hungarian pilots who had supported the rebels made a few sorties from Kunmadaras AB, attacking Soviet troops who had built pontoon bridges across the Tisza River. Soon, however, all Hungarian airbases were overrun by Soviet troops, and the rebels' flying activities stopped.

Another area where the Il-28 saw action in the autumn of 1956 was the Middle East. Egyptian Air Force (EAF) *Beagle*s first saw action during the Suez Crisis (26 October–7 November 1956). Great Britain was thoroughly displeased with President

4 OBAZ = *otdel'noye booksirovochnoye aviazveno* – independent [target-] towing flight.

Gamal Abdel Nasser's independent political course; when Egypt nationalized the Suez Canal on 26 July 1956, this was the last straw. In concert with France and Egypt's arch-enemy, Israel, Great Britain took action. According to the plan, Israel would start an armed conflict with Egypt, then Great Britain and France would interfere on the pretext of ensuring the safety of international traffic in the Suez Canal and occupy the area. Stage 1, Operation *Kadesh* ('cleansing' in Hebrew), was scheduled for 29 October–1 November, and Stage 2, Operation *Musketeer*, for 1–7 November.

By then the EAF had taken delivery of about fifty *Beagle*s but only one squadron operating twelve aircraft was fully combat-capable. Two other squadrons had only just been formed before the fighting began, and the crews had not yet mastered the new jet bombers. Consequently the Il-28 was used in the conflict on a small scale. For instance, on the night of 31 October one of the *Beagle*s bombed an Israeli kibbutz named Gezer. An Israeli Defence Force/Air Force (IDF/AF – *Heyl Ha'avir*) Gloster Meteor NF.13 took off to intercept the intruder but could not find the target in the darkness. On the same day a group of Il-28s raided Lod airbase but the bombs missed their target, exploding near the Jewish settlement of Ramat-Rachel.

The EAF top commanders fully realized that, with no qualified crews to fly them, the *Beagle*s would be sitting ducks and a lucrative target for the Anglo-French strike force. Hence President Nasser ordered the EAF's assets to be dispersed to remote bases or relocated to Syria and Saudi Arabia. (It was just as well that he did; on the night of 1 November Great Britain and France launched Operation *Musketeer* as planned. RAF bombers detached to Luqa, Malta, and Royal Navy strike aircraft from the carriers HMS *Albion*, HMS *Eagle* and HMS *Bulwark* attacked Egyptian airbases in the Suez Canal area.) Twenty Il-28s were flown to the Royal Saudi Air Force (RSAF) base at Riyadh by Soviet and Czech crews; the other 24 or 28 *Beagle*s moved to Luxor, Egypt's southernmost airbase, where they were supposed to be safe. This assumption turned out to be wrong; on 4 November RAF English Electric Canberras bombed Luxor, forcing the evacuation of eight more Il-28s to Saudi Arabia. On the same day the base was attacked by French Air Force (*Armée de l'Air*) Republic F-84F Thunderjet fighter-bombers; the French claimed the destruction of every single aircraft at the base but the EAF acknowledged the loss of only seven bombers.

Sporadic armed incidents between Egypt and Israel continued between the Arab–Israeli wars. Combat aircraft took part in these operations; for example, United Arab Republic Air Force (UARAF) Il-28s flew several night reconnaissance missions over the Israeli seaport of Eilat in December 1958.

In 1959 Chinese Il-28s saw action again when the government forces ruthlessly stamped out an ethnic minority uprising in Tibet. Apart from that, the *Beagle*s were used in numerous skirmishes with the Taiwanese Nationalists – mostly over the Strait of Taiwan. Some sources suggest that Il-28Rs and HZ-5s actually overflew the island on reconnaissance sorties; several of these aircraft fell victim to Nike Ajax missiles.

One Chinese *Beagle*, however, was lost in a different way. On 11 November 1966 pilot Li Hsien-pin, navigator/bomb aimer Li Tsai-wang and gunner/radio operator Liang Pao-sheng of the 22nd Bomber Regiment/8th Bomber Division defected to Taiwan in an Il-28 serialled 0195 Yellow. The three had conspired to defect long before the flight, joining the PLAAF and successfully passing the complex loyalty check system.

The aircraft took off at noon from Hangchow coastal airbase on a routine practice bombing sortie. After following the coastline for a while it turned and headed for Taiwan at full speed. Chinese fighters scrambled and gave chase – too late. The Il-28 was quickly spotted by Taiwanese air defence radars; ROCAF Lockheed F-104G Starfighters took off to intercept, escorting the bomber to Taoyuan air base after the pilot had made his intentions clear by rocking the wings. The aircraft overran on landing, collapsing the nose gear and damaging the nose glazing; all three crew members were injured, the gunner dying a day later.

The defection was timed to coincide with the centenary celebration of Sun Yat-sen, the 'father of the Chinese revolution' revered by both Communists and Nationalists, celebrated on 12 November. Sure enough, the Taiwanese and Western press created an almighty uproar. This was compounded by the pilot, who was the least injured in the crash landing, speaking at the Centennial Rally the next day and denouncing Red China and communism in general.

Meanwhile, the unfortunate event was promptly reported to the PLAAF HQ in Beijing, and retribution followed swiftly. The Air Force Vice-Commander Cheng Chung arrived at Hangchow on the same day and probably gave everyone a thorough dressing-down. All flights from Hangchow and other bases nearest to Taiwan were suspended until further notice.

Apart from the nose section, 0195 Yellow was virtually intact. The Nationalists repaired and test flew the aircraft, then reportedly used it for reconnaissance flights over mainland China (some sources say the aircraft was handed over to the USA for close examination). Shortly afterwards, the British model kit manufacturer Airfix released a 1/72nd scale model of the *Beagle*. (Speaking of which, another kit of the Il-28 to the same scale from the Chinese company Trumpeter has appeared on the market recently.)

In 1962 Nasser sent his combat aircraft (including Il-28s) to Yemen, extending military aid to the Republicans who had overthrown the king. At the same time the Soviet Union also supported the Republicans, supplying them with a number of *Beagle*s. The Il-28s attacked the Royalists' positions and flew reconnaissance sorties; the Western press reported that they were flown by both Yemeni and Soviet crews. (This may well be true. Soviet military personnel participated in many regional conflicts in which the Soviet Union was not formally involved, and not only in an advisory capacity, and that was something the public back at home was definitely not supposed to know!) Sometimes the bombers attacked the Saudi towns of Dhahran and Najran located next to the Yemeni border. In June 1966 a solitary Il-28 escorted by UARAF MiG-17Fs bombed the RSAF base at Khamis Mushayt; in the same month UARAF Il-28Rs flew reconnaissance missions over the Saudi seaport of Qizan. When the Six-Day War erupted, however, all Egyptian troops had to leave Yemen because things were bad enough back at home.

The Il-28 saw action in Africa as well. In April 1967 a *coup d'état* occurred in Nigeria and the corrupt government was toppled by Gen. Irons, C-in-C of the Nigerian Armed Forces. The next month, however, Irons was killed in a new *coup* organized by Col Ojukwu, governor of the Eastern province and one of the leaders of the Ibo tribe. The rebels declared their intention to secede, forming the so-called State of Biafra, named after a bight in the Gulf of Guinea. This immediately sparked a bitter three-year civil war between the separatists and the federal government.

The Federal Nigerian Air Force (FNAF) originally used six impressed Nigeria Airways Douglas DC-3s (ex-5N-AAN, 5N-AAP, etc.) and twelve Czech-supplied Aero L-29 Delfin advanced trainers against Col Ojukwu's rebels in the light bomber/paradrop and strike roles respectively. Pretty soon, however, it obtained real combat aircraft from Arab nations supporting the Islamic government in Lagos in its struggle against the Christian Ibo separatists. Egypt was the first to extend help, supplying 41 MiG-17Fs (misidentified as MiG-15s by some sources) and, together with Algeria, six second-hand Il-28s in 1969. The bombers were flown by Egyptian mercenary crews. Operating from Enugu and Kalabar, the *Beagle*s bore the brunt of the bombing missions but were reportedly found to be ineffective. They certainly did not venture near the Biafran capital, Uli, which was well protected by flak. Moreover, poor mission planning and the lack of a clearly defined forward

When the Il-28 was phased out, many of these bombers sat at Soviet airbases, awaiting disposal. *(Yefim Gordon archive)*

line of own troops (FLOT) sometimes resulted in friendly forces being bombed!

Sometimes the Il-28s were used to escort the DC-3s on bombing/paradrop sorties or for strafing Biafran positions. In February 1969 a group of DC-3s escorted by Il-28s and MiG-15s para-dropped supplies and ammunition for government forces surrounded at Owerri. When this didn't work and the DC-3s were temporarily unflyable through flak damage, the federal forces commandeered a Pan African Airways DC-4 which had landed at Port Harcourt, loaded it with ammunition and ordered the captain to fly to Owerri, escorted by an Il-28. However, the captain contrived an engine malfunction, forcing a return to Port Harcourt – which probably saved both aircraft and crew.

The war presented no great danger for FNAF fighter pilots and bomber crews, since the Biafran Air Force had no aircraft capable of air-to-air combat. All the enemy could put up was Malmö MFI-9B primary trainers converted into makeshift attack aircraft. Flown by mercenary pilots led by the Swedish Count Carl Gustav von Rosen, these aircraft were known locally as Minicons – probably a corruption of mini-COIN (counter-insurgency aircraft) – and could only attack ground targets, which they did with a measure of success. Still, the accident rate was rather high and all the *Beagle*s were soon grounded after being damaged in accidents. On 20 March 1969 one Il-28 struck trees during a low-level mission and suffered an engine failure, making a successful forced landing at Port Harcourt. Another *Beagle* veered off the strip at Port Harcourt on landing, burning out the brakes and tyres, but was later repaired. On another occasion an Il-28 was slightly damaged at Enugu by Minicons but was later repaired.

In 1967 there was trouble in the Middle East again when the third Arab–Israeli war, commonly referred to as the Six-Day War (5–10 June 1967), broke out. The Israelis had been planning this war long and carefully – right down to building five mock Egyptian airbases in the Negev Desert, where they constantly practised raids against the real thing. Within a year all IDF/AF combat squadrons had passed a training course at these facilities.

Building on the results of this training, the Israeli high command developed a pre-emptive attack plan known as the Moked Plan. The combined air forces of the Arab nations outnumbered the IDF/AF almost three times, so it was decided to destroy them on the ground rather than tangle with them in the air. The first wave of strike aircraft was to attack nineteen airfields deep in Egyptian territory, knocking out the aircraft based there, but it was decided to spare the runways at the four bases located on the Sinai Peninsula so that Israeli aircraft could use them, once the peninsula had been occupied. The first strike was scheduled between 08.35 and 09.10, when the Egyptian fighters were not expected to be out on combat air patrol and the base commanders were usually not on site. This would be followed by three more waves of strike aircraft which were to destroy the greater part of the Egyptian Air Force on the ground by 14.00. After that, the strike force would be redirected at airbases in Syria, Jordan and Iraq.

By the spring of 1967 it became clear that war was imminent; skirmishes on the Israeli–Syrian border in which both sides used heavy weapons and aircraft were becoming increasingly more frequent. On 17 May Egypt started concentrating troops on the Israeli border; four days later Egypt and Israel called a mobilization of the army reserve, and on 22 May President Nasser declared the Suez Canal closed to Israeli ships.

The Arab nations (Egypt, Syria, Jordan, Lebanon and Iraq) had a total of some 800 combat aircraft at the start of the conflict. This total included 49 to 56 Il-28s – 35 or 40 in Egypt, ten in Iraq and four to six in Syria. These aircraft and the Tu-16 *Badger-A* bombers (30 in Egypt, including some Tu-16KS-1 missile strike aircraft, and six in Iraq) were considered priority targets during the planned air strikes.

On the morning of 5 June a massive assault was launched against Arab airbases. Among other things, 28 EAF Il-28s were destroyed on the ground at Ras-Banas AB and Luxor. One more *Beagle* and its fighter escort (probably MiG-17Fs) were shot down by *Heyl Ha'avir* Dassault Mystère IVs while attacking Israeli troops advancing on at El'Arîsh. The Syrian Air Force lost two Il-28s on the ground.

In February 1968 the Il-28 first put in an appearance in Vietnam, when three *Beagle*s were deployed to Fukien AB, 30 km (18 miles) north-west of Hanoi. It was believed they were to support the large-scale Viet Cong offensive launched after the USA had stopped the first series of bombing attacks on Vietnam (the Tet offensive), but the Il-28s did not participate in this operation. Normally the *Beagle*s were based in southern China; if the US intelligence service reported the presence of these aircraft on any North Vietnamese airfield, the airfields in question would be pounded with cluster bombs loaded with pellets.

In 1971 the North Vietnamese Il-28s did see action, supporting the Vietnamese People's Army and the Pathet Lao guerrillas in Laos. Soviet airmen took part in these operations, too; pilot Berkootov and navigator/bomb aimer Khachemizov were even

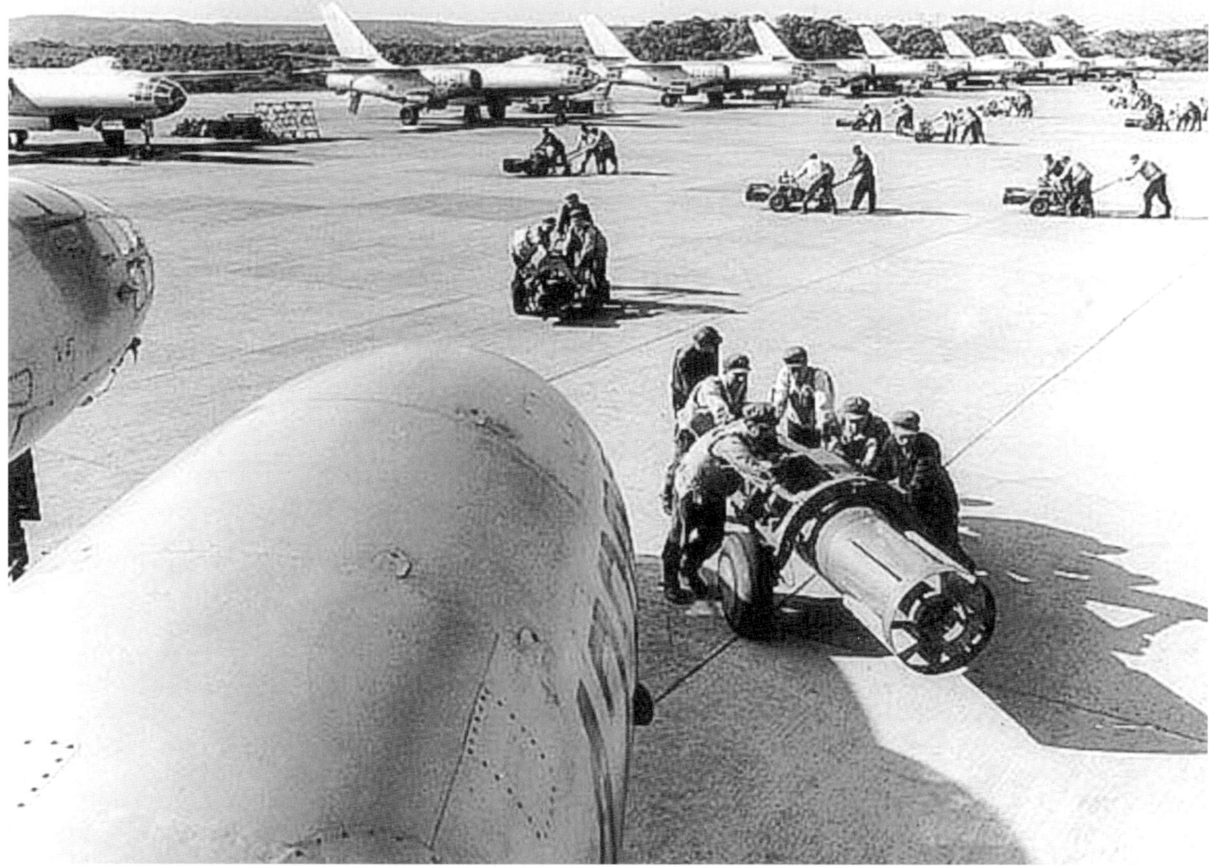

Armourers load large-calibre HE bombs into a regiment of PLAAF Il-28s. Chinese *Beagle*s also had their share of fighting. *(China Aircraft)*

awarded the title of Hero of the Vietnamese People's Army.

August 1968 added another shameful page to the Il-28's biography when *Beagle*s were used, along with other Soviet Air Force aircraft, to suppress the mutiny in Czechoslovakia. Specifically these were 7th FBAP bombers from Starokonstantinov, and possibly Il-28R reconnaissance aircraft from Schuchin (Belorussian DD).

Skirmishes between Israel and Egypt continued after the Six-Day War until 1970. EAF Il-28s participated actively in these clashes, flying reconnaissance missions over Israeli territory; two of them were shot down between 10 July and 1 August 1970. One more example was lost in a 'friendly fire' incident in March 1970 when an Il-28BM towing a sleeve-type target was destroyed by an S-125 Koob (Cube; NATO SA-3 *Gainful*) surface-to-air missile; the missile system was manned by a Soviet crew under N. M. Kootyntsev. Of course a scandal erupted; to make matters worse one of the airmen who had perished in the shootdown was a member of one of the Arab royal families. However, using the missile system's data recording equipment, Kootyntsev proved that the air defence crews had not been informed of the bomber's mission and the Il-28's IFF transponder was out of order. Furthermore, a group of four *Heyl Ha'avir* McDonnell Douglas F-4E Phantom IIs had crossed the Suez Canal, formating with the *Beagle*, then heading back at ultra-low level. As a result, the missile team misidentified the Il-28 as the leader of an Israeli strike group and opened fire. The Egyptians had to admit the Soviet officer was right.

Iraqi Air Force Il-28s were used operationally in the late 1960s and in the first six months of 1974 in Saddam Hussein's relentless war with the Kurdish minority living in the north of Iraq and striving for sovereignty. The Kurdish rebels claimed one bomber shot down in April 1974.

According to some reports, Soviet Air Force Il-28Sh strike aircraft were used operationally

A formation of PLAAF *Beagle*s during an exercise. *(China Aircraft)*

during the Sino-Soviet armed conflict around Damanskiy Island on the Amur River in the early 1970s.

In the late 1970s the bloody regime of Pol Pot used a handful of *Beagle*s (probably Chinese-built H-5s) against the opposition forces headed by Heng Samrin, who became head of the government after Pol Pot was ousted. One of the Il-28s was reportedly shot down; two more were captured intact at Pochentong AB near Phnom Penh on 7 January 1979 when the base was overrun by Vietnamese troops supporting the opposition.

The Afghan War was the last conflict in which the venerable bomber participated. Despite its age, it turned out to be well suited for this war, thanks to its rugged dependability in the harsh conditions of Afghanistan, with its ill-equipped airfields and pervasive dust. Unexpectedly, the seemingly archaic manned tail gunner's station turned out to be quite useful; the gunner would fire at enemy troops on the ground, discouraging attacks with shoulder-launched surface-to-air missiles. The efficiency of this tactic can be judged by the fact that not a single Afghan Air Force Il-28 was lost to the Mujahidin rebels' air defences. However, the *Beagle*s were lost one night in January 1985 in a way that was not uncommon during the Afghan War. Traitors among the Afghan personnel of Shindand AB who had been bought off by the rebels blew up eleven of the bombers; the flames quickly spread to the other aircraft and the 335th Composite Air Regiment ceased to exist.

In 1985 another Chinese Il-28 absconded, this time to South Korea. The crew was less lucky this time; the aircraft was totally destroyed while attempting a forced landing in a field, killing the gunner and a local farmer.

Finnish Il-28Rs were used a lot for snooping around the Soviet border. (Finland was on friendly terms with the Soviet Union, but that did not stop the Finns from spying!) The neighbour's *Beagle*s were a constant source of annoyance for the Soviet Air Defence Force (PVO – ***Pro****tivo****vozdooshn****aya* ***o****borona*) fighter regiments stationed in the area. As soon as the air defence radars detected an aircraft heading towards the border from Finland, fighters would scramble to intercept. Realizing they had been detected, the Finnish crew would fly along the border on their side, while the Soviet fighters would do the same on *their* side, firmly indicating that the neighbours should 'keep their pooch off our lawn'. Then the Il-28 would ostensibly give up and head into Finnish territory; as soon as the fighters, too, headed back to base, the spyplane would pop back up. By then the fighters would be getting critically low on fuel and had no choice but to head for home, the angry pilots radioing to base to urgently send a relief crew. The Il-28R's long endurance (thanks to its tip tanks) allowed the Finns to play this game of tag.

Survivors

As already recounted, huge numbers of Il-28s were wantonly destroyed because of Khruschev's missilization ideas or ended up as AAA and gunnery targets. Others simply rotted away at various bases, waiting to be scrapped; for instance, the hulk of an Il-28 was present at Kubinka AB near Moscow until at least 1997, and several dozen were dumped at Tambov when the TVVAUL re-equipped with the Tupolev Tu-134UBL *Crusty-B* trainer.

Fortunately several examples of this sleek bomber have been preserved for posterity. The collection of the Soviet Air Force Museum in Monino near Moscow includes Il-28 04 Red (c/n 53005771); interestingly, this aircraft originally sported ten mission markings on the nose. Another Moscow-built *Beagle* (10 Red, c/n 65010809) is preserved in the Soviet Armed Forces Museum in Moscow. An Omsk-built example (01 Red, c/n 36603807) is on display in the open-air aviation museum at Khodynka airfield in the centre of Moscow; at one time this aircraft featured crude nose art depicting Santa Claus and Cheburashka (a cartoon character) on the starboard side. An Il-28 coded 07 Red is on display at the Naval Air Arm Museum in Safonovo near Severomorsk-1 AB (Murmansk Region). An Omsk-built example coded 85 (c/n 56606201) is a ground instructional airframe at the Samara State Aviation University (SGAU — ***Samar**skiy gosoo**dar**stvennyy aviatsee**on**nyy ooniver**si**tet*; formerly KuAI – Kuibyshev Aviation Institute). One example coded 30 Red is displayed on a plinth outside the Air Force's Aircraft Overhaul Plant No. 712 in Chelyabinsk, which refurbished Il-28s. Others probably survive as gate guards on various Russian airbases. A few more Il-28s are on display in the aviation museums of Bulgaria, Czechia, Finland, Hungary, Poland and Romania.

***

The Il-28 has been aptly described by one Russian author as 'a successful design that was always out of luck'. Even though the Il-28's combat potential was not used to the full, it was this type that introduced jet aircraft and all-weather capability to the bomber element of the Soviet Air Force and several other air arms. The Il-28 helped to train hundreds of first-class naval pilots. Western aviation experts gave the *Beagle* due credit, describing it as a masterpiece of Soviet aircraft design.

4 •

BEAGLES WORLD-WIDE

The Il-28 was operated by 25 nations in Europe, Asia (including SE Asia), Africa and the Middle East. Second-hand aircraft were also exported, which incidentally saved a few Il-28T torpedo-bombers from the torch.

Afghanistan

A number of obsolete Il-28 bombers phased out by the VVS were delivered to the Royal Afghan Air Force in 1969. Reports on the number of aircraft supplied vary considerably, ranging from twelve aircraft (one squadron) to 45 aircraft (three squadrons). The *Beagle*s were mostly based at Mazar-e Sharif where most of the Soviet military advisers were stationed. The Il-28s were probably used operationally by the Afghan Republican Air Force (*Afghan Hanai Qurah*) at the opening stages of the Afghan civil war (i.e. prior to the Soviet invasion).

Only one aircraft wearing the serial 163 Black and early-style red roundels with yellow Dari script has been identified; it was operated by the 335th Composite Air Regiment at Shindand in the summer of 1979. All of the unit's Il-28s were destroyed on the ground in January 1985.

Albania

The Albanian People's Republic Air Force (*Forcat Ushtarake Ajore Shquipëtare*, later renamed *Aviacione Ushtarak Shquipëtare*) took delivery of an unspecified number of Chinese-built Harbin H-5s. Three aircraft serialled 026, 29 and 3608 have been identified to date; the last example belonged to the 4020th (formerly 7594th) Aviation Regiment based at Rinas AB near the Albanian capital, Tirana, and remained operational until 1993. (In some sources the Albanian name has been rendered as *Aviatika Militar e Republika Popullóre e Shquipërise*.)

Algeria

The Soviet Union began providing military assistance to Algeria in 1962, right after the country gained independence from France. Initially twelve Il-28 bombers were delivered to the Algerian Air Force (*Al Quwwat al-Jawwiya al-Jaza'eriya/Force Aérienne Algérienne*) via Egypt, with which Algeria was closely allied; direct deliveries might have caused unfavourable political consequences for the Soviet Union. These aircraft probably participated in the clash with Morocco in 1963. Another twelve *Beagle*s were delivered directly from the USSR after the 1965 military *coup* when the new government (which was even more pro-Soviet) requested additional military aid. Nearly all the *Beagle*s were unserviceable by 1979, and the few which remained operational were relegated to secondary duties.

Bulgaria

The Bulgarian Air Force (BVVS – *Bolgarski Voyenno Vozdooshni Seeli*) operated various versions of the *Beagle*. Around 36 Il-28s were based at Tolbukhin AB in the north-east of the country; these included four Il-28R reconnaisance aircraft, a few Il-28T torpedo-bombers and two Il-28U trainers. A dozen aircraft modified for electronic warfare duties were reportedly still operational in 1983.

Only one aircraft, coded 43 Red (c/n ...2504), has been identified so far; it is on display at the Bulgarian Air Force Museum (Graf Ignatiev AB, Plovdiv).

China

Communist China was by far the largest foreign operator of the type. Deliveries to the People's Liberation Army Air Force (PLAAF, or *Chung-kuo Shen Min Taie-Fang-Tsun Pu-tai*) started in 1952. By 1956 the PLAAF inventory included more than 250 Soviet-built Il-28s. This number was further expanded when production of the *Beagle* and *Mascot* as the H-5 and HJ-5 respectively started at Harbin. RAT-52 torpedoes for the Il-28 were also manufactured locally.

More than 300 Il-28s were in service by the end of 1964, not counting Il-28Us (a total figure of 400-plus has been reported in service with twelve tactical bomber regiments). Their principal role was to be on ready alert and intimidate the Taiwanese Nationalists. More than 100 Il-28s were transferred to the naval air arm (PLANAF) and converted into torpedo-bombers similar to early Soviet conversions. This was at a time when a marine assault from Taiwan was considered a distinct possibility in mainland China.

Known PLAAF Il-28s are listed in Table 16. The meaning of PLAAF serials is obscure, but in the case of five-digit serials the first two digits may be a code denoting one of the eleven defence districts, the fourth digit a unit code, while the third and fifth digits make up the individual number of the aircraft in the unit. Chinese Il-28s usually had dark green upper surfaces and pale blue undersurfaces, but whole units are known to have been equipped with natural metal (or silver-painted) aircraft.

The *Beagle* remained in service until the late 1990s (300 H-5s and HZ-5s were reportedly still on strength with the PLAAF and 150 torpedo-bombers with the PLANAF in 1997), though it was gradually superseded by Tu-16 bombers and Tu-16K-11-16 anti-shipping missile carriers. The latter type was built in Xian (without the benefit of a licence) as the H-6, and soldiers on with the PLANAF as the H-6 IV armed with C-601 Silkworm missiles – Chinese copies of the K-16/NATO AS-5 *Kelt*.

Czechoslovakia

The first three Il-28s were delivered to the Czech Air Force (CzAF, or ČVL – *Československé Vojenské Létectvo*) in January 1955; the type was intended to replace the obsolete Aero C-3 (the Czech designation of Siebel Si 204Ds used as bomber trainers). Four Soviet instructors (surnames Tsilin, Yershov, Lisitskiy and Salazkin) started training the first ten crews on 9 February. The Czechs were quick on the uptake, and the three aircraft participated in the VE-Day air parade on 9 May in the same year, flown by Czech crews (flight leader Maj. Končir).

On 17 September 1955 ten Il-28s escorted by fighters took part in the Aviation Day flypast in front of the Czech government, dropping live bombs on 'enemy fortifications' (!). However, the performance was almost overshadowed by a

A busy scene at a Chinese airbase, with numerous H-5s getting ready for the day's flight training. Note the serviceman in the foreground who has livened up his khaki attire with a decidedly non-regulation straw hat! *(China Aircraft)*

Table 16. Known PLAAF Il-28s

Serial	C/n	Version	Notes
61 Red	?	Il-28U	
0031 Red	?	Il-28	
0131 Red	?	Il-28	
0194 Red	?	Il-28	Natural metal
0195 Yellow	?	Il-28	Hangchow AB; green with blue undersurfaces. Defected to Taoyuan AB, Taiwan, 11-11-66; preserved
0986 Red	?	Il-28	Natural metal
1110 Yellow	?	Il-28	Green with blue undersurfaces
1206 Red	?	Il-28	Natural metal
1210 Yellow	?	Il-28	Green with blue undersurfaces
1400 Red	?	Il-28	Natural metal
1402 Red	?	Il-28	Natural metal
1403 Red	?	Il-28	Natural metal
1471 Red	?	Il-28	Green with blue undersurfaces
1510 Red	?	Il-28	Green with blue undersurfaces
1512 Red	?	Il-28	Natural metal
1513 Red	?	Il-28	Natural metal
1618 Yellow	?	Il-28	Green with blue undersurfaces; unconfirmed (drawing only)
1718 Red	?	Il-28	Natural metal
1801 Red	?	Il-28	Natural metal
10198 Red	?	Il-28	Natural metal. Preserved PLAAF Museum, Datangshan AB
10692 Red	?	HJ-5 (Il-28U)	Natural metal. Preserved PLAAF Museum
30518	?	Il-28*	
30710	?	Il-28*	
30711	?	Il-28*	
30712	?	Il-28*	
30713	?	Il-28*	
30714	?	Il-28*	
30715**	?	Il-28*	
30716**	?	Il-28*	
30717	?	Il-28*	
30718	?	Il-28*	
30719**	?	Il-28*	
30810	?	Il-28*	
30811	?	Il-28*	
30812	?	Il-28*	
30813**	?	Il-28*	
30814	?	Il-28*	
30815	?	Il-28*	
43050 Red	?	Il-28	Natural metal
43684 Red	?	H-5	Natural metal
43693 Red	?	H-5	Natural metal; sometimes reported in error as Il-28U
44690 Red	?	Il-28	Preserved PLAAF Museum, two-tone blue camouflage with white undersurfaces; non-standard nose
45552 Red	?	Il-28	Natural metal
63019 Red	?	HJ-5 (Il-28U)	
none	4149	Il-28 (H-5?)	Natural metal. Preserved PLAAF Museum
none	54120	Il-28 (H-5?)	Natural metal. Preserved PLAAF Museum

Notes:

* Exact version not known (may be H-5).

** Existence not proved but likely.

A Czech Air Force Il-28 (or Avia B-228) in pre-1957 markings. *(RART)*

formation of 33 C-3s shaped like a hammer and sickle. The organizers of the flypast had probably wanted to show that aircraft which had done sterling service make way for new types, but the implication was just the opposite – the old guard never surrenders, it only dies!

The bomber units equipped with Il-28s became fully operational by October 1955. Until the mid-1960s the Czechs had a habit of redesignating foreign military aircraft in Czech AF service. For example, the Messerschmitt Bf 109G was the S-99 (the Bf 109G-12 trainer was the CS-99), the MiG-15*bis Fagot-B* was built as the Aero S-102 (and the UTI-MiG-15 *Midget* as the CS-102), etc. As already mentioned, Czech-built Il-28 bombers and Il-28U trainers were designated B-228 and CB-228 respectively.

Besides the bomber version (sometimes referred to as the Il-28B by the Czechs) and the Il-28U trainer, the Czech AF had some Il-28RTR ELINT aircraft. The aircraft were progressively modified; e.g. the nose guns were removed and new avionics installed in 1959–60. Some aircraft were fitted with empty shell collector cases under the tail turret.

At least one bomber was converted locally into an ELINT or ECM aircraft. This was characterized by large cylindrical pods at the wingtips resembling the Il-28R's drop tanks. The front and rear portions of these pods were dielectric and painted dark blue.

Initially Czech military aircraft and helicopters had alpha-numeric serials consisting of one or two letters and two figures; the letters were a code denoting the squadron to which the aircraft belonged. Il-28s were allocated serials in the AD, BA, CD, DE, EB, FC, FH, GO, LB, PK, PU, PX, RL, TH blocks and possibly others. The serial was painted on the forward fuselage in huge characters. A different system was introduced in mid-1957, with four-digit serials matching the last four of the aircraft's construction number; the serial was now painted on the rear fuselage.

Until 1960 Czech *Beagle*s continued appearing at airshows. For example, the 1956 VE-Day parade featured a flypast by no fewer than sixteen Il-28s. The grand show staged in Prague-Ruzyne airport on 2 September 1956 was opened by a formation of three Il-28s led by Maj. Hájek and closed by another Il-28 escorted by four MiG-15s, followed by three vics of three *Beagle*s. Business comes first, however, and the crews kept training. Training was not limited to home ground: in June 1956 nine aircraft were deployed to Hungary and nine more to East Germany to participate in Warsaw Pact military exercises, acting as aggressor aircraft. To this

This Czech Air Force Il-28U (or Avia CB-228) carries no alpha-numeric serial on the forward fuselage, showing that the picture was taken after 1957, when the four-digit serials on the aft fuselage were introduced. *(RART)*

end they were suitably marked by a blue or red stripe around the rear fuselage. Czechoslovakia also served as a training ground for *Beagle* crews from Egypt, Syria, Indonesia, Nigeria and a few more countries.

The basic bomber was retired in 1965. The trainers and reconnaissance versions remained in service until 1973. By 1977 all Czech Il-28s, except four aircraft displayed at the Military Museum at Prague-Kbely airport, had either been scrapped or had ended up as target drones or gunnery targets at practice ranges.

Czech sportsmen also used the Il-28 for setting several world records. The idea was born when the Czechs won every possible medal at the 3rd World Skydiving Championship held at Moscow-Tushino in 1956; the catch-phrase of the day was 'The students have surpassed the teachers'. Of course, the winners were treated like national heroes. Among other things, they had an audience with the then President of Czechoslovakia, Antonín Zápotocký who asked them in a private conversation what he could do for them. Seizing the opportunity, absolute world champion Gustav Koubek said they would like to make a jump from high altitude in order to glorify their homeland, but only the Air Force had aircraft which could take them high enough – specifically the Il-28 bomber, which could accommodate a team of skydivers in the bomb bay. The President tasked the Minister of Defence Lomský with providing assistance; the minister gave appropriate orders to the Czech Air Force C-in-C, Lt-Gen. Josef Vosáhlo.

Apparently the military were not overjoyed about this unexpected task, let alone the prospect of letting civilians use their aircraft. Since this was a presidential task, they could not just give Koubek and his team the brush-off. Hence they tried to scare the unwanted guests off. At the first meeting with Lt-Gen. Vosáhlo the sportsmen got bawled out by his aides, who kept telling them they would get

Table 17. Known CzAF Il-28s

Serial	C/n	Version	Notes
AD-31	?	Il-28 (B-228?)	
A...-81	57019	Il-28 (B-228)	Reserialled 7019?
BA-10?	?	Il-28U (CB-228?)	
BA-11 (1)	56775	Il-28 (B-228)	Fate unknown; see next line
BA-11 (2)	56926	Il-28RTR (B-228)	**Reserialled to, see below**
6926			Preserved Czech aerospace museum (VM VHÚ)*, Prague-Kbely
CD-10	65010501?	Il-28U	C/n reported as 650100501 – misquote? **Reserialled to, see below**
0501			Preserved VM VHÚ
DE-50	?	Il-28 (B-228?)	
DE-51	?	Il-28 (B-228?)	
TH-14	?	Il-28 (B-228)	
PK-30	?	Il-28 (B-228?)	
PU-12	?	Il-28R (B-228?)	
1904	1904	Il-28	
2107	52107	Il-28 (B-228)	Preserved VM VHÚ
2303?	52303?	Il-28R (B-228)	Reported preserved VM VHÚ but possible confusion with 3303, see below
2309?	52309?	Il-28	Unconfirmed (drawing only)
2404	...2404?	Il-28RT	Preserved *Nadace Létecké Historické Společnosti Výškov* (Výškov Aviation Historical Society Collection), Slatina. Could be B-228 c/n 52404
3303	53303	Il-28RT (B-228)	Preserved VM VHÚ
6915	56915	Il-28 (B-228)	Engine testbed
not known	54665	Il-28 (B-228)	Possibly serialled 4665

Note:

* VM VHÚ = *Vojenské muzeum Vojenského historického ústavu* – Military Museum of the Military Historical Society.

incinerated by the engine exhaust, or freeze like rabbits at high altitude, or get smashed to death against the aircraft's fuselage by the slipstream, or their lungs would burst and they would suffocate. But Koubek and his team would not be put off that easily and demanded persistently that a test with a dummy be performed at first. Grudgingly the military had to agree.

The sportsmen got their first look at the Il-28's bomb bay at Mladá AB, Milovice, discussing the modifications which needed to be made to the aircraft with the local technicians. An Il-28 serialled TH-14 was equipped with a cine-camera mounted ahead of the bomb bay to check how the dummy would travel after leaving the bay. Later, live jumps were made by Air Force parachutists Bílek (first name unknown) and Leopold Ozábal.

Meanwhile, the sportsmen were preparing in earnest for the record attempt. Special heat-insulated and windproof clothing, including face masks of the kind worn by anti-terrorist troops, was made to protect them from the slipstream and the killing cold of the stratosphere. The parachutists trained in a pressure chamber, with physicians monitoring their health; two of the candidates failed to pass this test. Then the aircraft's bomb bay doors were lined with thick felt to reduce the risk of injuries, special suspension belts were installed as a safety measure to restrain the parachutists until the aircraft climbed to a safe altitude, and the bomb bay was fitted out with an oxygen system, an intercom, lights and additional cameras.

Prior to the record attempt the skydivers made two training jumps from 6,000 m (19,685 ft) and 9,000 m (29,527 ft). An unexpected complication arose on the latter occasion – the barographs which were to record the altitude during the jump froze and failed. A special frost-resistant lubricant had to be developed urgently and all of the parachutists' equipment (altimeters, barographs, chronometers, oxygen kits) were tested at –60°C (–76°F) and simulated altitudes up to 13,000 m (42,651 ft). Incidentally, each man's equipment, together with the PTCH-3 parachute, weighed 60 kg (132 lb).

An East German Il-28R about to begin its take-off run. *(RART)*

At 08.07 on 21 March 1957, Il-28 TH-14 piloted by Jaroslav Hájek took off from Mladá AB, accompanied by a UTI-MiG-15 *Midget* trainer as a camera ship. When the bomber climbed as high as it would go, doing 550 km/h (297 kt), at 08.55 the skydivers Jaroslav Jehlička, Zdeněk Kaplan and Gustav Koubek left the bomb bay at 12,850 m (42,158 ft) and fell 11,664 m (38,267 ft) before opening their parachutes.

Not satisfied with this remarkable achievement, the same trio decided to make a second stratospheric jump – at night. At 21.15 on 27 March they took off from Mladá AB in the same aircraft, leaving it at 21.56 at an altitude of 12,518 m (41,069 ft) and falling 12,082 m (39,639 ft) before opening their parachutes. Special searchlights were set up on the ground, shining vertically into the sky to tell the pilots when and where to drop the skydivers.

East Germany

The LSK/LV (*Luftstreitkräfte und Luftverteidigung der Deutschen Demokratischen Republik* – Air Force and Air Defence Force of the German Democratic Republic) used the Il-28 exclusively for target-towing duties. To this end the 3rd *Staffel* (squadron) of JFG 1 (*Jagdfliegergeschwader* – fighter wing) at Cottbus was reorganized in February 1959 as ordered by East Germany's minister of defence. The squadron's first and second flights continued to operate PZL Lim-5 (Polish-built MiG-17F *Fresco-C*) day fighters and Lim-5P (Polish-built MiG-17PF *Fresco-D*) all-weather interceptors,[1] while the third flight was initially equipped with two Il-28s serialled 190 Black and 196 Black. To this end four LSK/LV pilots took conversion training in Cottbus on 1 February–4 March, while two navigators and three radio operators underwent theoretical training at the Soviet Air Force's 11th ORAP (*o**tdel'**nyy raz**ved**yvatel'nyy* ***aviapolk*** – independent reconnaissance regiment) stationed at Neu-Welzow AB.

Shortly afterwards 3/JFG 1 was transformed into ZDS 21 (*Zieldarstellungsstaffel* – target-towing squadron).[2] The unit became fully operational in the

1 Lim = *licencyjny myśliwiec* – licence-built fighter.

2 Some German sources claim that the Il-28s remained on strength with JFG 1 until December 1959.

spring of 1960, providing target practice primarily for *Volksarmee* (People's Army) AA gunners firing anything from 14.5 mm (.57 calibre) machine-guns to 57 mm S-60 radar-directed automatic AA guns. The latter were noted for their high accuracy, often shooting the towed 'sock' right off. Target practice took place at the Zingst AAA range on the Baltic Sea coast.

Il-28 target tugs were used to train East German Navy (*Volksmarine*) gunners as well; their tasks included dropping flare bombs which were used as targets by AA gunners (!). LSK/LV fighter pilots were to join the fun later on, practising attacks on low-flying targets. Of course great care was taken to ensure the target tugs would not be hit by friendly fire.

A single Il-28U was delivered in 1961 for crew training. The location of ZDS 21 changed several times; at one time the unit operated from Drewitz AB, not far from Cottbus. Five more Il-28s were transferred from the 11th ORAP to ZDS 21 at this base in 1962. After 1972 the unit was permanently based in Peenemünde. In due time the unit was renumbered, becoming ZDS 33; on 1 December 1981 it was demoted to ZDK 33 (*Zieldarstellungskette* – target-towing flight).

Originally the East German Il-28s were painted silver overall, but some aircraft were later repainted in a camouflage scheme with dark green/dark earth upper surfaces and light blue undersurfaces. The Il-28s served without incident until 1982, when they were replaced by Czech-built Aero L-39V Albatros target tugs and KT-04 towed targets. The last aircraft, serialled 208, was retired on 20 October 1982 and preserved at the LSK/LV officers' flying school in Bautzen (*Offizierhochschule Franz Mehring*).

East German Il-28s were also used to test new models of parachutes. Before a test jumper could risk his life, a tin dummy filled with sand would be dropped from an Il-28 at various speeds and altitudes.

Egypt (United Arab Republic; Arab Republic of Egypt)

The Egyptian Air Force (EAF, or *al Quwwat al-Jawwiya il-Misriya*) took delivery of its first *Beagles* in December 1955, ordering about fifty B-228s and CB-228s from Czechoslovakia. The aircraft were based at Cairo-West AB. After the Suez Crisis of 1956, in which at least seven of these bombers were lost, President Gamal Abdel Nasser launched a major programme to re-equip his armed forces; this included the acquisition of more *Beagles*. In March

Table 18. East German Il-28s

Serial	C/n	Version	Notes
11???	...2002	Il-28	Serial as reported but doubtful; latest German publications do not confirm existence of this aircraft in East Germany!
180 Black	...901418	Il-28R	Ex DDR-ZZI (engine testbed, VEB Entwicklungsbau Pirna), transferred 1-11-61. WFU Oranienburg AB ?-?-76; SOC* 25-6-79, scrapped
184 Black	5901207	Il-28R	Ex DDR-ZZK (engine testbed, VEB Entwicklungsbau Pirna), transferred 1-11-61. WFU Oranienburg AB ?-?-77; SOC 25-6-79, scrapped
190 Black	55006937	Il-28	D/D 1959. SOC 12-10-82, scrapped
193 Black	65010311?	Il-28U	D/D 1961. C/n reported as 610311. Camouflaged. SOC 30-3-79, became a target at the gunnery range in Peenemünde
196 Black	55006944	Il-28	D/D 1959. Crashed 30-7-71
204 Black	4404426	Il-28	D/D 12-1-62. Crashed in Poland 12-10-63
205 Black	54006279	Il-28	D/D 1962. Crashed in the USSR ?-5-69; SOC 30-5-70
208 Red**	55006448	Il-28	D/D 1962. Camouflaged. SOC 13-10-82, preserved Bautzen Museum this date
224 Black	55006445	Il-28	D/D 1962. SOC 9-12-77, scrapped
226 Black	55006417	Il-28	D/D 1962. Crashed at Peenemünde 4-2-70; SOC 30-7-71

Notes:

* SOC = struck off charge.

** The red serial on 208 is noteworthy, as normally only single-seat fighters wore red serials in the East German Air Force; all other aircraft wore black serials.

The aircraft transferred from the Soviet Air Force have been referred to as Il-28Rs, which certainly seems logical, considering that they were transferred from a reconnaissance regiment. However, German sources say only two Il-28Rs were delivered; and indeed the other LSK/LV *Beagles* do not have the tip tanks characteristic of the reconnaissance version.

This Egyptian Air Force Il-28 was displayed in Cairo in 1956 together with other aircraft then operated by the EAF. The bomber carries pre-UARAF green and white national insignia. *(RART)*

1957 three Romanian ships brought the first ten Il-28s to Alexandria, among other things; by late June the EAF had about 40 on strength.

In his speech on 25 July 1957 on the occasion of Nasser's fifth anniversary as President, Egyptian Air Force Chief of Staff Air Vice-Marshal Mohammed Sidki stated that the EAF's first-line assets had doubled as compared to the time immediately before the Suez Crisis. To add weight to his words, a formation of no fewer than 100 combat jets was to pass over Cairo on the same day. However, the show of force fizzled because the technical staff had managed to prepare only 42 aircraft for the display – eleven MiG-15*bis Fagot-B*s, eighteen MiG-17F *Fresco-C*s and thirteen Il-28s. The watching crowd went wild all the same, but the message was clear: it would take years for the Egyptian Air Force to become fully combat-capable.

When Egypt and Syria joined forces against Israel, creating the United Arab Republic on 1 February 1958, the EAF Il-28s were included in the assets of the newly created United Arab Republic Air Force (UARAF). Three squadrons of *Beagle*s were formed; in addition to the basic bomber and Il-28U trainer, the UARAF reportedly operated Il-28R tactical PHOTINT aircraft and Chinese-built H-5s. Egypt reclaimed most of these aircraft in September 1961 when the United Arab Republic ceased to exist and Egypt and Syria (and their respective air forces) went their separate ways.

Reports on the number of Egyptian Il-28s vary widely, some sources stating as many as 72 aircraft in 1966. These included four second-hand Il-28T torpedo-bombers bought from the Soviet Navy in 1962 with a supply of 90 RAT-52 torpedoes. Other sources claim that 27 of 30 (!?) aircraft on strength in 1967 were destroyed on the ground by Israeli air strikes during the Six-Day War (5–11 June 1967). Two Il-28s were resold to Nigeria and six to Syria; it makes you wonder where the remaining 34 aircraft went! Anyway, by the beginning of the Holy Day War (6 October 1973) Egypt had a *Beagle* force of 35 or 40 aircraft in four bomber squadrons and one reconnaissance squadron. The Il-28s were now based at Aswan. No more than four or five remained airworthy by 1983; two aircraft were

Egyptian Air Force Il-28 1733 at Kom Anshim AB; the aircraft wears camouflage introduced after the Six-Day War of 1967. *(Yefim Gordon archive)*

written off on 25 April 1970 under unknown circumstances (possibly a mid-air collision or ground collision).

Only two aircraft, serialled 1733 and 1778, have been positively identified so far; both wore sand/brown camouflage. A drawing exists of one more aircraft in natural metal finish serialled 1731. Speaking of which, Egypt was one of the few air arms to have camouflaged Il-28s (most operators had silver-painted aircraft); the camouflage was introduced as a result of lessons learned in the Six-Day War.

Another camouflaged EAF *Beagle*, 1778, at Cairo-West with a Soviet-built KrAZ-255B 6×6 truck in the foreground. *(RART)*

Finland

The Finnish Air Force (*Ilmavoimat*) received one Il-28 bomber and one Il-28R photo reconnaissance aircraft in 1960–1; two more Il-28Rs followed in 1966. Strangely enough, all four *Beagle*s were operated by the Finnish Air Force's transport squadron (*Kuljetuslentolaivue*, or KuljLLv) at Utti.

NH-2/3/4 were later converted to target tugs according to the Soviet Il-28BM standard; they worked with various types of targets, including a conventional sock and a large dart-shaped glider. The aircraft were silver overall, with the detachable engine cowlings originally painted green on NH-1; later, the cowlings, wingtips (or tip tanks, in the case of the Il-28Rs) and stabilizer tips were painted dayglo orange. The aircraft carried a dayglo orange pennant outlined in red on the fin, possibly to mark them as target tugs.

Table 19. Finnish Air Force Il-28s

Serial	C/n	Version	Notes
NH-1	...5706	Il-28	D/D* 28-1-60; retired after heavy landing 30-11-76; full c/n 53005706?
NH-2	...1710	Il-28R	D/D 24-6-61; WFU 6-81; full c/n 5901710?
NH-3	...1713	Il-28R	D/D 1-66, WFU 30-6-81; full c/n 5901713?
NH-4	...1106	Il-28R	D/D 1-66, WFU 30-6-81, preserved *Suomen Ilmailu Museo*, Tikkakoski; **not** Moscow-built (see Soviet section/Il-28T!), full c/n 5901106?

Notes:
* D/D Delivery Date

Il-28R NH-2 (c/n 1710) with camouflaged wraps on the tip tanks to hide the dayglo finish. *(Yefim Gordon archive)*

Another Finnish Il-28 target tug, NH-4 (c/n 1106); this aircraft apparently does not have the characteristic dayglo markings. *(Yefim Gordon archive)*

Hungary

The Hungarian Air Force (MHRC – *Magyar Honvedseg Repülö Csapatai*) introduced the Il-28 in late 1954/early 1955. Thirty-seven examples were initially on strength, with one regiment based at Kunmadaras; at least some of them (possibly all) were Czech-built B-228s and CB-228s. A second *Beagle* regiment, the 82nd *Végyes Repülö Hadosztaly* (bomber regiment) at Kécskemet, was established later. Little else is known, except that the last Il-28s were retired in 1972.

Table 20. Hungarian Air Force Il-28s

Serial	C/n	Version	Notes
10 Red	?	Il-28	
19 Red	?	Il-28RTR	Often reported in error as a Romanian Air Force aircraft
20 Red	?	Il-28	Preserved *Ozigetvar Muzeum*, Vécses, in fake Soviet Air Force markings
34 Red	56424	Il-28 (B-228)	
50 Red	?	Il-28	Preserved *Magyar Repülöstörteneti Muzeum*, Szolnok
55 Red	56455	Il-28 (B-228)	Preserved, location unknown
71 Red	?	Il-28	
72 Red	?	Il-28	
T1 Red	69420?	Il-28U (CB-228?)	

34 Red, a Hungarian *Beagle*, in flight. *(Yefim Gordon archive)*

Czech-built Hungarian Air Force Il-28 55 Red in a local museum. *(RART)*

Indonesia

When President Sukarno was in office, Indonesia was on fairly good terms with the Soviet Union and enjoyed Soviet military aid. In 1961 the Indonesian naval air arm (*Tentera Nasional Indonesia – Angkatan Laut*, or TNI-AL) took delivery of more than thirty overhauled Il-28T torpedo-bombers serialled from M-841 onwards, together with a suitable complement of RAT-52 torpedoes, and six Il-28U trainers (M-801–M-806). The aircraft were supplied via Czechoslovakia, which also served as a training base for the crews, and equipped No. 1 and No. 21 squadrons at Surabaya. Quite possibly the aircraft were reserialled later on, as a photo exists of TNI-AL *Beagle*s serialled 504, 506 and 508, plus Il-28Us serialled 511 and 512.

In 1966, however, Dr Sukarno was overthrown

Indonesian Navy Il-28T M-842 taxies out for take-off, with M-844 and M-847 visible beyond. *(RART)*

Another Indonesian Navy *Beagle*, now wearing TNI-AL insignia and the new-style serial 506. *(RART)*

M-803, one of four Indonesian Navy Il-28Us, immediately after take-off. *(RART)*

Another *Mascot* in new-style TNI-AL insignia, apparently withdrawn from use. Note the double ace of spades nose art, presumably a squadron badge. *(RART)*

by the staunchly anti-Communist Gen. Suharto. A wave of repressions against Communists swept through Indonesia, and Soviet support was promptly cut off. Predictably, all Soviet-built aircraft were soon grounded by lack of spares. The last *Beagle*s were retired in June 1972.

Iraq

Prior to the Six-Day War the Iraqi Air Force (*al Quwwat al-Jawwiya al-Iraqiya*) operated a single light-bomber squadron equipped with ten Il-28s and two Il-28Us. The aircraft were supplied via Egypt in 1958, replacing de Havilland Venom FB.50 fighter-bombers. Interestingly, the *Militair'82* handbook reported **ten Il-28Us** in service with the IrAF in 1982.

Kampuchea

A handful of Il-28s (probably Chinese-built H-5s) were operated by the National Khmer Aviation

A Federal Nigerian Air Force Il-28 undergoing minor maintenance. *(RART)*

This Federal Nigerian Air Force *Beagle* is photographed in an intriguing setting – possibly after an off-field landing; though none were lost to enemy action, several Il-28s were damaged in accidents. *(RART)*

(NKA) when the country was run by the dictator Pol Pot.

Morocco

The Royal Moroccan Air Force (*al Quwwat al-Jawwiya al-Malakiya Marakishiya* or *Aviation Royale Chérifienne*) operated a mere two Il-28s, probably supplied by Egypt.

Nigeria

In 1969 Nigeria, which had been in the throes of a civil war since May 1967, bought three second-hand Il-28 bombers (two from Egypt and one from Algeria); some sources, though, claimed that the Federal Nigerian Air Force (FNAF) had at least six of the type. The aircraft wore wraparound green/dark brown camouflage. Only one Nigerian Il-28, NAF 635, is known; a drawing of an example serialled NAF-158 has been published, but this appears doubtful.

North Korea

An unknown number of Il-28s were delivered to the Korean People's Army Air Force before the end of the Korean War; at any rate, ten *Beagle*s took part in the victory parade in Pyongyang on 28 July 1953. In the early 1960s Communist China began rebuilding North Korea's air force in an attempt to strengthen its military presence in the region. Obsolete ex-PLAAF equipment was exported to North Korea in violation of the ceasefire treaties; this included 70 Il-28s delivered by sea. Deliveries continued until the mid-1960s, when relations between China and North Korea deteriorated. Only three examples have been identified to date; two of these are bombers – Harbin H-5 45 Blue in dark green camouflage with natural metal undersurfaces and red rudder, and Il-28 314 Red in overall natural metal finish. The third aircraft is an Il-28R serialled 0220 Red, once again in natural metal finish.

Pakistan

In 1965 China signed a contract with Pakistan on the delivery of combat jets, mainly Chengdu FT-5 trainers (a MiG-17 derivative) and Shenyang F-6 (Chinese-built MiG-19SF) fighters to the Pakistani Air Force (PAF, or *Pakistan Fiza'ya*). The deal also included fourteen Soviet-built Il-28 bombers which were delivered in 1966 to form a light-bomber squadron. Pakistan denied Indian claims that it was using the type operationally.

The reason for this deal was that the USA had withdrawn all military support in the wake of the Indo-Pakistani conflict of 1965. The PAF was entirely equipped with US aircraft, including Martin B-57Bs (a spin-off of the Canberra), and as no spares were forthcoming the force was faced with the daunting prospect of being grounded entirely – or finding replacement aircraft.

Thus, the Soviet 'Canberra' was selected as a possible replacement for the US Canberra since it was readily available from China. Moreover, Pakistan was even negotiating the delivery of 30 to 40 Il-28s directly from the USSR in 1969. Had the deal gone through it would inevitably have caused a rift in the Indo-Soviet relationship. Eventually, however, Pakistan arranged to buy an adequate supply of Wright J65 turbojets for the B-57s in France, so the Il-28s were put in storage and never flown.

Poland

The first Il-28s for the Polish Air Force (PWL – *Polskie Wojsko Lotnicze*) arrived at Warsaw-Okęcie airfield (which is now the city's international airport) on 20 July 1952. The type attained initial operating capability (IOC) early the following year, allowing the long-serving Tu-2 and Petlyakov Pe-2 bombers to be retired. Thus the second stage of upgrading the PWL was completed; the first was the replacement of piston-engined fighters with MiG-15 *Fagot-A/B*s and MiG-17 *Fresco*s which were later licence-built by the PZL Mielec factory as the Lim-1/Lim-2 and Lim-5/Lim-6 series respectively. Apart from the baseline bomber version, the PWL also had Il-28Rs equipping several long-range reconnaissance units.

A small number of Il-28U trainers was also

Polish Air Force Il-28 11 Red just before landing. *(Wojskowa Agencja Fotograficzna)*

62 Red, another PWL *Beagle*, in cruise flight. Unlike 11 Red, this one has a late-model SRO-2 *Odd Rods* IFF transponder. *(Wojskowa Agencja Fotograficzna)*

A senior officer gives last-minute instructions to the crew of a Polish Il-28R, 03 Red. *(Wojskowa Agencja Fotograficzna)*

delivered; starting in 1955, they served alongside regular Il-28s at the WOSL (*Wyższa Oficerska Szkoła Lotnicza* – Officers' Higher Flying School) – popularly known as Szkoła *Orląt* (Eaglets' School) – at Dęblin. The *Mascot*s were known locally as SIł-28, the S standing for [*samolot*] *szkolny* (trainer), and had alpha-numeric serials commencing with S. The PWL's Il-28s were of both Soviet and Czech origin.

Polish pilots quickly grew familiar with the type and performed well during national and Warsaw Pact manoeuvres. The most striking demonstration of their skill, however, came at the 1966 military parade in Warsaw commemorating the 1,000th anniversary of Polish statehood. Until the 1970s it was quite common to sky-write by flying in special formations, and messages like 'Peace' or '50 years of

Maintenance work on PWL Il-28U S5 Red. Note the non-standard dipole aerial mounted on the rear fairing. *(Wojskowa Agencja Fotograficzna)*

A publicity shot of seven Polish Air Force Il-28s. *(Wojskowa Agencja Fotograficzna)*

Table 21. Known Polish Air Force Il-28s

Serial	C/n	Version	Notes
1 Red	?	Il-28	
2 Red	?	Il-28	Air Force Technical Institute (ITWL), brake parachute testbed
3 Red	?	Il-28	
4 Red	...1910	Il-28	Soviet-built but factory unknown. Preserved *Muzeum Wyzwolenia Miasta Poznania* (Poznań City Liberation Museum)*
5 Red	?	Il-28	
7 Red	?	Il-28	
03 Red	...2905	Il-28R	Soviet-built but factory unknown
09 Red	?	Il-28	
11 Red	?	Il-28	
17 Red	?	Il-28	
20 Red	?	Il-28	
22 Red	56729	Il-28 (B-228)	Preserved *Muzeum Wojska Polskiego* (Polish Armed Forces Museum), Warsaw, with fake serial 65 Red **(see below)**
30 Red	41302	Il-28R (B-228?)	**Reserialled to, see below**
32 Red (a)			
32 Red (b)	?	Il-28	
33 Red	?	Il-28	
34 Red	?	Il-28	
39 Red	?	Il-28	
40 Red	?	Il-28	
41 Red	56729	Il-28 (B-228)	
42 Red	?	Il-28	
43 Red	?	Il-28	
46 Red	?	Il-28	
50 Red	56538	Il-28 (B-228)	Converted to target tug. Preserved *Muzeum Braterstwa Broni* (Comradeship-in-Arms Museum), Drzonów near Zielona Góra**
52 Red	?	Il-28	See five lines below
54 Red	?	Il-28	
57 Red	...2308	Il-28	Soviet-built but factory unknown
58 Red	?	Il-28	
59 Red	?	Il-28	
62 Red	?	Il-28	
64 Red	...2113	Il-28	Soviet-built but factory unknown. **Reserialled to, see below**
52 Red			Preserved *Muzeum Oręża Polskiego* (Polish Arms Museum), Kołobrzeg
65 Red	...2212	Il-28	Soviet-built but factory unknown. Preserved WOSL, Dęblin
68 Red	?	Il-28R	
69 Red	?	Il-28	Preserved *Muzeum Marynarki Wojennej* (Navy Museum), Gdynia
72 Red	41909	Il-28R (B-228?)	Preserved *Muzeum Lotnictwa i Astronautyki* (MLiA – Aerospace Museum), Kraków; full c/n may be 430511909
001 Red	?	Il-28	ITWL, brake parachute testbed
021 Red	?	Il-28	
030 Red	?	Il-28R	
101 Red	?	Il-28	
111 Red	?	Il-28	
119 Blue	?	Il-28	Converted to, see below
		Il-28H	*Instytut Lotnictwa*, engine testbed
133 Red	?	Il-28	
S1 Red?	?	Il-28U	Existence not proved but likely
S2 Red?	?	Il-28U	Existence not proved but likely
S3 Red	69216	Il-28U (CB-228)	Preserved MLiA, Kraków
S4 Red	?	Il-28U	
S5 Red	?	Il-28U	
not known	41906	Il-28 (B-228)?	Could be an Il-28R (full c/n 430511906?)

Notes:

* Aka *Muzeum Cytadeli Poznańskiej* (Poznań Fortress Museum)

** Some sources state this aircraft as preserved *Muzeum Ziemi Lubuskiej* (Lublin Region Museum).

something-or-other' made up of aircraft were almost obligatory at airshows. Yet the Poles went one better and created an eagle – the Polish national symbol – out of no fewer than 33 Il-28s. The impressive formation was led by Lt-Col Jerzy Wójcik.

By the mid-1970s the Polish Il-28s had been withdrawn from first-line service and used as target tugs with fabric sleeve-type targets, just as in East Germany. Yet again the Poles went one better, developing targets with acoustic hit detectors. The last PWL *Beagle* was retired on 29 December 1977.

The Il-28 contributed a lot to the progress of parachuting in Poland. On 4 September 1957 the parachutist Tadeusz Dulla made a jump from an Il-28 flying at 12,500 m (41,010 ft),[3] setting a national record. Later, other Polish skydivers made single and group jumps from Il-28s in a similar fashion.

Romania

This was one Socialist country that was paranoid about security, so little was known about Romanian Il-28s until recently. The type was introduced into the Romanian Air Force (*Forţele Aeriene ale Republicii Socialişte Române*) service in early 1955, when the *Regimentul 282 Aviaţie Bombardament* (282nd Bomber Regiment) at Ianca AB, 40 km (25 miles) south-west of Galati, took delivery of the first three aircraft – two bombers and one Il-28U trainer.[4] Soon afterwards the unit moved to Mihail Kogălniceanu AB. As it often did, the Soviet Union sent a team of instructors to train the customer's personnel *in situ*; the group which came to Romania to assist in mastering the Il-28 was led by Capt. Mikhail Boykov. It remained with the unit until 5 May 1955, whereupon the 282nd Bomber Regiment relocated to Otopeni (now Bucharest's international airport).

Two years later the unit moved yet again, this

Table 22. Known Romanian *Beagle*s

Serial	C/n	Version	Notes
001 Red	?	Il-28U	
002 Red	?	Il-28U	
003 Red	?	Il-28U	
014 Red	?	Il-28	
015 Red	?	Il-28	
018 Red	?	Il-28U	
125 Red?	?	?	Existence not confirmed
301 Red?	?	B-5	Existence not confirmed
307 Red	?	B-5	Target tug conversion
308 Red	?	B-5	
309 Red	?	B-5	
310 Red	?	B-5	Repainted in grey/blue camouflage by 7-01 as 310 Black. Damaged beyond repair at Borcea-Feteşti AB 21-7-01
402 Red	?	Il-28R	Preserved *Museul Aviaţiei*, Bucharest-Otopeni airport
403 Red	?	Il-28R	Target tug. Crashed at Bacău AB 1-8-55
405 Red	?	Il-28R	Preserved *Museul Aviatiei*, Baneasa section
407 Red	?	Il-28U (BT-5?)	D/D 1979. Stored Bacău AB
408 Red	?	Il-28U (BT-5)	D/D 1979
433 Red	?	Il-28	Target tug
443 Red	?	Il-28	
462 Red?	?	B-5	Existence not confirmed
491 Red?	?	B-5	Existence not confirmed
501 Red	?	Il-28U	
543 Red?	?	B-5	Existence not confirmed
701 Red	?	B-5	
703 Red	?	B-5	Stored Bacău AB
704 Red	?	B-5R	
706 Red	?	B-5	Stored Bacău AB
707 Red	?	B-5	
708 Red	?	B-5	
709 Red	?	B-5	
710 Red?	?	B-5	Existence not confirmed

A long row of VVS *Beagles* on the flight line, headed by Il-28U 03 Blue. *(Yefim Gordon archive)*

time to Boteni, and was transformed into the *Regimentul 282 Aviaţie Cercetare* (Reconaissance Regiment). In 1960 it was demoted to squadron status, becoming the *Escadrila 282 Aviaţie Cercetare*, and relocated for the last time to Borcea AB, near Cocargeaua, where it remains at the time of writing. Two of the bombers (433 Red and 443 Red) were used for target-towing duties at Mihail Kogalniceanu AB in the 1960s; it is not known whether they were standard Il-28BMs or local conversions. The original Soviet-built *Beagles* (unofficially designated Il-28B in Romanian Air Force service) and Il-28U trainers were later supplemented and gradually replaced by Chinese-built B-5s delivered in 1972. One of them, 307 Red, was also converted for target-towing duties; target practice took place at the Cap Midia gunnery range.

Starting in 1961, all Romanian *Beagles* and their engines were refurbished at the Bacău aircraft overhaul plant (URA Bacău).[5] In due time the unit was renumbered, becoming *Escadrila 38 Aviaţie Cercetare*; also, the original natural metal finish of the H-5s gave way to an overall light grey colour scheme (except for the tail turret, which is white) and the new Romanian roundels replacing the Socialist-era star-type insignia. Romania is the last European nation to operate the type. Incidentally, the Romanians have given the *Beagle* a nickname, *Blândul Ben* ('Gentle Ben', after a good-natured bear in a TV series), reflecting the aircraft's easy and forgiving handling.

A minor sensation (and a major treat for warbird enthusiasts) was planned for 27–29 July 2001, when a Romanian Air Force H-5 was to participate in the 30th Royal International Air Tattoo at RAF Cottesmore, Rutland, making the type's first-ever visit to the West. Unfortunately these plans were dashed to the ground (literally) just a few days before the show when the aircraft (310 Black) crash-landed during a training flight on 21 July, losing its entire starboard wing. Since all other surviving H-5s were non-airworthy at the time (or in less than showcase condition anyway), the trip had to be cancelled.

Somalia

In the late 1960s the Somalian Aeronautical Corps (*Dayuuraduha Xoogga Dalka Somaliyeed*) reportedly operated ten Il-28s. Unfortunately no details are known.

Soviet Union

The Soviet Air Force (VVS) was the largest operator of the type. Unfortunately, because of the system of tactical codes described earlier, the only way of positively identifying an aircraft is by the construction number, of which only a few are known.

3 Other reports state a height of 11,900 m (39,041 ft)

4 Some sources claim that **all three** aircraft delivered initially were trainers.

5 Later renamed IAv Bacău (*Intreprenderia Avioane* – aviation enterprise); now Aerostar SA.

Table 23. Soviet *Beagle*s

C/n	Tactical code/ registration	Version	Notes
a) Moscow production			
50301104	none	Il-28T*	Prototype, Ilyushin OKB
50301106	not known	Il-28T*	Prototype, Ilyushin OKB. **Converted to, see below**
	4 Red	Il-28TM	Prototype, Ilyushin OKB
50301408	not known	Il-28	
50301801	not known	Il-28	
430512301	not known	Il-28R	
61003001?	not known	Il-28U	C/n reported as 63001
6*003501?	not known	Il-28U	C/n reported as 63501
52003701	not known	Il-28	VK-5-powered version/first prototype, Ilyushin OKB
52003714	none	Il-28RM	Prototype, Ilyushin OKB
52003719	not known	Il-28	VK-5-powered version/second prototype, Ilyushin OKB
53005005	not known	Il-28	
53005112	12 Red	Il-28LSh	Ilyushin OKB, ski landing gear testbed
54005217	38 Red	Il-28	Year in c/n out of sequence – delivered late?
53005710	10 Blue	Il-28LL	LII, ejection seat testbed
53005717?	09 Red	Il-28T	Nikolayev Minelayer and Torpedo-Bomber Flying School
53005771	04 Red	Il-28	Preserved Soviet (Russian) Air Force Museum, Monino
55006424	26 Blue	Il-28	
55006445	not known	Il-28	Transferred to the East German AF as 224 Black
55006448	not known	Il-28	Transferred to the East German AF as 208 Red
55006542	11 Red	Il-28	GSVG, Oranienburg AB (until 1975)
55006937	not known	Il-28	Transferred to the East German AF as 190 Black
55006968	03 Red	Il-28	
65009706	42 Blue	Il-28U	
65009807	100 Red	Il-28U	
65010311?	not known	Il-28U	C/n reported as 0311. Transferred to the East German AF as 193 Black
65010809	16 Red	Il-28	Moscow-built. **Recoded to, see below**
	10 Red		Preserved Armed Forces Museum, Moscow (currently resprayed as 10 Red outline)
b) Voronezh production			
6450001	not known	Il-28	
6450301	not known	Il-28	
2402101	01 Red	Il-28	LII, refuelling system testbed
3402209	12 Blue	Il-28	
3402701	not known	Il-28	
c) Omsk production			
0016601	not known	Il-28	
0416601	not known	Il-28	
36603509	not known	Il-28	
36603807	01 Red	Il-28	Preserved Moscow-Khodynka
56605702	33 Red	Il-28	Preserved Civil Aviation Museum, Ulyanovsk, as Il-20 (no tactical code, Soviet flag on tail, Aeroflot logo on fuselage)
56606201	85 Red	Il-28	Preserved/GIA Kuibyshev Aviation Institute (KuAI)**
d) unknown factories			
...1905	not known	Il-28	Probably Moscow-built (c/n 50301905)
...2007	not known	Il-28	Probably Moscow-built (c/n 50302207). Development aircraft, Ilyushin OKB, brake parachute tests
...3513	not known	Il-28	Full c/n 52003513 or 36603513
...4702	not known	Il-28T	Full c/n 52004702 or 46604702
...4705	not known	Il-28T	Full c/n 52004705 or 46604705
?	2 Red	Il-28-131	

Table 23 (continued). Soviet *Beagles*

C/n	Tactical code/ registration	Version	Notes
?	7 Red	Il-28T*	Pacific Fleet/567th MTAP
?	08 Blue	Il-28	57th VA/63rd BAD/408th FBAP, Cherlyany AB, 1957
?	19 Red	Il-28Sh	
?	22 Red	Il-28	Preserved *Rígas Aviacijas Múzejs*, Riga-Spilve
?	21 Red	Il-28Sh	
?	25 Red	Il-28Sh	
?	29 Red	Il-28Sh	
?	30 Red	Il-28	Preserved as gate guard at a Russian airbase
54005777	CCCP-Λ	Il-20	
54006104	CCCP-Λ...538	Il-20	Ie, SSSR-L...538
?	CCCP-Λ2035	Il-20	Ie, SSSR-L2035; existence not confirmed

Notes:
*   The purpose-built Il-28T with a long weapons bay.
**   Now Samara State Aviation University (SGAU).

A typical publicity shot from a Soviet airfield, with Il-28 crew chiefs reporting to the pilots. At least one aircraft, 35 Red, has red-painted cowlings. Note the Il-28U trainer (03 Red) at the end of the row. *(Yefim Gordon archive)*

A typical Soviet Air Force Il-28 cruising at high altitude. *(Yefim Gordon archive)*

This Il-28, 67 Red, carries an 'Excellent aircraft' badge on the nose, an award to the ground crew for maintaining the bomber in perfect condition. *(Yefim Gordon archive)*

Syria

The Syrian Air Force (*al Quwwat al-Jawwiya al-Arabiya as-Suriya*) took delivery of six ex-Egyptian Il-28s. Two of them were destroyed by Israeli attacks during the Six-Day War (5–11 June 1967).

Taiwan (Republic of China)

The Republic of China Air Force operated a single ex-PLAAF Il-28 which fell into Nationalist hands when its crew defected on 11 November 1966. The aircraft was reportedly used for spy missions over mainland China, retaining its PLAAF stars-and-bars insignia and the serial 0195 Yellow. It is now on display at the ROCAF museum at Taoyuan AB.

Vietnam (North)

Having established fairly close ties with North Vietnam in the mid-1960s, Communist China started foisting its obsolete military aircraft, including *Beagle*s, on the Vietnamese. China served as a training and maintenance base for the Vietnamese People's Air Force (VPAF, or *Không Quan Nham Dan Viêt Nam*). For instance, Vietnamese Il-28s (obviously ex-PLAAF but Soviet-built aircraft) are known to have been repaired at Mengtse airbase in Yunnan province. In 1968 the VPAF inventory included eight or ten Il-28s based in Hanoi. Only three serials, 1817 Red, 2210 Red and 3256 Red, have been reported, but the former two are unconfirmed.

VPAF Il-28s probably supported North Vietnamese ground troops during the Vietnam War but did not intrude into South Vietnam in order to hit Republic of Vietnam Air Force or USAF bases.

Yemen

Both North and South Yemen operated the *Beagle* on a small scale in the mid-1960s. The Yemen Arab Republic (North Yemen) had six Il-28s, while the People's Democratic Republic of Yemen (South Yemen) had twelve. Unfortunately no serials or base details are known.

5 •

THE IL -28 IN DETAIL

The following structural description applies to the basic bomber version of the Il-28.

The Il-28 is an all-metal monoplane with shoulder-mounted unswept trapezoidal wings, two turbojet engines in underwing nacelles and a conventional swept tail unit with a low-mounted tailplane. The crew includes three persons: pilot, navigator/bomb aimer and tail gunner/radio operator.

The airframe is made chiefly of D-16T duralumin, with flush riveting used throughout. AK6 aluminium alloy is used for the wing/fuselage attachment fittings and grade 30KhGSA steel for the tail unit/fuselage attachment fittings. The frames of the cockpit canopy, navigator's station and tail gunner's station glazing frames are made from cast ML5-TCh magnesium alloy, as are the frames of the navigator's and tail gunner's entrance hatches.

Fuselage: Circular-section stressed-skin semi-monocoque structure built in four sections for ease of assembly. The skin panels are 0.8–2.0 mm (0.03–0.78 in.) thick and are supported by 50 frames (1–17, 17A, 18, 18A, 18B and 19–47), including 14 mainframes, and 38 stringers, 7 of which are reinforced. Maximum fuselage diameter between frames 17 and 20 is 1.8 m (5 ft 10.86 in.).

The ***forward fuselage*** (***section F1***, frames 1–11A)

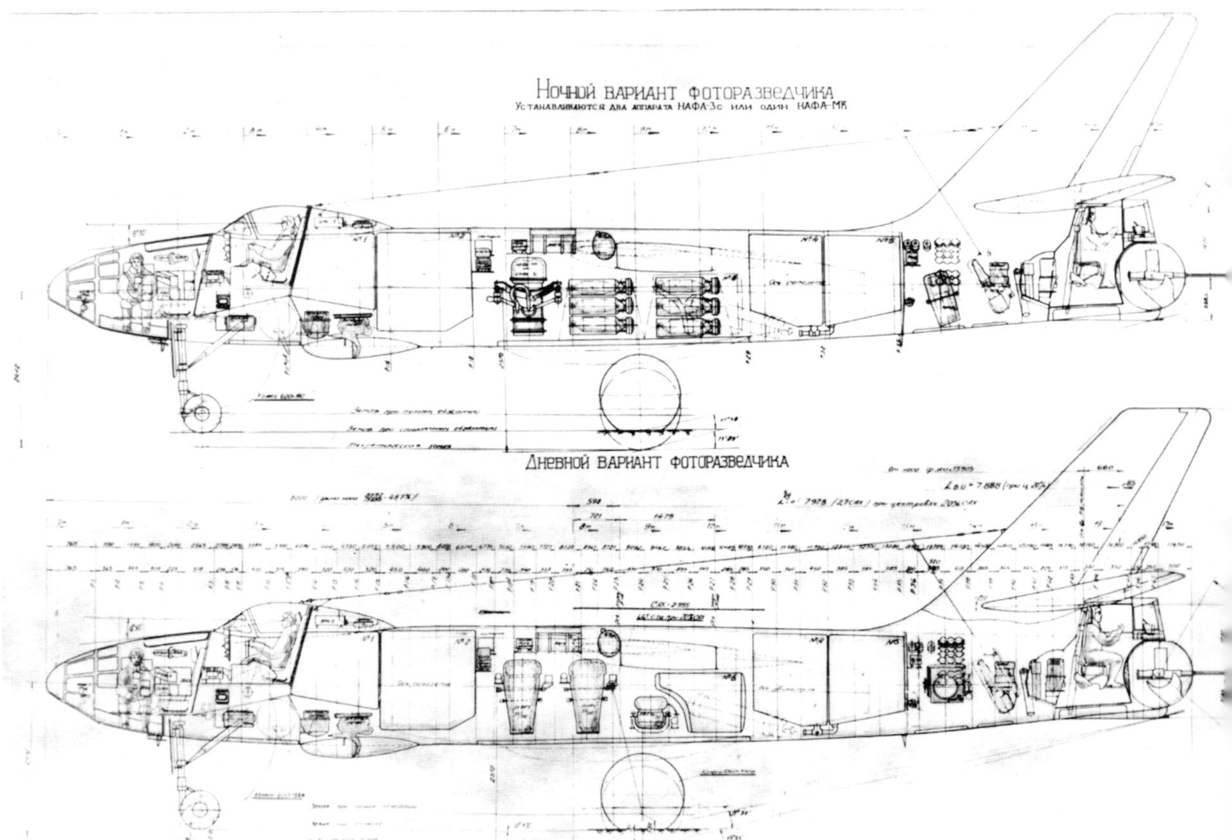

A diagram from the manufacturer's drawings showing the internal layout of the Il-28R configured for night (above) and day (below) reconnaissance missions. *(Yefim Gordon archive)*

This photo shows some of the removable access panels which made the *Beagle* so easy to service. *(Yefim Gordon archive)*

incorporates a pressurized cockpit (frames 6–11A) and a pressurized navigator's compartment (frames 0–6), both of which have sloping rear bulkheads. The navigator's compartment features extensive Plexiglass glazing, with an optically flat Triplex lower forward panel 13–15 mm (0.51–0.59 in.) thick. The entrance hatch (frames 3–6) located in front of the cockpit canopy is offset to starboard and hinged to port; the navigator's ejection seat is immediately below. For bomb aiming by means of the optical sight the navigator uses a folding jump seat attached to frame 2.

The cockpit canopy consists of a fixed windshield with an elliptical flat Triplex forward panel 13–15 mm thick and two curved sidelights, and a rear section hinged to starboard with a one-piece blown Plexiglass transparency. The cockpit is equipped with a control column featuring a W-shaped control wheel, hinged rudder pedals, port and starboard consoles with throttles and other controls. The forward fuselage incorporates the nosewheel well (frames 4–11A) and the nose cannon ammunition boxes (frames 7–8).

The ejection seats have back plates of 10 mm (0.39 in.) steel armour and dished seat pans of 6 mm (0.23 in.) steel. Additional duralumin armour sheets 10–30 mm (0.39–1.18 in.) thick are installed under the navigator's seat. The pilot's windshield does not incorporate bulletproof glass. Total weight of the armour is 454 kg (1,000 lb).

The ***centre fuselage*** (***section F2***, frames 11B–38A) is unpressurized, incorporating the bomb bay (frames 18–29) and the avionics bay for the search radar (frames 11B–16). It also accommodates the wing centre section (frames 23–27) and the fuel cells are located in the fuselage forward and aft of the wings. The bomb bay is closed by two pneumatically actuated doors powered by the pneumatic system, with an emergency air bottle.

The ***rear fuselage*** (***section F3***, frames 38B–42A) is

The navigator's station glazing. *(Yefim Gordon archive)*

The cockpit canopy. Note that Il-28 crews still wore leather helmets and flying goggles. *(Yefim Gordon archive)*

The forward fuselage of an Il-28U. *(Yefim Gordon archive)*

also unpressurized, incorporating an avionics bay (with ventral access hatch) and tail unit attachment fittings located at frames 38, 40 and 42A. Il-28s built by Plant No. 64 in Voronezh have sections F2 and F3 combined into a single whole, so that the fuselage is built in **three** sections with manufacturing joints at frames 11 and 42.

The ***aft fuselage*** (***section F4***, frames 42B–47) is the tail gunner/radio operator's pressurized cabin accessed from below via a forward-opening hatch located between frames 42B and 45. The tail turret is mounted on frame 47. The gunner's station has a 106 mm (4.17 in.) bulletproof rear window and 68 mm (2.67 in.) bulletproof side windows; additionally, the gunner and the ammunition boxes of the Il-K6 turret are protected by 8 mm (0.31 in.) steel armour.

Wings: Cantilever shoulder-mounted two-spar structure built in three sections. The centre section is integrated into the fuselage and the detachable one-piece wing panels carry the engine nacelles. The wings employ a TsAGI SR-5S (P11-1) aerofoil with

The aft fuselage and tail unit of an Il-28R (c/n 2905), showing the gunner's entry hatch, which doubles as an escape slide/slipstream deflector. *(Wojskowa Agencja Fotograficzna)*

a thickness-to-chord ratio of 12%. Dihedral 1°12′, incidence 3°, aspect ratio 7.55, taper 2.08.

The wing box formed by the two spars (attached to the fuselage at frames Nos. 23 and 27), reinforced skins and multiple ribs and stringers accepts the aerodynamical loads. The wing skins are 2–4 mm (0.07–0.15 in.) thick. At the tips, the trailing edge is occupied by ailerons, the starboard aileron incorporating a trim tab. The rest of the trailing edge is occupied by two-section hydraulically actuated slotted flaps inboard and outboard of the engine nacelles. The flaps are deflected 20° for take-off and 48° for landing; total flap area is 7.45 m^2 (80 sq. ft). Both the ailerons and the flaps are horn-balanced to reduce control/actuator forces.

Tail unit: Conventional swept tail surfaces with cantilever tailplanes. The fin and the stabilizers have a two-spar structure and are attached to the fuselage by three pairs of bolts.

The fin is swept back 41° at quarter-chord (leading-edge sweep is 45°). The stabilizers have 33° leading-edge sweep and 7° dihedral. The tail unit utilizes symmetrical NACA aerofoils with a thickness-to-chord ratio of 12–10% for the vertical tail and 11–10% for the horizontal tail. Stabilizer span is 7.36 m (24 ft 1.77 in.), stabilizer area is 10.82 m^2 (116.34 sq. ft); fin area is 7.8 m^2 (83.87 sq. ft).

Landing gear: Pneumatically retractable tricycle type, with oleo-pneumatic shock absorbers on each unit. The aft-retracting nose unit has twin wheels – originally 600 × 155 mm (23.6 × 6.1 in.), later 600 × 180 mm (23.6 × 7.08 in.) or 600 × 185 mm (23.6 × 7.28 in.). The main units with single 1,150 × 355 mm (45.27 × 13.97 in.) wheels retract forward into the lower portions of the engine nacelles, the wheels turning through 90° by means of mechanical linkages to lie flat under the jetpipes. The nosewheel well is closed by a forward door segment attached to the nose gear oleo and two lateral doors; each mainwheel well is closed by twin lateral doors and a small rear door hinged on the inboard side. All wheel well doors remain open when the gear is down.

The Il-28R has a hydraulically retractable landing gear 1,260 × 390 mm (49.6 × 15.35 in.) mainwheels featuring a hydraulic spin-up system to prolong tyre life. Wheel track 7.4 m (24 ft 3.3 in.), wheelbase 6.677 m (21 ft 10.8 in.). Nosewheel tyre pressure 4.5 kg/cm^2 (0.315 psi), mainwheel tyre pressure 7–8 kg/cm^2 (0.49–0.56 psi).

Powerplant: Two Klimov VK-1A non-afterburning turbojets, each rated at 2,700 kgp (5,952 lb st) for take-off and 2,400 kgp (5,291 lb st) for cruise. The VK-1A has a single-stage centrifugal

This view of Il-28U 42 Blue (c/n 65009706) shows how the Il-28's two-piece annular cowlings are removed to expose the engine completely.

compressor, nine straight-flow combustion chambers, a single-stage axial turbine and a subsonic fixed-area nozzle. The engine features an accessory gearbox for driving fuel, oil and hydraulic pumps and electrical equipment. Starting is electrical by means of an ST2 or ST2-48 starter.

The engines are installed in area-ruled underwing nacelles and fitted with long extension jetpipes. Each engine is mounted on a bearer via four attachment points: two trunnions on the right and left sides of the compressor casing below the axis of the engine and two mounting lugs in the upper part of the engine. The forward part of each nacelle consists of two annular cowling sections, the front section incorporating a parabolic centrebody carried on a straight-through vertical pylon; when these are detached, the engine is exposed almost completely for maintenance or removal.

To reduce the take-off run, two PSR-1500-15 jet-assisted take-off (JATO) rockets with a thrust of 1,650 kgp (3,637 lb st) and a burn time of 13 sec. could be fitted to the centre fuselage sides under the wing roots.

Control system: Manual controls throughout. One-piece ailerons for roll control, one-piece elevators for pitch control and one-piece rudder for directional control; the rudder and elevators are horn-balanced to reduce control forces. The starboard aileron, rudder and both elevators incorporate trim tabs. The elevators and rudder have cable control runs, while the ailerons are controlled by push-pull rods. The elevator trim tabs are mechanically operated by means of cables, while the starboard aileron and rudder trim tabs are electrically actuated.

Fuel system: Five self-sealing fuel cells (bladder tanks) located in the fuselage ahead and aft of the wings (No. 1, frames 11A–15; No. 2, frames 15–18; No. 3, frames 18–21; No. 4, frames 29–32; No. 5, frames 32–36). The cell walls are 3.3–10.8 mm (0.12–0.42 in.) thick. The total capacity of the fuel system is 7,908 lit. (1,739 imp. gal.) on the standard bomber and 6,600 lit. (1,452 imp. gal.) on the Il-28U trainer. The Il-28R reconnaissance version features modified internal tankage and 950 lit. (209 imp. gal.) drop tanks at the wingtips, which gives a total of 9,550 lit. (2,101 imp. gal.).

Electric system: Two GSR-9000 (later STG-12000) starter-generators driven by the engines and two 12-A-30 lead-acid batteries installed in the fuselage.

Hydraulic system: The hydraulic system operates the flaps, wheel brakes and, on the Il-28R, the landing gear actuators and mainwheel spin-up drives. Hydraulic power is provided by a GNP-1 hydraulic pump driven by the port engine, with two hydraulic accumulators as a back-up.

Pneumatic system: The hydraulic system operates the landing gear (on all versions except the Il-28R), bomb bay doors, gunner's station entry hatch, and inflatable canopy/hatch seals. In an emergency it is also used to deploy the flaps, operate the wheel brakes and jettison the navigator's hatch cover. Compressed air is stored in several spherical bottles which are charged on the ground and topped up by engine bleed air in flight.

De-icing system: The wings, tail unit and engine air intakes are de-iced by engine bleed air.

Armament: The defensive armament comprises four 23 mm (.90 calibre) Nudelman/Richter NR-23 cannon. Two of them, with 100 rpg, are rigidly mounted in the nose, the other two, with 225 rpg, are carried in the Il-K6 tail turret installed in the rear fuselage and controlled by the gunner.

The normal bomb load of the Il-28 consists of 1,000 kg (2,204 lb) of bombs carried internally. The maximum bomb load is 3,000 kg (6,612 lb) – i.e. one FAB-3000 HE bomb.

Avionics and equipment

The Il-28 features a comprehensive avionics suite enabling the aircraft to operate at night and in any weather.

a) piloting and navigation equipment: SD-1 VOR receiver, AP-5 electric autopilot, OSP-48 instrument landing system (comprising an ARK-5 Amur automatic direction finder (in a dielectric fairing immediately aft of the cockpit), an RV-2 Kristall low-altitude radio altimeter and an MRP-48 Dyatel marker beacon receiver), RV-10 high-altitude radio altimeter.

b) communications equipment: RSU-5 (on early production aircraft) or RSIU-3 Klyon (Maple) UHF command radio; RSB-5 communications radio with antenna cable stretched between fin top and antenna mast immediately aft of the cockpit; SPU-5 intercom (*samolyotnoye peregovornoye oostroystvo*).

c) flight instrumentation: AGK-47B artificial horizon, GPK-46 gyro compass, DGMK-3 remote gyromagnetic compass indicator, KI-11 compass, AB-52 navigation display, KUS-1200 airspeed indicator (ASI, *kombineerovannyy ookazahtel' skorosti*), VD-17 altimeter, RV-2 radio altimeter indicator, EUP-46 electric turn and bank indicator (*elektricheskiy ookazahtel' povorota*), VAR-75 vertical speed indicator (VSI, *variometr*), UP-2 turn indicator (*ookazahtel' povorota*), MA-095 Mach meter, AVR-M and AChKhO chronometers, etc.

Table 24. Specifications

Overall length	17.65 m (57 ft 10.88 in.)
Span	21.45 m (70 ft 4.48 in.)
Height	6.7 m (21 ft 11.77 in.)
Wing area	60.8 m^2 (653.76 sq. ft)
Empty operating weight	12,890 kg (28,417 lb)
Normal gross weight	18,400 kg (40,564 lb)
Maximum gross weight	21,000 kg (46,296 lb)
Gross weight in overload condition	23,200 kg (51,146 lb)
Maximum landing weight	14,750 kg (32,517 lb)
Normal bomb load	1,000 kg (2,204 lb)
Maximum bomb load	3,000 kg (6,612 lb)
Top speed: at S/L	800 km/h (444.4 kt)
at 4,500 m (14,763 ft)	902 km/h (501 kt)
at 10,000 m (32,808 ft)	855 km/h (475 kt)
Unstick speed: with an 18,400 kg (40,564 lb) TOW	235 km/h (130.5 kt)
with a 23,200 kg (51,146 lb) TOW	260 km/h (144.4 kt)
Landing speed	185 km/h (100.0 kts)
Rate of climb	15 m/sec (2,952 ft/min)
Service ceiling: with an 18,400 kg (40,564 lb) TOW	12,500 m (41,010 ft)
with a 23,200 kg (51,146 lb) TOW	10,750 m (35,269 ft)
Time to height*: 5,000 m (16,404 ft)	6.5 min
10,000 m (32,808 ft)	18.0 min
2,500 m (41,010 ft)	31.0 min
Time to service ceiling: with an 18,400 kg (40,564 lb) TOW	40.7 min
with a 23,200 kg (51,146 lb) TOW	45.4 min
Range**	1,930 km (1,198 miles)
Endurance**	3 hrs 7 min
T/O run*: concrete strip, unstick speed 220 km/h (122.2 kt)	875 m (2,870 ft)
dirt strip, unstick speed 235 km/h (130.5 kt)	1,290 m (4,232 ft)
T/O run***: concrete strip, unstick speed 260 km/h (144.4 kt)	1,720 m (5,643 ft)
dirt strip, unstick speed 260 km/h (144.4 kt)	2,350 m (7,709 ft)
Landing run	1,170 m (3,838 ft)

Notes:

* with an 18,400 kg (40,564 lb) TOW.

** with a 20,750 kg (45,745 lb) TOW and cruising at 9,700–11,500 m (31,824–37,729 ft).

*** with a 23,200 kg (51,146 lb) TOW.

d) targeting equipment: PSBN-M 360° ground-mapping and search radar, OPB-6SR optical computing bomb sight (on radar-equipped aircraft only; substituted by OPB-5s on aircraft with the radar removed), PKI collimator gunsight (for the pilot) and a collimator gunsight for the gunner. The revolving radar antenna is covered by a teardrop fairing made of PVC.

e) IFF equipment: Bariy-M (Barium) IFF transponder in rear fuselage, later replaced by SRO-2M Khrom (Chromium) IFF transponder (*samo**lyot**nyy **rah**diolokatsee**on**nyy ot**vet**chik*) with triple rod aerials ahead of the nose gear unit.

Rescue equipment: In an emergency, the pilot and navigator/bomb aimer use upward-firing ejection seats. The tail gunner/radio operator bales out downwards via the entrance hatch; the hatch cover is actuated by twin pneumatic rams, doubling as a slipstream deflector.

Il-28T torpedo-bombers carried an LAS-3 inflatable rescue dinghy; one was also carried by reconnaissance aircraft and bombers on overwater missions.

Exterior lighting: port, starboard and tail navigation lights; retractable landing lights in the outer faces of the engine nacelles.

Appendix I •

Acronyms and Glossary

AD – air defence.
ADP – advanced development project.
AFA – ***aerofotoapparaht*** – *aerial camera.*
AM – [***pushka***] *Afanas'yeva i Makahrova* – Afanas'yev/Makarov cannon.
AMD – *aviatsionnaya mina desanteeruyemaya* – air-dropped [anti-shipping] mine.
ARK – *avtomaticheskiy rahdiokompas* – automatic direction finder (ADF) used in conjunction with ground beacons
ASW – anti-submarine warfare.
AUW – all-up weight.
AVMF – *Aviahtsiya voyenno-morskovo flota* – Naval Air Arm.
BAD – *bombardeerovochnaya aviadiveeziya* – bomber division (= group).
BD – *bahlochnyy derzhahtel'* – beam-type [weapons] rack (as distinct from bomb cassettes for small-calibre bombs).
Bleed air – excess air piped from the compressor section of a gas turbine engine for various uses (pressurization, de-icing etc.).
CG – centre of gravity.
C-in-C – Commander-in-Chief.
COIN – **co**unter-**in**surgency (role or aircraft), i.e., for use against guerrillas; typically, this applies to light fixed-wing attack aircraft, often adapted from general aviation designs.
DD – Defence District (*voyennyy okroog*) – one of the large areas into which the territory of the Soviet Union (Russia) was (is) divided with respect to the MoD's control of the Armed Forces.
DF – direction finder.
DK – *distantsionno* [*oopravlyayemaya*] *kormovaya* [*strelkovaya oostanovka*] – remote-controlled tail barbette.
ECM – **e**lectronic **c**ounter**m**easures (disrupting the operation of enemy radios and the like).
Elevating angle – angle of vertical motion of a trainable gun.
ELINT – **el**ectronic **int**elligence (reconnaissance).
FBAP – *frontovoy bombardeerovochnyy aviapolk* – tactical bomber regiment (= wing).
FFAR – folding-fin aircraft rocket – unguided rocket designed to be launched from a podded or retractable launcher and having foldaway stabilising fins to fit into its launch tube.
FOD – foreign object damage (damage to a jet engine caused by ingestion of foreign objects, usually on the ground).
Free-fall weapons – i.e., with no provision for guidance to the target.
GHQ – General Headquarters.
GKAT – *Gosoodahrstvennyy komitet po aviatseeonnoy tekhnike* – State Committee on Aviation Hardware (ex/to MAP, which see; demoted during the Khruschchov years but then reinstated).
GSVG = *Grooppa sovetskikh voysk v Ghermahnii* – Group of Soviet Forces in [East] Germany (1945–89); renamed ZGV (*Zahpadnaya grooppa voysk* – Western Group of Forces, i.e., Soviet/Russian Armed Forces contingent in East Germany and then reunited Germany in 1988–94).
HDU – hose drum unit (a powered drum installed on a flight refuelling tanker from which the fuel transfer hose is deployed).
HF – high frequency (radio).
IFF – identification friend-or-foe (usually by means of interrogators and transponders sending coded signals when interrogated to identify the aircraft as 'friendly').
IFR (1) – instrument flying rules.
IFR (2) – in-flight refuelling.
ILS – instrument landing system (system of ground-based and airborne radio navigation aids permitting blind runway approach and landing at night or in adverse weather).
IMC – instrument meteorological conditions (when the pilot has no external visual references for judging the aircraft's attitude and altitude and has to rely solely on the flight instruments).
JATO – jet-assisted take-off (by means of rocket boosters to shorten the take-off run).
KP-14 – *kislorodnyy preebor* – individual oxygen breathing apparatus.
KU – *kormovaya* [*strelkovaya*] *oostanovka* – tail barbette.
LII – *Lyotno-issledovatel'skiy institoot* – Flight

Research Institute named after Mikhail M. Gromov in Zhukovskiy near Moscow.
LL – *letayuschchaya laboratoriya* – lit. 'flying laboratory' (testbed or research/survey aircraft).
Localizer (LOC) – a radio beacon indicating the landing approach heading (part of the ground component of an ILS).
Mach buffeting – vibration at high Mach numbers caused by disruption of the airflow over the tail surfaces.
Mach number – the aircraft's speed in relation to the speed of sound (333 m/sec) which is Mach 1.0.
MAP – *Ministerstvo aviatseeonnoy promyshlennosti* – Ministry of Aircraft Industry.
MMZ No. *** – *Moskovskiy mashinostroitel'nyy zavod* – Moscow Machinery Plant No. ***.
Mock-up review commission – a commission consisting of customer (in this context, Air Force) and aircraft industry representatives which inspects a full-scale mock-up of a new aircraft and reviews the advanced development project in order to eliminate any obvious shortcomings before prototype construction begins.
MOP – *Ministerstvo oboronnoy promyshlennosti* – Ministry of Defence Industry.
MRP – *markernyy rahdiopreeyomnik* – marker beacon receiver.
MTAP – *minno-torpednyy aviapolk* – minelaying and torpedo-bomber regiment.
MTOW – maximum take-off weight.
Never-exceed speed (V_{NE}) – the speed limit determined for an aircraft due to structural strength limits; exceeding it may cause the aircraft to break up due to ram air pressure.
NII – *naoochno-issledovatel'skiy institoot* – research institute (any kind).
NII VVS – *naoochno-issledovatel'skiy institoot voyenno-vozdooshnykh seel* – (Soviet) Air Force Research Institute named after Valeriy P. Chkalov.
NKPB – *nochnoy kollimahtornyy pritsel bombardirovochnyy* – collimator bomb sight for night use.
NR – [*pushka*] *Noodel'mana i Rikhtera* – Nudelman/Richter cannon.
NS – [*pushka*] *Noodel'mana i Soorahnova* – Nudelman/Sooranov cannon.
OKB – *optyno-konstrooktorskoye byuro* – experimental design bureau.
OMTAP – *otdel'nyy minno-torpednyy aviapolk* – independent minelaying and torpedo-bomber regiment.
OPB – *opticheskiy pritsel bombardirovochnyy* – optical bomb sight.
ORAP – *otdel'nyy razvedyvatel'nyy aviapolk* – independent reconnaissance regiment.
OSP – *oboroodovaniye slepoy posahdki* – blind landing equipment (ILS).
PHOTINT – **phot**ographic **int**elligence (reconnaissance).
PO – *preobrazovahtel' odnofahznyy* – single-phase AC converter.
PSBN – *pribor slepovo bombometahniya i navigahtsii* – blind-bombing and navigation device.
PSR = *porokhovaya startovaya raketa* – solid-fuel rocket booster.
PZL – Panstwowe Zaklady Lotnicze – State Aircraft Factories concern (Poland).
RAT – *reaktivnaya aviatsionnaya torpeda* – air-dropped rocket-propelled torpedo.
Radar cross-section (RCS) – a measure of how visible an aircraft is to ground radars.
RB (in RB-17 designation) – *reaktivnyy bombardirovschchik* – jet bomber.
RBP – *rahdiolokatseeonnyy bombardirovochnyy pritsel* – 'radar bomb sight' (bomb-aiming radar).
RD – *reaktivnyy dvigatel'* – jet engine.
RDS – the meaning of this acronym designating early Soviet nuclear munitions (RDS-3, RDS-4 etc.) is not known but some sources have deciphered it as *reaktivnyy dvigatel' Stahlina* – 'Stalin's jet engine'!
REB – *rahdioelektronnaya bor'bah* – ECM.
RP – *rahdiopreetsel* – 'radio sight' (i.e., fire control radar).
rpm – a) revolutions per minute (rotation speed of a shaft etc.); b) rounds per minute (rate of fire of a machine-gun or an automatic cannon).
RTR – *rahdiotekhnicheskaya razvedka* – ELINT.
RV – *rahdiovysotomer* – radio altimeter.
SAM – surface-to-air missile.
Self-sealing fuel tanks – flexible tanks with a special protective rubber layer. The rubber swells when it comes into contact with jet fuel if the tank is punctured by bullets, thereby closing the bullet holes and stopping the leak.
SP – [*sistema*] *slepoy posahdki* – blind landing system (ILS).
SPU – *samolyotnyy dahl'nomer* – distance measuring equipment (DME)
SPU – *samolyotnoye peregovornoye oostroystvo* – intercom.
ss (as a suffix to numbers of official documents) – *sovershenno sekretno* – top secret.
State acceptance trials – in the Soviet Union/Russia, trials in order to determine whether a military aircraft is suitable for service.

For civil aircraft, State acceptance trials are basically certification trials.

TKRD – ***toor**bokom**pres**sornyy reak**tiv**nyy **dvig**atel'* – lit. 'turbo-compressor jet engine' (an early Soviet term for turbojets).

Traversing angle – angle of sideways motion of a trainable gun.

TsAGI – *Tsen**trahl'**nyy **a**ero- i **ghid**rodina**mee**ch-eskiy insti**toot*** – Central Aerodynamics & Hydrodynamics Institute named after Nikolay Yegorovich Zhukovskiy.

U (i.e., U-19) – *ooskor**it**el'* – booster.

UB (1), e.g., UB-2F Chaika – *oopravl**ya**yemaya **bom**ba – guided bomb.*

*UB (2), e.g., UB-16-57 – ooniver**sahl'**nyy blok* – versatile [rocket] pod, i.e., one that can be carried by various aircraft types.

VA – *voz**doosh**naya **ar**miya* – air army (= air force).

VEB – *Volkseigener Betrieb* (German) – people's (i.e., state-owned) enterprise in former East Germany.

VHF – very high frequency (radio).

VMC – visual meteorological conditions (more or less clear weather when the pilot can judge the aircraft's attitude and altitude by using external visual references).

VVS – *Vo**yen**no-voz**doosh**nyye seely* – Air Force (in this instance, Soviet/Russian Air Force).

• Appendix II

Detail Plans

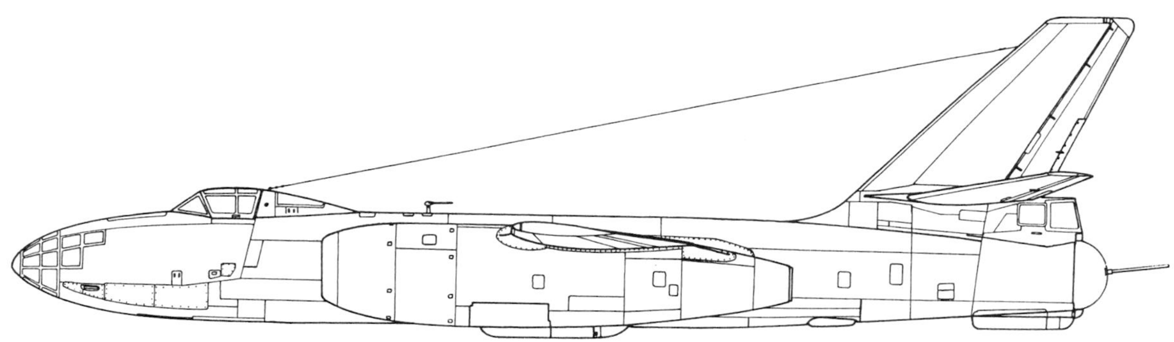

The Rolls-Royce Nene-powered first prototype Il-28.

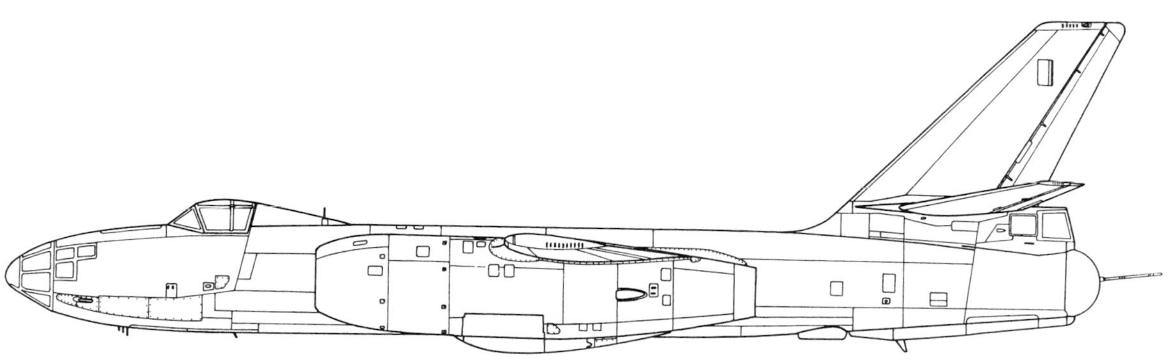

The second prototype powered by RD-45F engines.

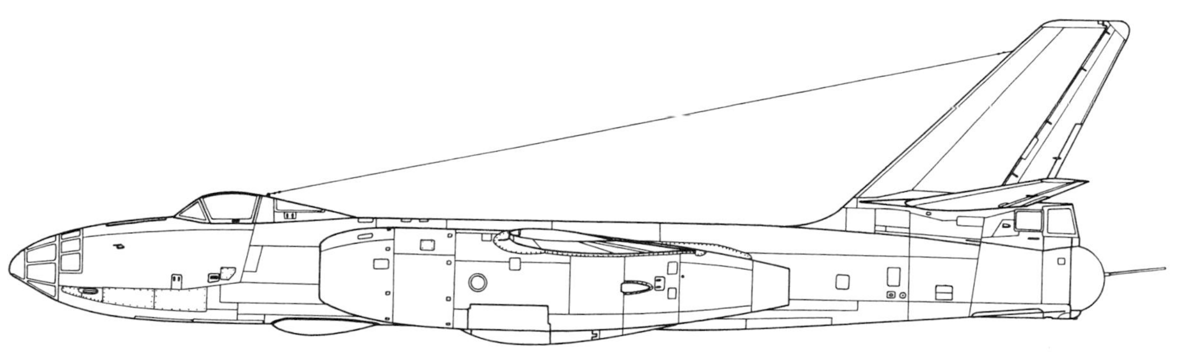

An early-production Il-28; note the redesigned canopy and the addition of landing lights.

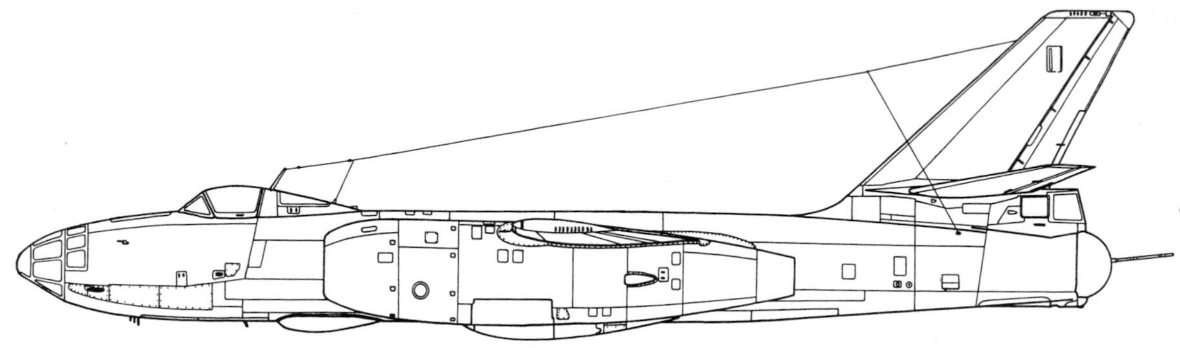

A later Il-28 bomber; note the relocated landing lights.

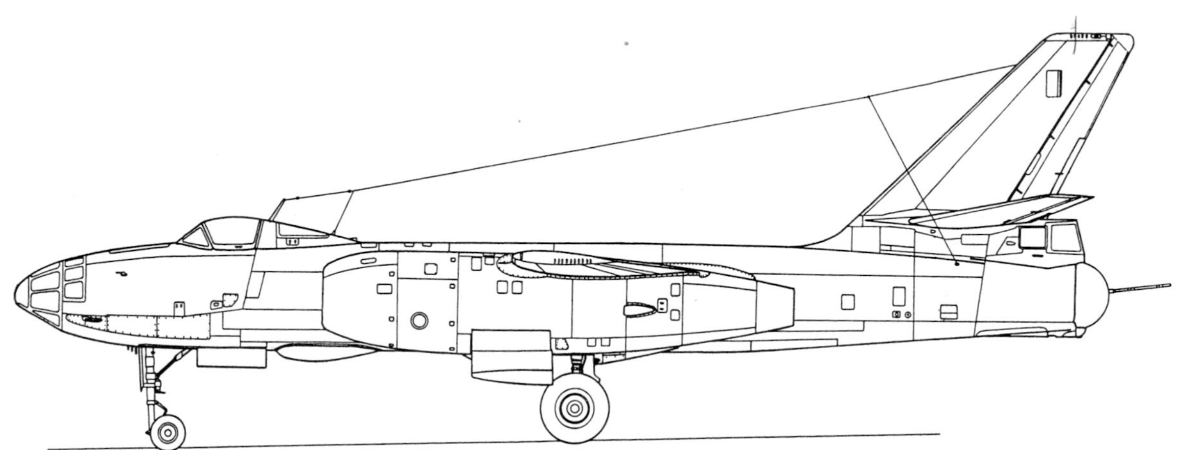

Above, below and opposite: A three-view illustration of a typical production *Beagle*.

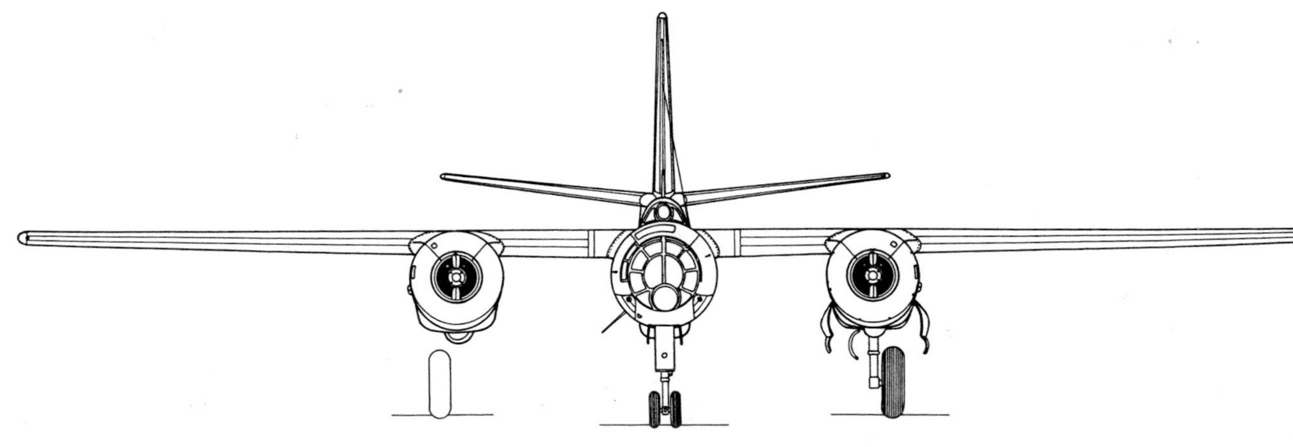

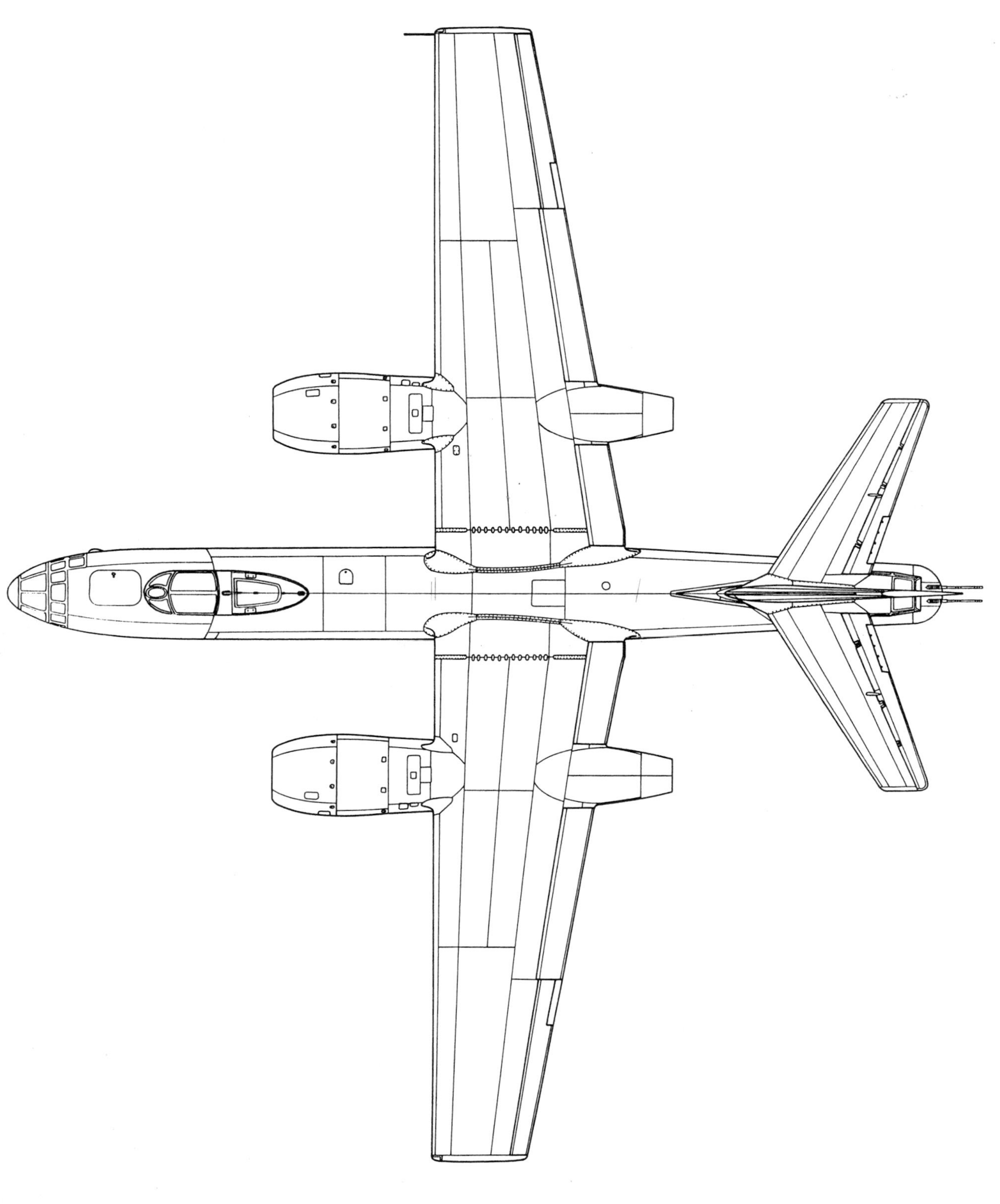

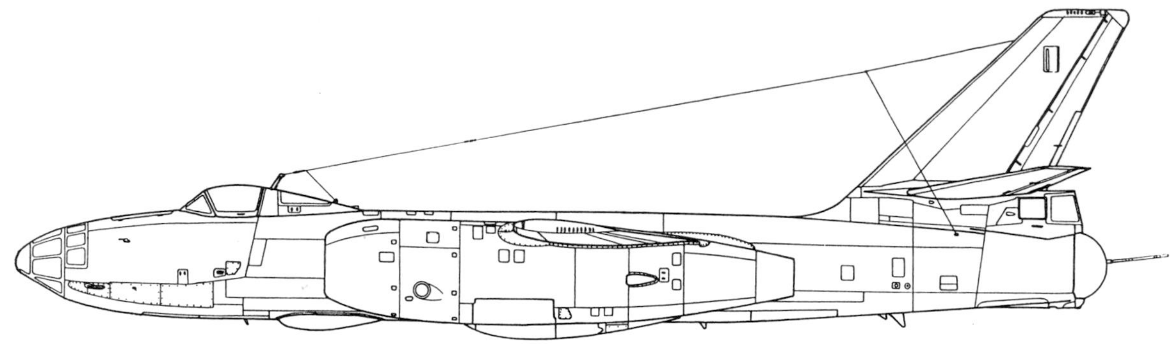

An Il-28 fitted with non-standard communications equipment; note the additional aerials under the rear fuselage.

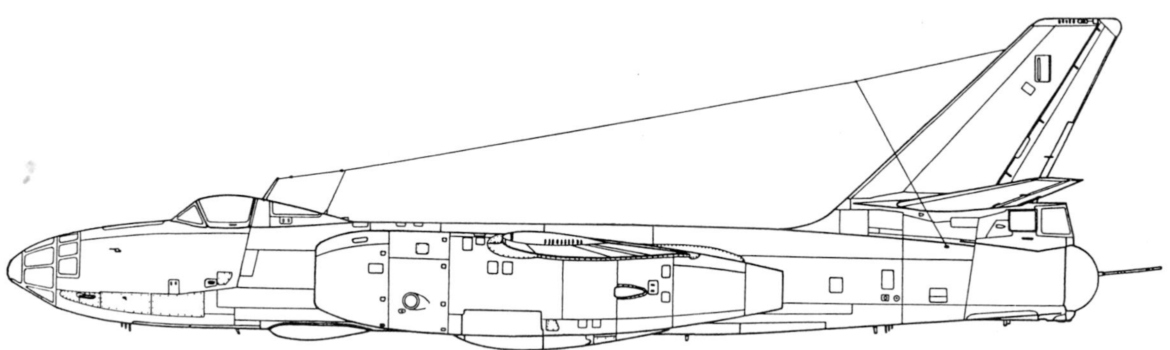

Another *Beagle* with non-standard communications equipment and a different antenna array.

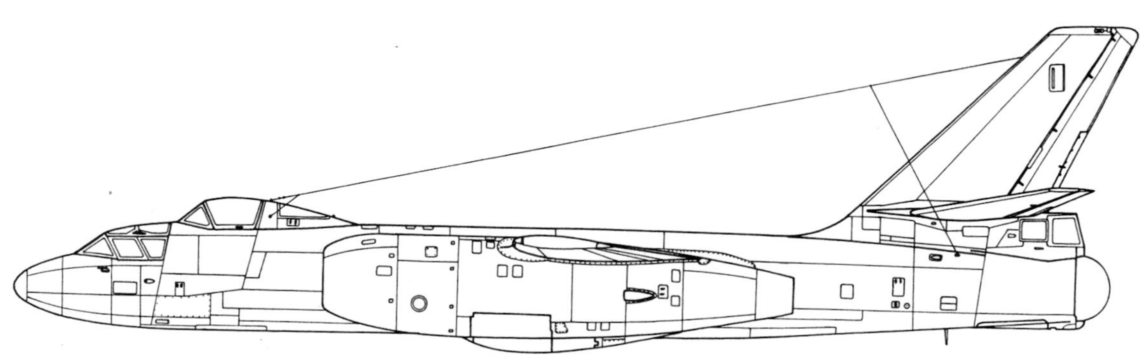

The Il-28U trainer prototype.

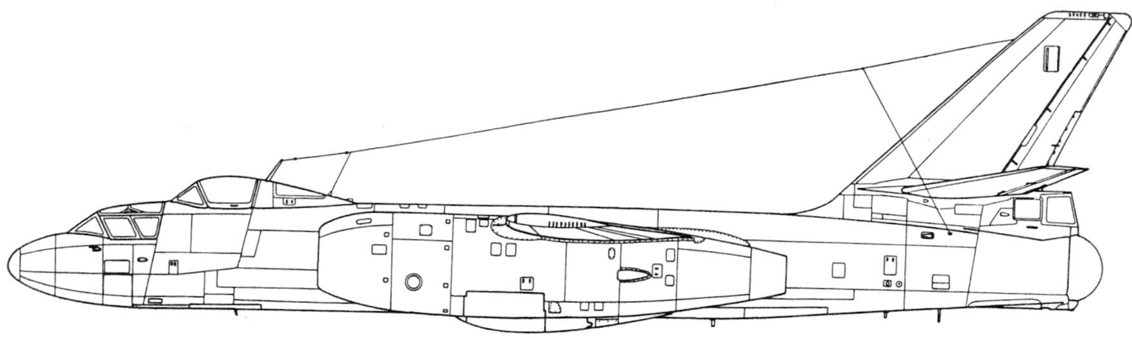

A typical production Il-28U.

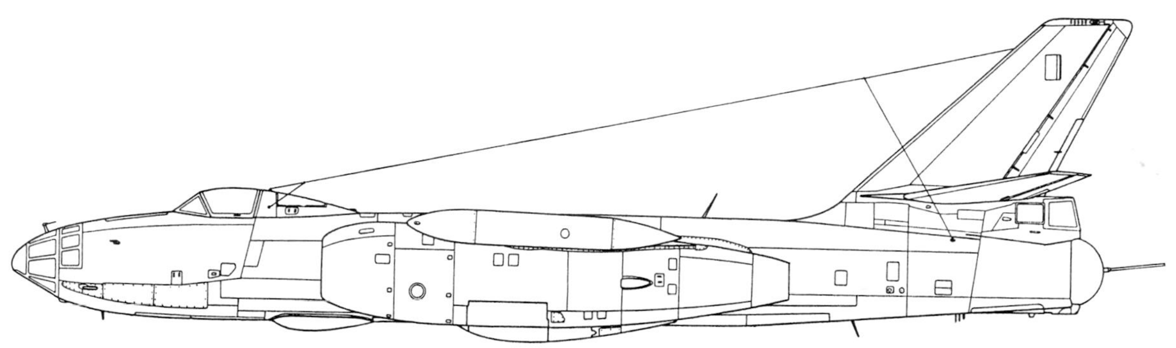

A prototype of the Il-28R reconnaissance aircraft; note the aerial atop the extreme nose.

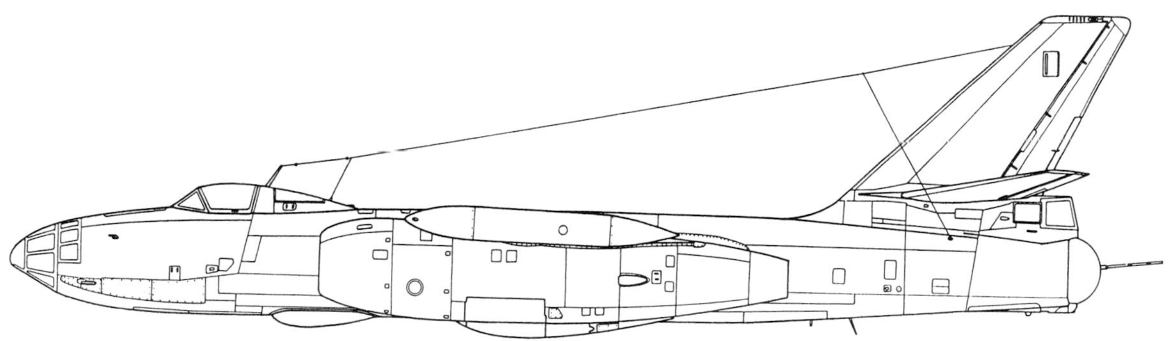

A production Il-28R with early-model communications equipment (note the wire aerial from cockpit to fin).

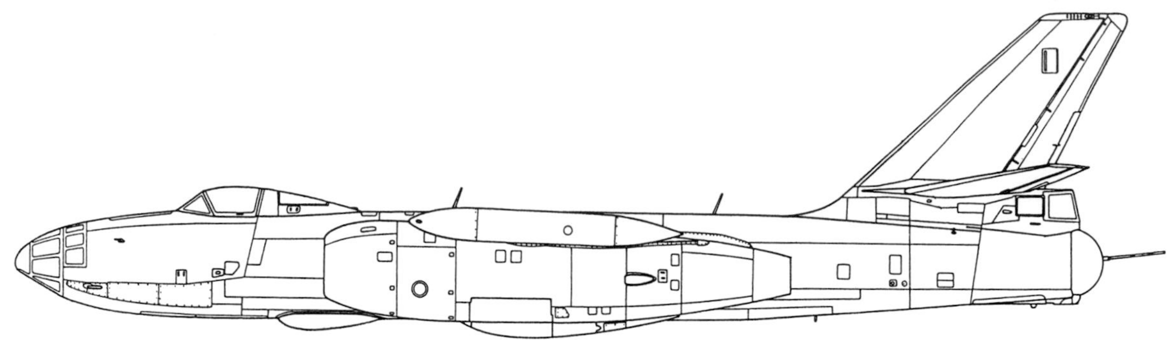

An updated Il-28R with a blade aerial for the communications radio.

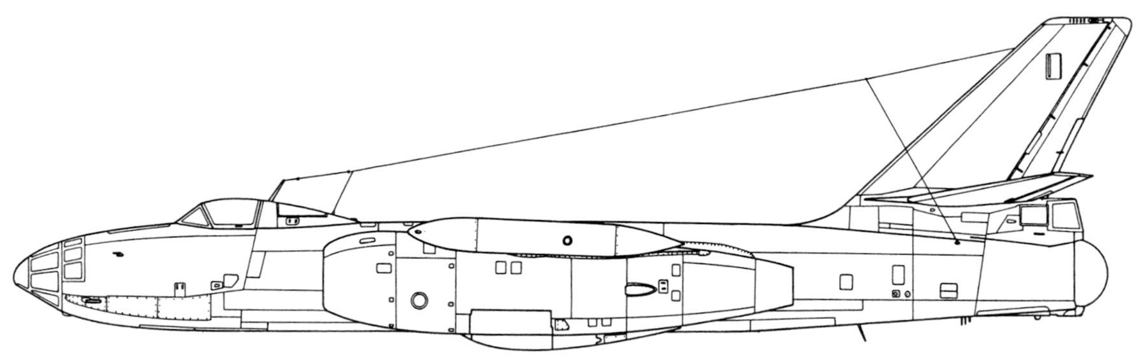

One of the two Il-28Rs delivered new to East Germany in its latter days as East German Air Force 180 Black or 184 Black. The aircraft is converted for target-towing duties; note the lack of radar and cannon.

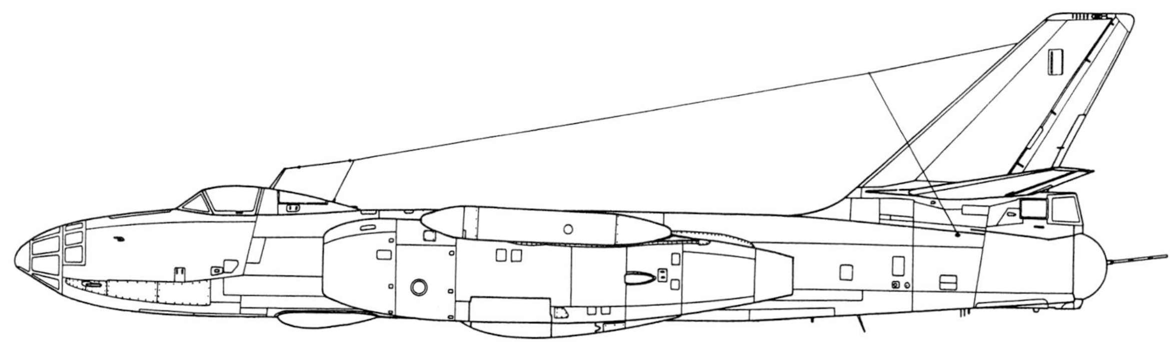

A Polish Air Force Il-28 in ECM configuration with wingtip jammer pods.

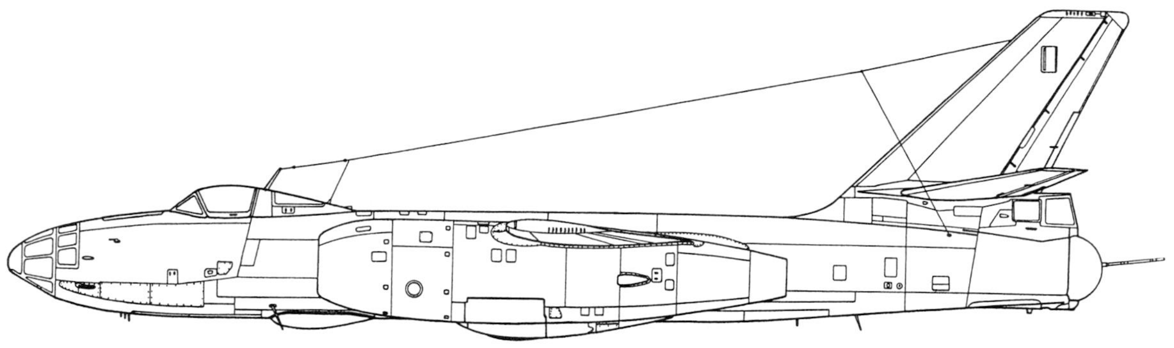

The Il-28RT ELINT version.

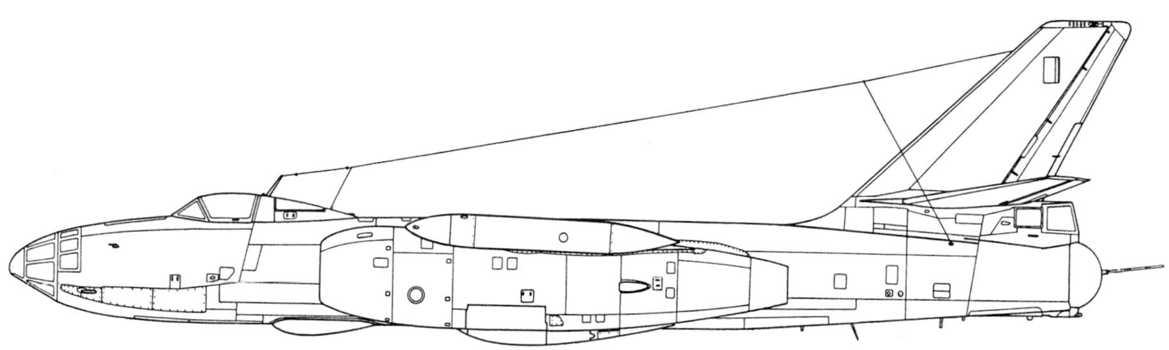

An Il-28T torpedo-bomber conversion.

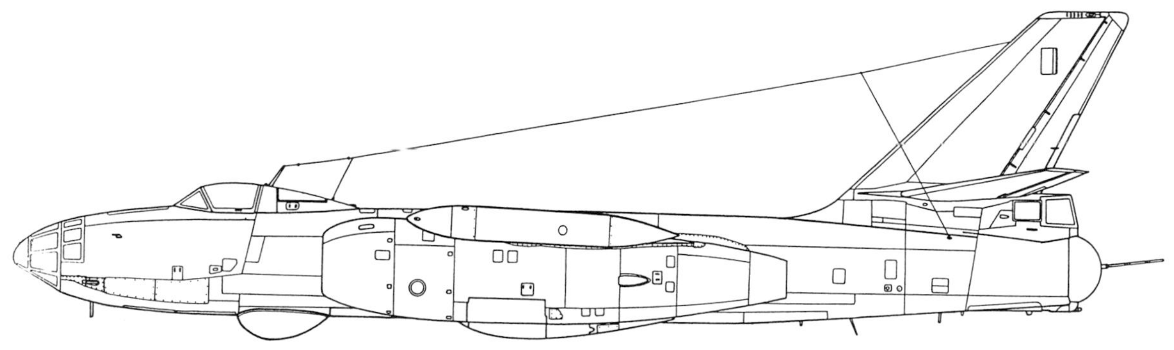

Presumably the Il-28N nuclear-capable bomber.

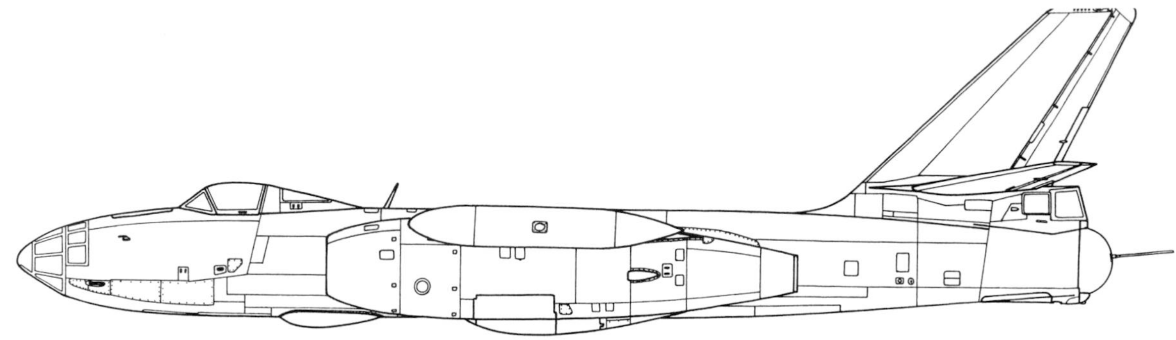

The Il-28RM prototype.

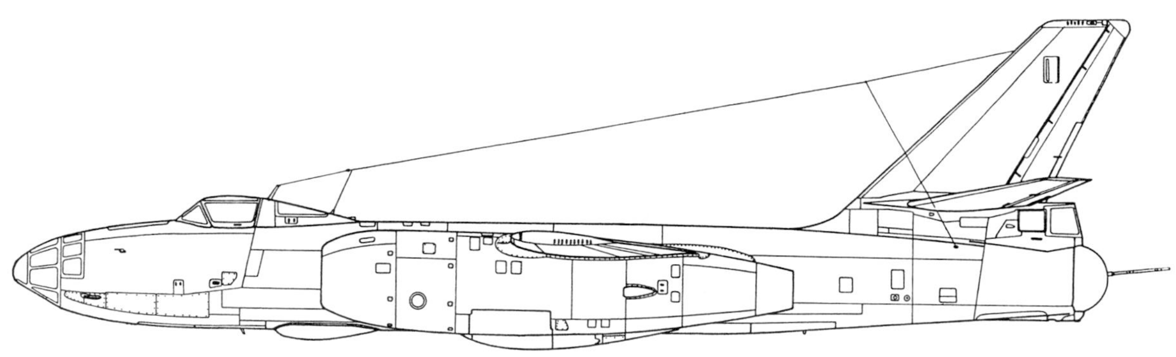

The experimental Il-28 bomber with VK-5E engines; note the non-standard cockpit glazing.

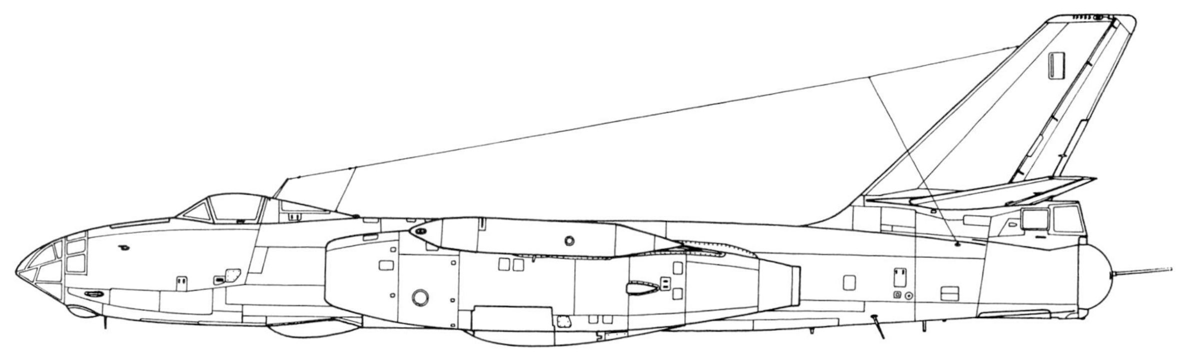

4 Red, the Il-28TM prototype (c/n 50301106).

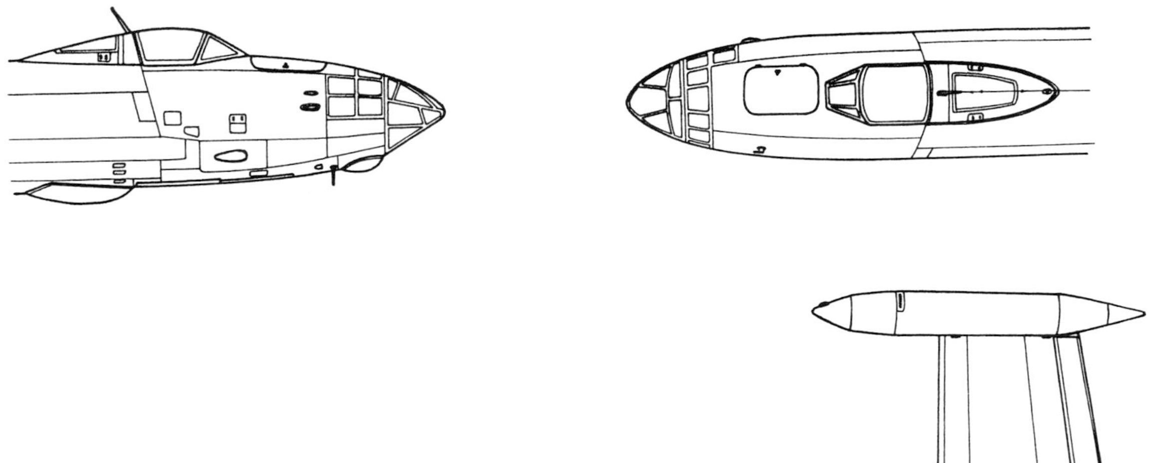

Scrap views of the Il-28TM's modified nose glazing and tip tanks.

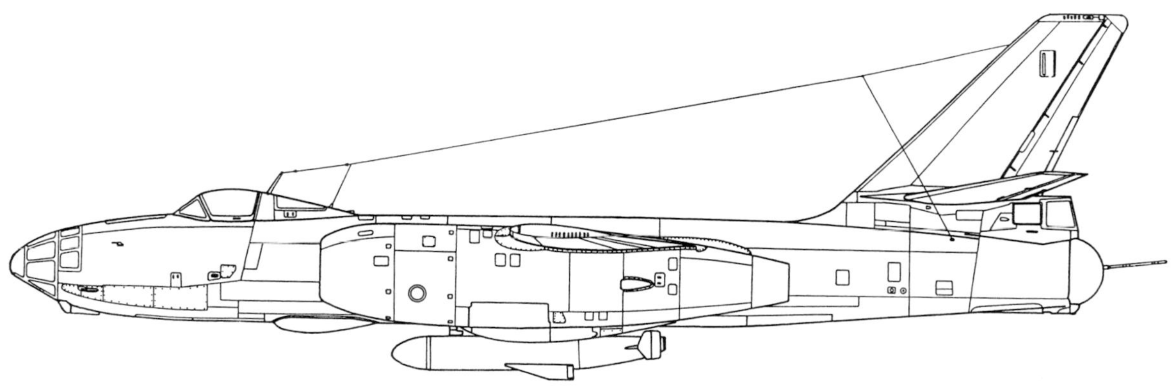

An Il-28-131 with a UB-2F Chaika guided bomb under the fuselage.

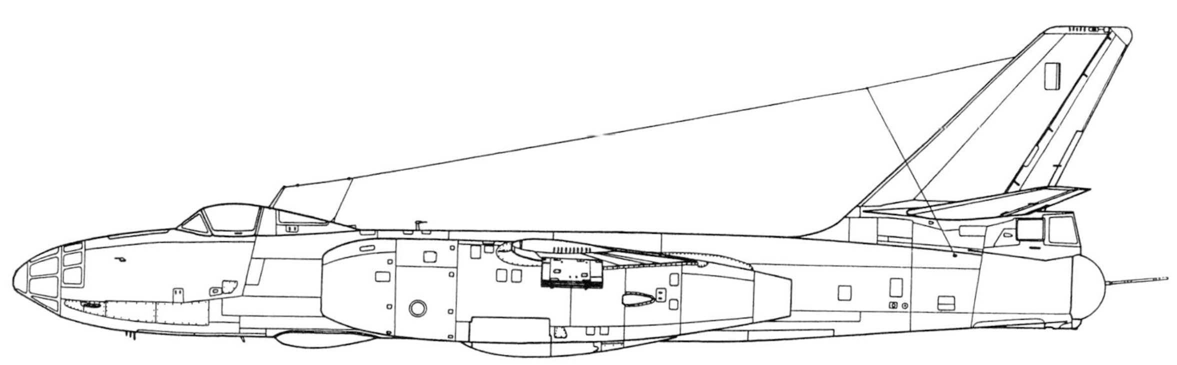

An Il-28Sh attack aircraft.

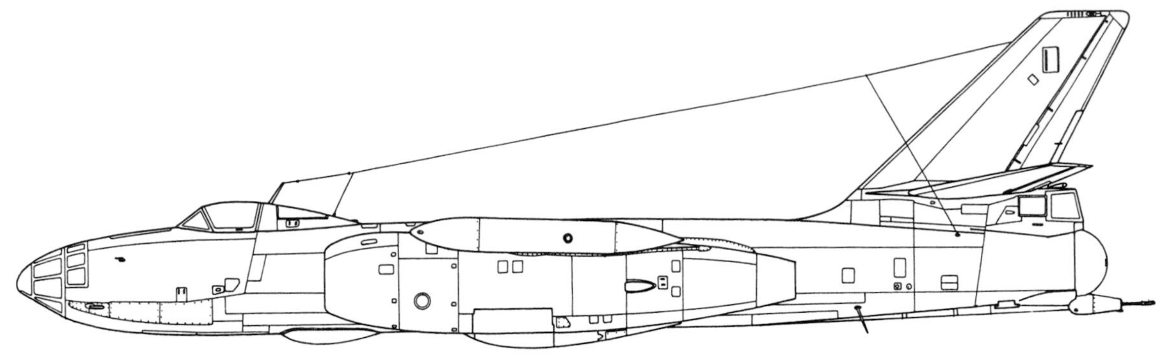

An Il-28BM target tug.

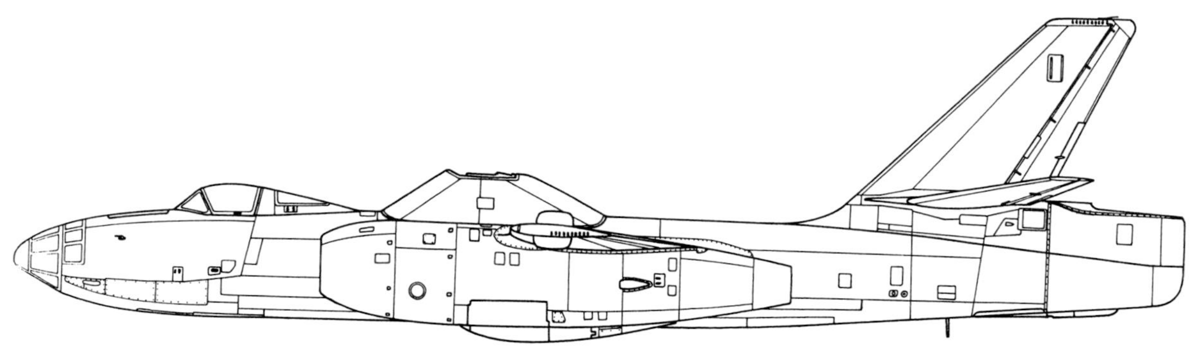

Il-28LL 10 Blue (c/n 53005710), LII's ejection seat testbed used in the Vostok manned-spacecraft programme.

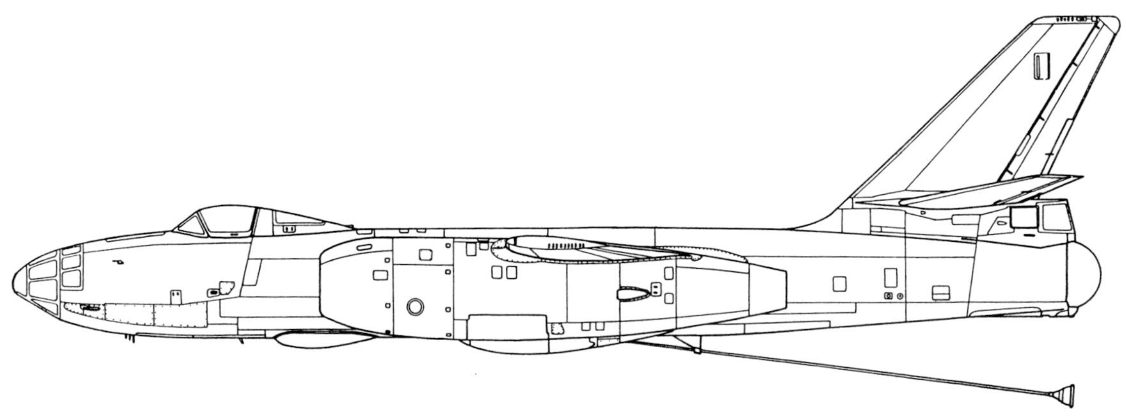

01 Red (c/n 2402101), the Il-28 used by LII as a tanker trainer.

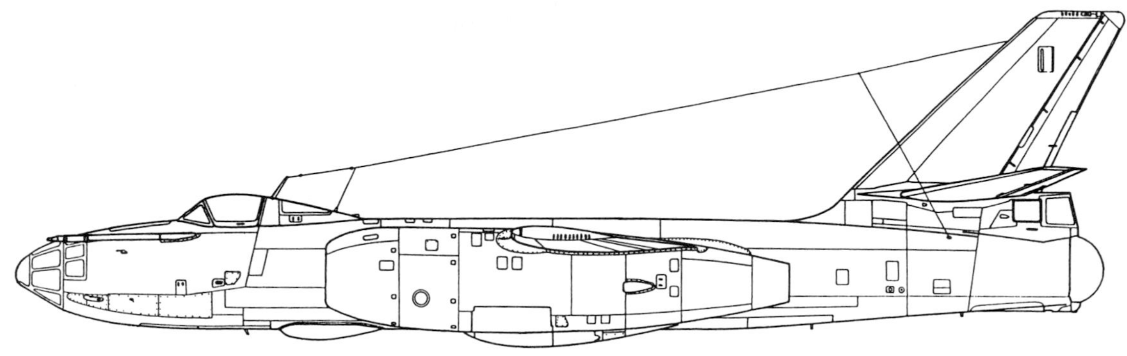

The Il-28 refuelling system testbed with a fixed refuelling probe.

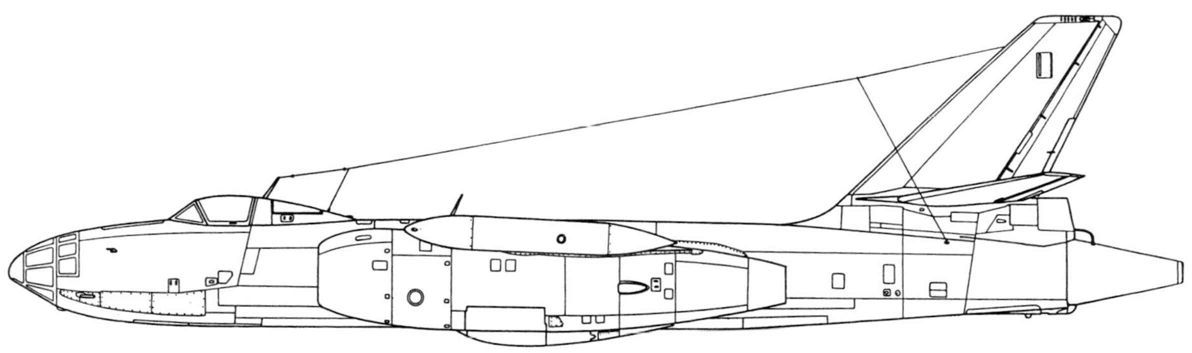

The Soviet Il-28R used as a testbed for a Dooshkin liquid-propellant rocket engine.

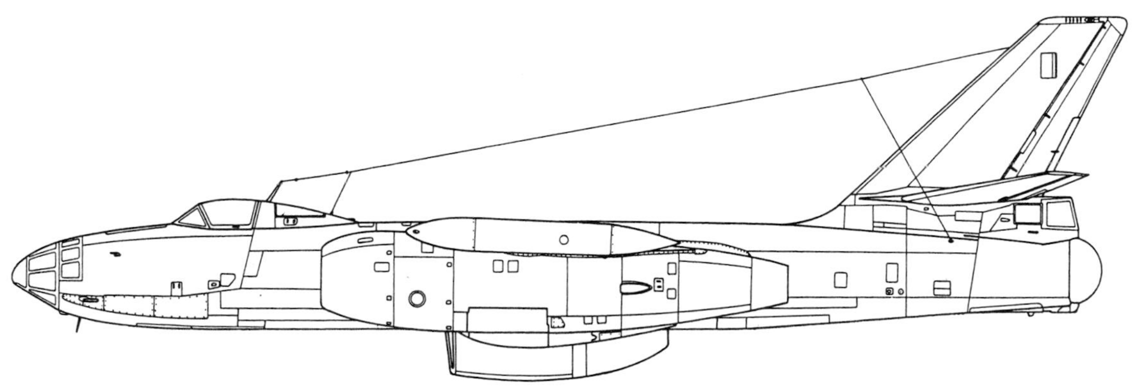

DM-ZZI (c/n 1418) or DM-ZZK (c/n 5901207), one of two Il-28Rs used as testbeds for the East German Pirna 014A-1 turbojet.

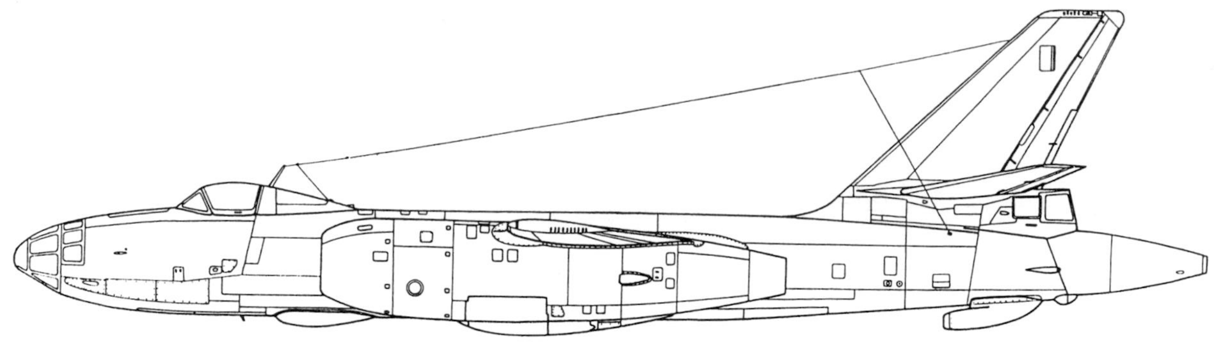

Avia B-228 6915 (c/n 56915) as originally used to test the Walter M-701 turbojet.

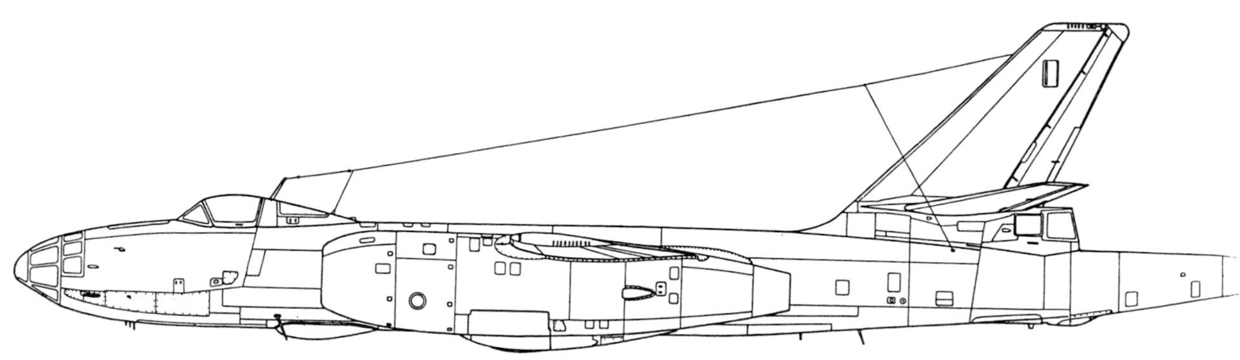

The same aircraft in a later configuration with the Ivchenko AI-25TL (Walter Titan) turbofan.

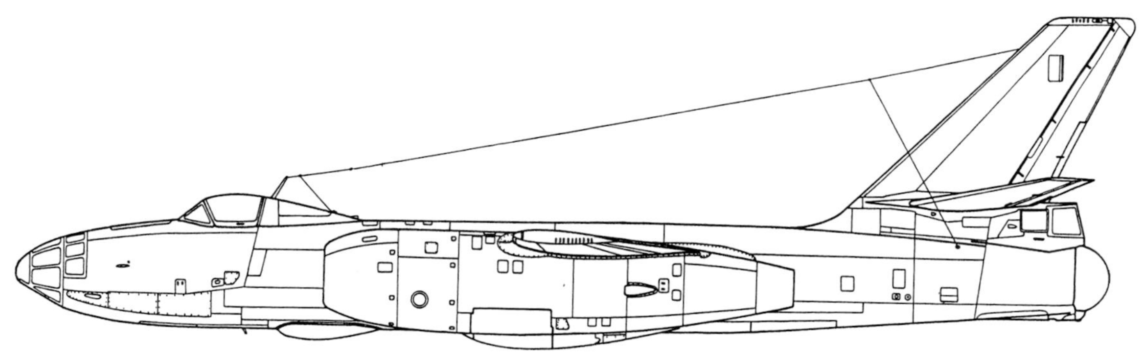

An Il-20 mailplane used by Aeroflot.

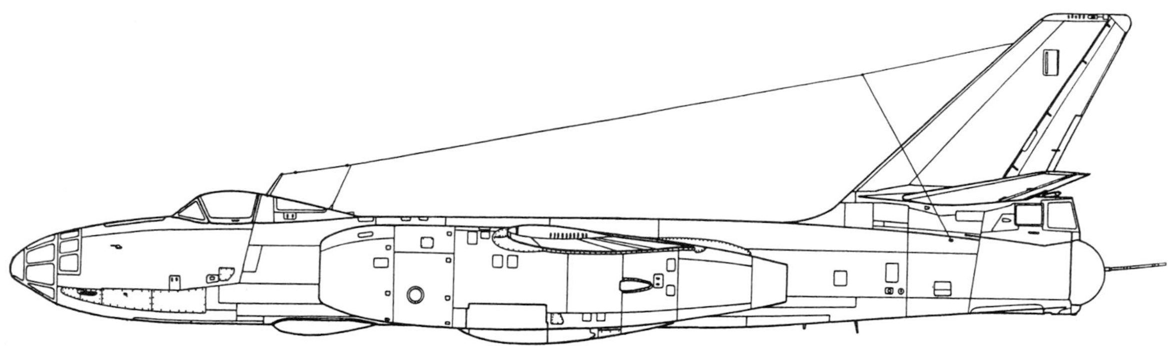

A standard Czech Air Force Avia B-228 (BA-11, c/n 56775) with a Sirena radar warning receiver.

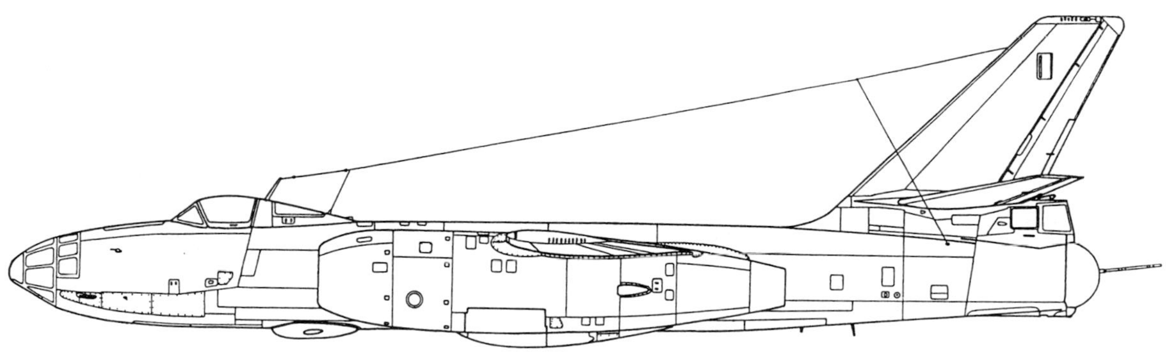

An early-production Harbin H-5.

INDEX

Page numbers in *italics* refer to illustrations